Praise for EATING THE

"Witty and clever."

—*Entertainment Weekly*

"Mr. Klosterman's relentlessly thoughtful prose makes a case that our arts and entertainment are more suffused with meaning than ever before. Even as he's fretting over the direction of the culture, his writing stands as an eloquent defense of it."

—*The Wall Street Journal*

"*Eating the Dinosaur* [is] a gutsy, irreverent, wonderful read. . . . Klosterman is a gifted essayist. . . . Klosterman exhibits a deep knowledge and a deft touch on an expansive list of topics, and his insights are sometimes enlightening, sometimes educational and always entertaining."

—*BookPage*

"Funny, irreverent and fascinating—Klosterman at his best."

—*Kirkus Reviews*

"Chuck Klosterman . . . is a pop-culture philosopher."

—*Fort Worth Star-Telegram*

"Klosterman once again zeroes in on disposable culture—and in doing so, points out everything indispensable about it. *Dinosaur* contains some of Klosterman's best work."

—*The Portland Mercury*

"Mr. Klosterman's discourses, though topically random, are engrossing and worthwhile. He has built a career on extrapolating meaning from trivialities, and his latest creation does that. It is a work of depth about shallow things."

—*The Washington Times*

Praise for Chuck Klosterman

"One of America's top cultural critics."

"Mr. Klosterman makes good, smart company."

"The reigning Kasparov of pop culture wits-matching."

"Klosterman is like the new Hunter S. Thompson."

ALSO BY CHUCK KLOSTERMAN

Fargo Rock City:
A Heavy Metal Odyssey in Rural Nörth Daköta

Sex, Drugs, and Cocoa Puffs:
A Low Culture Manifesto

Killing Yourself to Live:
85% of a True Story

Chuck Klosterman IV:
A Decade of Curious People and Dangerous Ideas

Downtown Owl:
A Novel

EATING THE DINOSAUR

CHUCK KLOSTERMAN

SCRIBNER
New York London Toronto Sydney

SCRIBNER

A Division of Simon & Schuster, Inc.
1230 Avenue of the Americas
New York, NY 10020

First Scribner trade paperback edition July 2010

SCRIBNER and design are registered trademarks of The Gale Group, Inc.,
used under license by Simon & Schuster, Inc., the publisher of this work.

For information about special discounts for bulk purchases,
please contact Simon & Schuster Special Sales at 1-866-506-1949
or business@simonandschuster.com.

The Simon & Schuster Speakers Bureau can bring authors to your live event.
For more information or to book an event contact the Simon & Schuster Speakers Bureau
at 1-866-248-3049 or visit our website at www.simonspeakers.com.

DESIGNED BY THE DESIGNOSAUR

Manufactured in the United States of America

1   3   5   7   9   10   8   6   4   2

Library of Congress Cataloging-in-Publication Data

Klosterman, Chuck, 1972–
Eating the dinosaur / by Chuck Klosterman.—1st Scribner hardcover ed.
p. cm.
1. Popular culture—United States. 2. Consumption (Economics)—Social aspects—
United States. 3. Sports—Social aspects—United States. 4. United States—
Civilization—1970– I. Title.
E169.12.K555 2009
973.92—dc22
2009018719

ISBN 978-1-4165-4420-3
ISBN 978-1-4165-4421-0 (pbk)
ISBN 978-1-4391-6848-6 (ebook)

There is something insane and self-contradictory
in supposing that things that have never yet been done
can be done except by means never tried.

—Francis Bacon, *The New Organon*

That's not the way the world really works anymore.
We're an empire now, and when we act, we create our own reality.
And while you're studying that reality—judiciously, as you will—
we'll act again, creating other new realities, which you can
study too, and that's how things will sort out.

—Unnamed George W. Bush senior adviser,
speaking to *New York Times* reporter Ron Suskind in 2002

Don't Believe the Truth—*I don't know what the title means.*
It's a pothead thing, innit?

—Liam Gallagher of Oasis, discussing his own album

Contents

EATING THE DINOSAUR

Something Instead
of Nothing

1 For the first twelve years of my adult life, I sustained a professional existence by asking questions to strangers and writing about what they said.

"Why did you do it?" I would ask these strangers. It did not matter what *it* was. "What were you thinking while you did that? Did it satisfy you? What does it mean to be satisfied? Do you consider yourself to be famous? How does it feel to be famous? How did this experience change you? What elements didn't change? What will never change? What drives you? Are you lying to me right now? Why should I care about what you are saying? Is this all a construction? Are you constructed? Who constructed you? What was their purpose? Does God exist? Why or why not? Thank you very much. It was great meeting you in the lobby of this unnecessarily expensive hotel."

This has been a tremendous way to earn a living. Who wouldn't enjoy getting paid for being curious? Journalism allows almost anyone to direct questions they would never ask of their own friends at random people; since the ensuing dialogue exists for commercial purposes, both parties accept an acceleration of intimacy. People give emotional responses, but those emotions are projections. The result (when things go well) is a dynamic, adversarial, semi-real conversation. I am at ease with this. If given a choice between interviewing someone or talking to them "for real," I prefer the former; I don't like having the social limitations of tact imposed upon my day-to-day interactions and I don't enjoy talking to most people more than once or twice in my lifetime.

2 For the past five years, I've spent more time being interviewed than conducting interviews with other people. I am not complaining about this, nor am I proud of it— it's just the way things worked out, mostly by chance. But the experience has been confusing. Though I always understand why people ask me the same collection of questions, I never know why I answer them. Frankly, I don't know why anyone answers anything. The obvious explanation is that the interviewee is hoping to promote a product or a concept (or the "concept of themselves," which is its own kind of product), but that's reductive and often untrue; once a media entity makes the decision to conduct and produce an interview with a particular somebody, the piece is going to exist regardless of how the subject responds to the queries. The interviewee can say anything, even if those sentiments contradict reality. They can deliver nothing but clichés, but the story will still run. On three occasions I've consciously (and blatantly) attempted to say boring things during an interview in the hope of killing the eventual article. It only worked once. But this type of behavior is rare. Most of the time, I pretend to be interesting. I try to frame my response in the context in which the question was asked, and I try to say things I haven't said before. But I have no clue as to why I do this (or why anyone else does, either).

During the summer of 2008, I was interviewed by a Norwegian magazine writer named Erik Moller Solheim. He was good at his job. He knew a lot of trivia about Finland's military history. We ate fried pork knees and drank Ur-Krostitzer beer. But in the middle of our playful conversation, I was suddenly paralyzed by an unspoken riddle I could not answer: Why was I responding to this man's questions? My books are not translated into Norwegian. If the journalist sent me a copy of his finished article, I could not read a word of it. I don't even know what the publication's name (*Dagens Naeringsliv*) is supposed to mean. I will likely never go to Norway, and even if I did, the fact that I was interviewed for this publication would have no impact on my time there. No one would care. The fjords would be underwhelmed.

As such, I considered the possible motives for my actions:

1. **I felt I had something important to say.** Except I did not. No element of our interaction felt important to me. If anything, I felt unqualified to talk about the things the reporter was asking me. I don't have that much of an opinion about why certain Black Metal bands burn down churches.
2. **It's my job.** Except that it wasn't. I wasn't promoting anything. In fact, the interaction could have been detrimental to my career, were I to have inadvertently said something insulting about the king of Norway. Technically, there was more downside than upside.
3. **I have an unconscious, unresolved craving for attention.** Except that this feels inaccurate. It was probably true twenty years ago, but those desires have waned. Besides, who gives a fuck about being famous in a country I'll never visit? Why would that feel good to anyone? How would I even know it was happening?
4. **I had nothing better to do.** This is accurate, but not satisfactory.
5. **I'm a nice person.** Unlikely.
6. **When asked a direct question, it's human nature to respond.** This, I suppose, is the most likely explanation. It's the crux of *Frost/Nixon*. But if this is true, why is it true?

What is the psychological directive that makes an unanswered question discomfiting?

Why do people talk?

3 Why do people talk? Why do people answer the questions you ask them? Is there a unifying force that prompts people to respond?

Errol Morris[1]: Probably not, except possibly that people feel this need to give an account of themselves. And not just to other people, but to themselves. Just yesterday, I was being interviewed by a reporter from the *New York Observer,* and we were talking about whether or not people have privileged access to their own minds.

Privileged access?

EM: My mind resides somewhere inside of myself. That being the case, one would assume I have privileged access to it. In theory, I should be able to ask myself questions and get different answers

---

1. Errol Morris is the most recognized American documentary filmmaker of the modern era and arguably the finest American nonfiction director of all time. His movies include *Gates of Heaven, The Thin Blue Line, The Fog of War,* and *Standard Operating Procedure.* For two years, he had a TV series called *First Person* that was composed of intense one-on-one interviews with random, unfamous weirdos. What makes Morris such a brilliant artist is the simplicity of his technique: He simply asks people questions, films their response, and then finds (or creates) stock footage that accentuates the import and context of what his subject is saying. He does this through the use of the "interrotron," a self-designed camera that allows the interview subject to see a live image of Morris's face in the eye of the recording camera.

than I would from other people, such as you. But I'm not sure we truly have privileged access to our own minds. I don't think we have any idea who we are. I think we're engaged in a constant battle to figure out who we are. I sometimes think of interviews as some oddball human relationship that's taking place in a laboratory setting. I often feel like a primatologist.

Do you feel like you know the people that you interview? Because I feel as though I never do. It seems like a totally fake relationship.

EM: I don't feel like I know myself, let alone the people I interview. I might actually know the people I interview *better* than I know myself. A friend of mine once said that you can never trust a person who doesn't talk much, because how else do you know what they're thinking? Just by the act of being willing to talk about oneself, the person is revealing something about who they are.

But what is the talker's motive? Why did you decide to talk to the *New York Observer*? Why are you talking to me right now?

EM: Well, okay. Let's use the example of Robert McNamara.[2] Why does McNamara feel the need to talk to me—or to anyone—at this point in his life? Because there's a very strong human desire to do so. It might be to get approval from someone, even if that person is just me. It might even be to get a sense of condemnation from people. Maybe it's just programmed into us as people. McNamara also had this weird "approach-avoidance" thing: He

---

2. McNamara was the controversial U.S. secretary of defense during the Vietnam War and president of the World Bank from 1968 to 1981. He was the subject of Morris's Academy Award–winning 2003 film *The Fog of War: Eleven Lessons from the Life of Robert S. McNamara.*

agreed to do the interview because he assumed I was part of the promotion of his [then new] book.[3] I called him around the same time his book was coming out, and he thought it was just part of that whole deal. When he realized it was not, he became apprehensive and said he didn't think he was going to do it. But then he did, and it went on for well over a year. In fact, I continued to interview him for a long time after that movie was finished, just because I found it very interesting.

But why did McNamara keep talking?

EM: He said he enjoyed talking to me. That was his explanation.

2A While working for newspapers during the 1990s, I imagined that being interviewed by other reporters would be fun. I assumed answering questions would be easier than asking them. This proved completely untrue. The process of being interviewed is much more stressful than the process of interrogating someone. If you make a mistake while you're interviewing someone else, there is no penalty (beyond the fact that it will be harder to write a complete story). But if you make a mistake while *being* interviewed—if you admit something you'd prefer to keep secret, or if you flippantly answer a legitimately serious question, or if you thoughtlessly disparage a peer you barely know, or if you answer the phone while on drugs— that mistake will inevitably become the focus of whatever is writ-

---

3. *Wilson's Ghost: Reducing the Risk of Conflict, Killing, and Catastrophe in the Twenty-first Century.*

ten. As a reporter, you live for those anecdotal mistakes. Mistakes are how you isolate hidden truths. But as a person, anecdotal mistakes define the experience of being misunderstood; anecdotal mistakes are used to make metaphors that explain the motives of a person who is sort of like you, but not really.

4 "The people who come on *This American Life* have often never heard of our show, or have never even heard of NPR, so they have no idea what the conversation is going to be. It's very abstract. And we're on the frontier of doing journalism that's so personal, no normal journalist would even consider it. That's part of it. It's hard to resist whenever someone really wants to listen to you. That's a very rare thing in most of our lives. I'm a pretty talky person who deals with lots of sensitive people every single day, but if someone really listens to me and cares about what I say for ten minutes in the course of a day—that's a lot. Some days that doesn't happen at all."

[These are the words of Ira Glass, host of *This American Life*, the tent-pole program for most National Public Radio stations. It was later turned into a television show for Showtime. Glass has an immediately recognizable interviewing style: amicable, intellectual, nerdy, and sincere.]

"Sometimes I will be talking to journalism students and they will ask how I get people to open up to me, and the answer is that I'm legitimately curious about what those people are saying. I honestly care about the stories they are telling. That's a force that talks to the deepest part of us. There is something that happens during therapy when the therapy session is going well: If someone is talking to a therapist about something unresolved—something they don't understand—and they suddenly start talking about it, it just flows out in this highly narrative, highly detailed form. Most people are not articulate about *everything* in their life, but they are articulate about the things they're still figuring out."

[What makes Glass and *TAL* successful is the instantaneously emotive quality of the work—the stories told on the show are typically minor moments in people's lives, but they hinge on how those seemingly minor moments are transformative. The smallest human details are amplified to demonstrate realizations about what it means to feel profound things. I ask Glass why his interview subjects trust him, particularly since their stories will inevitably be used on a radio show, mostly for the entertainment of people they'll never meet.]

"They can tell by my questions that I'm really, really interested and really, really thinking about what they're saying, in a way that only happens in nature when you're falling in love with someone. When else does that experience happen? If you're falling in love with someone, you have conversations where you're truly revealing yourself . . . I think small intimacy that doesn't extend beyond a single conversation is still intimacy. Even if the basis behind that conversation is purely commercial, there can be moments of real connection with another person. In an interview, we have the apparatus of what generates intimacy—asking someone to bare himself or herself. And if you're the person being asked the questions, and if you're normal, it's hard not to have it work on your heart."

[Since Glass understands that interviewing is an inherently manipulative process, I ask what motivates him to talk whenever a reporter asks him a question.]

"I really try to do a good job for the interviewer. The first time I was ever interviewed was in the mid-nineties. It was for *Chicago* magazine, about the radio show. I had never been interviewed before. It was a woman reporter, and she was very experienced. But I had never been interviewed before, even though I had conducted and edited thousands of radio interviews over the previous seventeen years. I experienced the entire interview as her: She would ask me a question, and I would listen to myself giving the answer, and I would think, 'That's not going to work. That's not going to work. That's not the lead.' I was editing my interview as I produced it. I related more to her than I did to myself. That happened for a long time. But there is a vestige in that. I want to give a good quote. I so often demand a good quote from other people, so I want to do the same for other reporters. I want to be sincere and actually answer the question I've been asked, and I want to say it in a way that's sparkly and interesting. I want to get an A in the class. The whole thing is a projection."

[I ask Glass how much of his own self-identity is based around being good at interviewing other people. He says, "None at all," but that it was when he was younger. He offhandedly mentions that it's difficult to discuss his self-identity. He says his self-image is not very good. I ask him what his self-image is.]

"Well, this kind of takes us outside the realm of what you were originally asking about . . . I'm not sure if I want to talk about this, but . . . [*pause*] . . . People who really know me, there's probably not a huge gap between my own self-image and their perception. I mean, I don't think of myself as a bad person . . . I don't know how to answer this . . . [*very long pause*] . . . I'm coming out of a four-year period[4] where I was so overwhelmed by what I had to do that

_____

4. This interview was conducted on August 6, 2008.

I don't really feel like *anybody* anymore. I used to completely identify myself through the work I did. It completely absorbed me. But
these last four years have been so frantic that I've barely been able
to work on things that are my own. A lot of what is on the show
is now completely done by other people, and it's great work—but
then I have the added weird experience of getting credit for things
I haven't done. Since the TV show started and I've really worked
two jobs nonstop for four years, I've kind of forgotten what I used
to be like. I feel like I'm doing hand-to-hand combat with editing
and writing all day long, and I don't even feel *anything* about it.
This is a huge problem, and I'm trying to deal with it."

[I ask him if the expansion of *This American Life* to television—
and the growth of the *TAL* brand in the mainstream culture—
has made him a less happy person.]

"Yes."

[I ask if he likes the idea of that information eventually appearing in a book. I ask if the public recognition of this realization
will make him feel better.]

"No, I won't feel better about it. I'll feel bad about it. But I'm trying to do right by the person who's interviewing me."

4A I don't agree with Ira Glass. I used to, but I don't
anymore. He makes a valid point, and I certainly
understand why he would argue that it's hypocrit-
ical for a journalist to decline answering another reporter's ques-

tion; the degree of empathy Glass feels toward rival interviewers indicates that he's a giving person. But I never feel this way. I don't feel it's my obligation to respond to anything, and as a reporter, I never felt anyone else owed me a response. And yet I still provide answers to every question I encounter, even if I don't know what I should say.

Sometimes I openly lie.

This morning, I was interviewed by a reporter from a magazine based in New York. He was asking me about a novel I'd written, specifically about one passage where a character says something negative about human nature. The reporter said to me, "This character sounds exactly like you speaking. That specific sentiment sounds like something you would say." And he was correct. In this specific instance, the interior thoughts of the character were an exact reflection of my personal thoughts about the world at large. The reporter was totally right. But I refuted his suggestion. "No, that's not true," I said. "I don't feel that way at all."

Now, why did I do this?

When I wrote those words on my computer, my goal was for every reader to come to the same conclusion that this reporter did. My intention was that people would read this sentence and instantly recognize that the character was a proxy for my own worldview and that this narrative device would allow me to directly write about the way I felt. But I didn't want to admit that. I didn't want to say, "Yes, this is how I feel." I just wanted people to *suspect* that this was true. So when I was asked if this sentence represented who I was, I said no. In other words, I gave an answer that completely undercut my own artistic intentions—and if asked this same question again, I would repeat the behavior. I feel no compulsion to do right by the people who interview me. In fact, I sometimes want to do wrong, even if the only person who suffers is myself.

3A

How skeptical are you about the things people tell you during interviews?

Errol Morris: I'm skeptical about *everything* I hear. I *am* in the business of deciding what is or isn't true, and in figuring out which accounts are accurate and which are inaccurate, but I'm also in the business of creating a story, and that is something different. When I did *The Thin Blue Line,*[5] there were all these separate first-person interviews that I eventually stitched together into one story line. I found all these so-called eyewitnesses who had testified at the trial, and I interviewed them one by one by one. I was principally interested in two questions. The first was: How reliable was their testimony in this capital murder case? The second was: Who in the hell is this person that I am talking to? If you have this presumption that every person sees the world in a different way, how do you capture that? What you're trying to do with any interview is to capture the way a person sees the world.

What's more interesting to you: someone who lies consciously, someone who lies unconsciously, or someone who tells a relatively mundane version of the truth?

EM: Conscious mendacity! Actually, that's a very difficult question. The whole idea of lying as it applies to personhood is an important problem. I'll give you an example: I read a piece about modern forms of lie detection—methods that go beyond the polygraph. The writer's idea was that we can actually record activity inside the brain that proves who is or who isn't lying. It suggests

---

5. This is a documentary about the 1976 murder of a policeman.

that the brain is some kind of 'reality recorder' and that we *know* when we are lying. But I think those kinds of lies represent a very small piece of the pie. I think the larger sect of liars are people who think they are telling the truth, but who really have no idea what the truth is. So the deeper question is, what's more important: narrative consistency or truth? I think we're always trying to create a consistent narrative for ourselves. I think truth always takes a backseat to narrative. Truth has to sit at the back of the bus.

That's interesting, but I disagree. I think truth tends to usurp narrative every single time. If it turned out that even one person in your nonfiction film *Vernon, Florida* had been a hired actor, your entire career would be called into question. Or look at someone like James Frey[6]: Here was a guy who wrote a book that everyone seemed to appreciate as a narrative construction—but the moment they realized it was fake, his talent as a stylist no longer mattered. The perception of its value was dependent on the veracity of the story.

EM: When you talk about a James Frey–type of situation, you're talking about a person who has been outed. That was more like, "We caught you! We caught you! And we as a society are going to make you pay for deceiving us!" But that's an egregious example. Most lying is just an accepted part of the world . . . if you don't want to know something, can you not know it? Can you convince

---

6. Frey is the disgraced author of *A Million Little Pieces*, a bestselling nonfiction book that purported to be about the author's drug and alcohol addictions, his life of crime and depravity, and how he overcame these vices with his own sheer willpower. The book proved to be partially—and perhaps mostly—untrue. In fact, Frey initially attempted to sell the book as a novel, only (it seems) to realize it was more commercially viable if he claimed all the events had happened to him in real life.

yourself that you *don't* know it? Can you actually *not* know it, in some real sense? Can you form a barrier to knowing things?

Probably. But doesn't that change when a conversation becomes "an interview"? Does the import of the truth change when the situation is specifically designed for the purposes of truth finding?

EM: That's a crazy idea. Why does an interview change anything? Have I sworn to tell the truth? Have I put my hand on a Bible?

No, but the difference is distribution. If you were to make a film about me, I'm not just talking to you. I'm talking to a public audience.

EM: But what if you have no idea what the truth is? What if you're convinced that your lies are what really happened?

I wouldn't classify that as lying. I'd classify that as being wrong.

EM: I'm a great believer in self-deception. If you asked me what makes the world go round, I would say self-deception. Self-deception allows us to create a consistent narrative for ourselves that we actually believe. I'm not saying that the truth doesn't matter. It does. But self-deception is how we survive. I remember this crazy-ass journalist from Dallas who once interviewed me, and he asked if I Mirandized my documentary subjects before putting them on film. I was like, "What?" I should read my interview subjects their Miranda rights because their words might be used in the court of public opinion?

Well, that *is* crazy. But tell me this—have you ever been in a situation where you were interviewing someone, and you knew

the subject did not understand the consequences of what they were saying?

EM: All the time!

Is there an ethical problem with that?

EM: Is there an ethical problem with the possibility of people not knowing what they're saying? Or with *why* they're saying it?

No, a problem in the sense that a subject might not realize that this interview is going to galvanize how she's perceived. Or a problem in the sense that someone might be talking to you without realizing the consequence of what he's saying.

EM: Well, it's possible you're assigning too much importance to yourself [*sarcastically*] "Do these people not realize that this interview is going to *transform* how they are seen by others? Do they not realize it will *transform* how they see themselves?" If people were entirely reasonable, they would avoid all interviews, all the time. But they don't.

And why don't they?

EM: Because perhaps something interesting will transpire. They think, "Maybe this person will present me in a way that will be interesting. Maybe this person will present me in a way that I would like to be seen."

4B During most of the 1980s and much of the '90s, Prince declined almost every interview request he received. On those rare occasions he granted an interview, he always made a curious demand: The reporter could not use a tape recorder or take written notes. The reporter just had to memorize whatever Prince happened to be saying that day. At the time, it was assumed that Prince did this because he was beavershit crazy and always wanted to be in a position to retract whatever was written about him. However, his real motive was more reasonable and (kind of) brilliant: He wanted to force the reporter to reflect only the *sense* of the conversation, as opposed to the specific phrases he elected to use. He was not concerned about being misquoted; he was concerned about being quoted accurately. Prince believed that he could represent himself better as an abstraction—his words could not be taken out of context *if there was no context.* He could only be presented as the sum total of whatever was said, devoid of specifics.

Do I grant interviews because I want to be presented in a way that will be interesting? Maybe. Except that the things that would be most interesting to other people might be potentially humiliating to me. Do I want to be presented in a way that I would like to be seen? Of course, but "the way I would like to be seen" would almost certainly be an inaccurate, delusional depiction of who I actually am. It strikes me that the two objectives mentioned by Morris are inherently contradictory: Presenting a subject in an interesting way inevitably means said subject is unable to control how that perception will be received.[7] The interviewee is not able

---

7. A textbook example is blues guitarist John Mayer's 2010 interview with Rob Tannenbaum in *Playboy.* Mayer was totally unguarded in the conversation, speaking candidly about race, pornography, and the complexity of his own romantic

to compose the way they want to be seen. Here again, it becomes easy to see the media savvy of Prince. By making it impossible to quote him directly, he was able to satisfy both of Morris's contradictory desires—he would always come across as interesting (in that the reporter would be forced to essentially fictionalize a narrative from a conversation that was almost impossible to reference), but he'd still be presented in the way he wanted to be seen (which is to say, enigmatically).

It was a good idea.

5 "If a question is interesting, it is very difficult to resist answering it, because you will usually find your own answer interesting to yourself. If you have any ego at all, or a desire to share your experience and thought processes, then you may also imagine your answer will be of interest to other people." This is Chris Heath talking (or, more accurately, this is Chris Heath writing—I posed my questions to him via e-mail). Heath[8] has done hundreds of deep celebrity profiles for *GQ* and *Rolling Stone*, first emerging as a journalistic superstar during that brief,

---

life. One of the central elements of the dialogue was Mayer's surprising popularity within the black community. However, because Mayer verbally acknowledged a racial epithet and mentioned that he was not physically attracted to black women (despite citing several black women he *did* find attractive), he was immediately crucified by public opinion. As Tannenbaum himself tweeted the day after the piece was published on the Internet, "The Web is a series of filters. Each filter narrowed the story more & more, until, in some sectors, it turned into, *John Mayer is a racist.*" Mayer was eventually forced to apologize for being honest and interesting. It has been said that pretty much everything about John Mayer is fascinating, except for his music.

8. A British writer, Heath started at the UK magazine *Smash Hits* and has also written two books on the Pet Shop Boys and a third on Robbie Williams.

bizarre stretch of the middle nineties when *Details* was the most interesting magazine in America. "But that lure and appeal would quickly break down in a real conversation without a second factor: the person asking the question must be interested in hearing the answer. There's no single bigger reason why people answer questions. Here, of course, lies the biggest difference between a successful interviewer and an unsuccessful one: the successful one makes the interviewee feel as though he or she is interested in the answers. The unsuccessful interviewer—and I have sat in or listened to enough interviews to know, unfortunately, and disappointingly, how common they are—does not."

Taken at face value, Heath's analysis is obvious, undeniable, and Glass-like—it's hard to resist talking to someone who cares about what you are saying. It's a seductive experience, even if you're simply sitting next to someone at a dinner party who happens to be an especially intriguing bozo. But there's a difference between being listened to by a stranger at a party and being listened to by Chris Heath, and everyone understands what that difference is: No matter how captivating Heath may seem, the conversation is happening for a practical, nonpersonal purpose. The banter may be pleasurable, but you're not bantering for pleasure.

Unless, of course, giving interviews to reporters is the closest you ever come to the kind of day-to-day dialogue normal people have all the time—and that's often the case for the superfamous. One of the underappreciated complexities to success is that it makes every interpersonal conversation unbalanced; I assume the only people Jennifer Aniston can comfortably talk with about her career problems are Courteney Cox and Lisa Kudrow (to anyone else, her problems would seem like bragging). In all likelihood, interviews are the only situations when a woman like Aniston can openly talk about the central issues occupying her mind.

"I detect that there's a prevalent notion in the media that it's next to impossible to interestingly interview a celebrity, because they do so many interviews that they're drained and leeched dry of any interest or motivation," writes Heath. "I have a feeling that the opposite is more often true. Celebrities do so many short, pointless, bad interviews—weeks of talking in which it must be impossible to maintain the delusion that one is being understood or accurately depicted in any way—that when they find themselves in a conversation in which, maybe subconsciously, they feel the possibility of being somewhat understood, and that the reality of their life will be somewhat realistically portrayed, the interview may begin to feel less like wasted time and more like an antidote to all that other wasted time. And so when asked a good question, they'll answer."

But how does this apply to normal people? How does this affect people who didn't marry Brad Pitt or popularize a type of haircut?

"It's an uncomfortable leap, but this question led me to consider how different (or similar) that motivation is to people's desire to appear on *Jerry Springer*–type shows or in various reality TV situations," Heath continued. "We are used to the idea of giving witness to one's life as an important and noble counterpoint to being unheard, especially when applied to people in certain disadvantaged, oppressed or unacceptable situations. But in a slightly more pathological way, I'm not sure that we aren't seeing the emergence of a society in which almost *everyone* who isn't famous considers themselves cruelly and unfairly unheard. As though being famous, and the subject of wide attention, is considered to be a fulfilled human being's natural state—and so, as a corollary, the cruelly unheard millions are perpetually primed and fired up to answer any and all questions in order to redress this awful imbalance."

There's a lot of truth in that last bit. I fear that most contemporary people are answering questions not because they're flattered by the attention; they're answering questions because they feel as though they *deserve* to be asked. About everything. Their opinions are special, so they are entitled to a public forum. Their voice is supposed to be heard, lest their life become empty.

This, in one paragraph (minus technology), explains the rise of New Media.

4C Because this essay will appear in a book that I will have to promote through the media, reporters who interview me will ask questions about this essay. They will ask if I have come to understand why I (or anyone else) answer interview questions. I will initially say, "No." But I will still guess at the explanation, and my verbalized guess will go something like this: People answer questions because it feels stranger to do the opposite. And the next time I interview someone, I will try to remember this.

3B How different were your conversations with Robert McNamara when you weren't filming him? Is he a different person when he's not on camera? Are *you* a different person when you're not interviewing or being interviewed?

Errol Morris: That's a whole set of questions. One of the things that really interests me is that filming people for a movie has become very crazy. I usually have a crew of thirty people in the studio. That created a big question during the making of *The Thin Blue Line*—can you really investigate something with a camera? Are you able to hear something you would normally miss in a normal conversation? Are people going to disclose something to a camera with a bunch of strangers in the room? The self-serving answer for someone in my position is, of course, "Yes." I think that you can. I think something strange happens when you put a person in a formal interview setting and they realize they are expected to talk. *They do talk.* But why do people submit themselves to this? That's more complex. It's crazy. I mean, why am I talking to you right now?

That's precisely what I'm trying to figure out. With someone like McNamara, I can imagine a motive—he's a historic figure, and his identity is built around his life's work and the consequence of that work. But what about those people you interviewed in that *First Person* series for the Independent Film Channel? Those were nonfamous private citizens. Publicity got them nothing. There was a person you interviewed in an episode of *First Person*—Rick Rosner[9]—whose personal story was that he purposely repeated his senior year in high school several times and then lost on the game show *Who Wants to Be a Millionaire*. For him, what is the value of being interviewed?

EM: Well, Rick Rosner now tells other people that if they want to understand him, they should watch that one-hour program about his life that I made.

---

9. Rosner is believed to have one of the highest IQ scores ever measured. Through an elaborate system of disguises and false identification, he inexplicably repeated twelfth grade four times. After losing on *Who Wants to Be a Millionaire,* he attempted to sue the program over the phrasing of the $16,000 question he got wrong. He has also worked as a male stripper and twice subsisted on dog food. Years later, he would appear in a commercial for Domino's Pizza.

Why do you think he feels that way?

EM: I can't speak for Rick Rosner, but I can kind of imagine why he would like it. I imagine that he is a pretty complicated character who doesn't understand himself that well. He's in the grip of all this *stuff* that he cannot control. So the interview allows him to scrutinize himself in a different way. There are two ways to look at this. There are two different models. The first model is that we all have this black box inside ourselves that is filled with our secrets, and we would never want to allow any interviewer to open that box. But the second model is that even we don't know what's inside that black box, and being interviewed allows us to open it and sort through the contents.

Do you enjoy being interviewed?

EM: I don't mind talking. I think talking has been very important to me. For a long time I had writer's block and all I could do was talk. Then I was able to make movies that involved other people talking. Recently I've started writing, and that's changed things. For a long time, I thought my constant talking was an impediment to my writing, but now I don't know if that was true or not. I'm envious of writers, because a writer leaves this trail of detritus. As a writer, you have this trail of writing that is an account of yourself and who you are. For years, I was deprived of that opportunity, because I couldn't write. So the talking was essential. It was a way to do something instead of nothing.

6 More than a year after meeting in Boston, Errol Morris was gracious enough to record his bits of dialogue from this essay for the book's eventual audio version. Much to my surprise, he took issue with one of his own sentences from our interview.

At the beginning of section 3A, there's a line that now reads, "I *am* in the business of deciding what is or isn't true." This is not how the sentence read in the original transcript, nor is it what I vividly remember from our conversation. What Morris originally said was, "I'm *not* in the business of deciding what is or isn't true." However, this is not what he meant to say, nor is it a sentiment he wanted to imply. As such, I immediately changed it (I would be a bad interviewer if I consciously published a statement the subject did not agree with, regardless of whether or not that statement had been inadvertently expressed). But this dispute accidentally proves the point I've been making all along: It's hard to fathom why people allow themselves to be interviewed. Even when you're simply transcribing a person's direct dialogue, you will rarely capture how they actually feel.

Here's what (I think) happened: When Morris originally said "I'm not in the business of deciding what is or isn't true," he was essentially saying, "I am not a cop. I'm not part of the executive branch of government. My job is to make a nonfiction movie, not to define anyone's guilt or innocence." Now, there's absolutely nothing wrong with that objective. But when Morris reread those literal words on the page, they felt totally alien to him; they seemed to suggest he didn't even care what the truth was. "Why would I spend three years trying to right a miscarriage of justice and solve a murder case in Texas, if I was truly indifferent to the business of deciding what is or isn't true," Morris later wrote me in an e-mail. "And why would I ask the question about the reliability of the testimony of various witnesses if I didn't care about truth?" I completely understand his perspective. I've had the same thing happen to me. It does not matter how diligent or well-intentioned the reporter is—the inherent distortion of the process inevitably overrides accuracy.

So what does this tell us? Should we just journalistically surrender? Should we stop answering questions *and* stop asking them altogether? Of course not. There is no alternative. The defective practice of trying to understand the world by asking other people how they see it is still the best means we have for establishing a reality we can all agree to be real. We have to do it, because it's better than nothing. It is, in fact, something. But that's *all* it is: Something. Instead of nothing.

Q: Who is your favorite singer of all time?

A: Oh, that's impossible. I'm not even sure what my answer would mean. A lot of the best singers are the bad singers, and it seems wrong to reward somebody simply for being singular. I mean, is Dylan a good singer or a bad singer? That's the essential question of all criticism, right? If I were to pick my favorite vocalist, I'd really just be selecting whatever voice best fits a specific song for a specific purpose, so it wouldn't be any reflection of how good they are in other scenarios. It would just be a manifestation of their raw talent in one situation. It would have almost nothing to do with them.

Q: Do you have a favorite guitarist?

A: No, that's even harder. That's more of a question of virtuosity versus feel. Somebody like Jeff Beck has a high level of both, I suppose, but sometimes that works to his disadvantage. Clapton and Page are both good, but I think we've taken the blues as far as they can go. The blues get in the way now. I don't see the need for any new blues.

Q: Well, whom would you classify as the greatest lyricist?

A: Jimi Hendrix.

Q: Why?

A: Highest degree of aesthetic accuracy.

Oh, the Guilt

1 It's fascinating and stupid to watch adults destroy things on purpose. It's a sensation that applies to a multitude of stimuli: monster truck shows, the dynamiting of sports arenas, race riots, Van Halen's musical legacy, eggs, governments, and temporary gods. And guitars. Always guitars. You absolutely cannot destroy enough guitars within the course of your career; Pete Townshend tried, but that still didn't stop him from getting wrongly accused of pedophilia or thinking that "Squeeze Box" was clever. People wreck guitars to illustrate how important guitars are supposed to be, aggressively reminding us that these are the machines that kill fascists. Sadly, this axiom has proven to be mostly inaccurate; according to the most recent edition of the *World Book Almanac,* the number of fascists killed in guitar-related assassinations continues to hover near zero.

"It seemed like Nirvana *had* to smash their instruments," Mudhoney front man Mark Arm supposedly said about Kurt Cobain. "It was really dumb. A roadie would remove all of the mics from the drum kit so they wouldn't get hurt. What the fuck?" Arm was talking about the '92 version of Nirvana, a group who had not yet begun recording *In Utero* but who'd already begun to lose track of how rich they were. However, the band had been preoccupied with destroying their own equipment long before their fiscal windfall: Nirvana annihilated their set at a show at Evergreen College way back in 1988.[1]

---

1. Twenty-one years after the fact, one of the guitars Cobain smashed at a 1989 show in Hoboken, New Jersey, sold on eBay for $100,000.

They would regularly wreck their own possessions while touring in support of *Bleach,* an album that (initially) sold thirty-five thousand copies and only appealed to slow-witted stoners and big-picture A & R representatives. "When we started smashing our equipment it was out of frustration, because I felt like we weren't playing very well," Cobain explained. "People expect it also. Give the kids what they want."

This is true. This is true, sort of.

2 *In Utero* was the first album actively promoted as a product I needed to buy *because* I was not going to like it. The wanting and the hating were somehow related. That's all I remember about waiting for the release of that record: Over and over again, I was informed about how much I was going to hate this album and how I would never want to play it, supposedly because it would be so challenging and corrosive that it wouldn't sound like music. It would have no relationship to melody or metal or capitalism. There seemed to be a lot of people arguing about this possibility in public (and they were always the same people), and they would all inevitably say the exact opposite of whatever they had allegedly argued in the past (in fact, it always seemed like their contradictory statements could only be found retrospectively in the denials). Following a lead in the *Chicago Tribune, Newsweek* raised doubt over whether Geffen Records would allow the album to be released as it was recorded. This was during an era when people still cared what *Newsweek* reported about rock music. The vortex of the controversy stemmed from Cobain's selection of Steve Albini as the *In Utero* producer—an abrasive, ethical man whose legacy is built on crafting sonically authentic records that normal people hate. The word that kept being connected to the project was *unlistenable*. The vocals were going to be "low in the mix" (which meant nothing to me at the time) and everything was apparently going to sound like the Jesus Lizard covering a Pixies album inside Mechagodzilla (except not good). Cobain insisted *In Utero* would sell "a quarter as much" as 1991's *Nevermind,* a non-arbitrary estimate that could be taken to mean Cobain figured 75 percent of his audience did not care about incendiary sonic experiences. "The grown-ups don't like it," he told Nirvana biographer Michael Azerrad, the assumption being that "the grown-ups" were the faceless executives at Geffen who had (somehow) hoped that Nirvana was going to bring in twelve new songs that sounded like Aerosmith's "Crazy." The accuracy of this assertion remains unclear. Later, in 1994, Cobain delivered an uncharacteristically lucid and relaxed interview to a French video outlet called *Metal Express* where he merely said, "I think the general consensus was that the album may not sell as much, so they were concerned with that. But they never, ever once put any pressure on us. They just basically told us their feelings about the record. Most people don't like the record. A lot of my friends don't even like the record." He seemed intellectually satisfied by that distaste. And while I'm sure the label would have been happier if Cobain had written a bunch of power ballads and asked Bob Rock to make them sparkle, it's not like the grown-ups hammered him in the press—David Geffen personally called *Newsweek* to complain about the accuracy of their report. My suspicion is that the label merely wanted an album that large numbers of people might like, and they did not think such a desire precluded the band from making an album that was valid.

But Nirvana (or at least Cobain, and possibly bassist Krist Novoselic) did not agree. They could not reconcile the dissonance between mass success and artistic merit; interestingly, they assumed combining mass success *with* dissonance was the only way to salvage any merit at all. And this reality requires some

very weird questions: Why did *In Utero* need to be convention-
ally "bad" in order for it to be exceptionally good? And—perhaps
more importantly—why did that fraction of badness only matter
if people knew *that the badness was intentional*?

3 Nirvana began recording *In Utero* in February of 1993, the
same month the Bureau of Alcohol, Tobacco and Firearms
raided the Mount Carmel compound in Waco, Texas, the
home of self-styled doomsday prophet David Koresh and his disci-
ples in the Branch Davidian cult. The raid resulted in the death of
six Davidians and four agents, spawning a fifty-one-day siege that
ended with over seventy people dying in a fire that was started
(or inadvertently created) by a military assault on the compound,
ordered by U.S. attorney general Janet Reno. This armed offensive against private U.S. citizens was seen as the last resort against
Koresh and his followers after the ATF had run out of alterna-
tives, one of which was bombarding the compound with high-
volume recordings of rabbits being slaughtered. I have never
listened to the sounds of dying rabbits, so I don't really know
what that sounds like; I suspect the vocals are not low in the
mix. "We will never know whether there was a better solution,"
Reno eventually testified in 1995, although one could argue that
any solution that did not involve the government burning people
alive might have been worth considering.

Koresh was a provocative public orator who could quote any
passage of the Bible verbatim, instantly connecting it with whatever subject he happened to be discussing at the time. He had a
lot of Cobainesque qualities: He had shoulder-length hair, played
guitar, had a bad childhood, often complained of stomach problems, and had troubling taste in women. (He is alleged to have

slept with a woman who was sixty-eight and a girl who was twelve, although the state of Texas never had enough evidence to press statutory rape charges. It should also be noted that neither of those females was crazy enough to let a total stranger suckle their nipples in a Wendy's.) Like Cobain, he became obsessed with guns, appealed to disenfranchised eccentrics who felt cast out by society, and played the central role in his own demise; unlike Cobain, he was dangerously self-confident and (at least a little) insane. Writing about Koresh for *The Washington Post* in the wake of the Waco disaster, neuropsychiatrist Richard Restack cited Karl Menninger's chief indicators of psychosis: "preoccupation with persecution, usually associated with grandiosity; more or less continuous erratic, disorganized excitement accompanied by irascibility; bizarre delusional ideas coupled with obvious indifference to social expectations; and pervasive convictions of evil or wickedness in self or others." These were indeed the qualities of David Koresh, and the reason we classify him as "insane" is because he cultivated those qualities himself. But those were also the core qualities of Cobain; the difference is that they were mostly manufactured by society (and were therefore real). Cobain trusted almost no one. He felt like people were viewing him as messianic; he thought they were searching for symbolism in his most minor actions. All of this was true. He was expected to entertain thousands of people in a cathartic, chaotic musical explosion and then answer inane questions about what that performance meant. He was a heavy drug user who could not comprehend why people liked his music, or even that he was under no social obligation to continue producing it. He saw "wickedness" in things that were not wicked in any significant way (the music of Pearl Jam, generally positive coverage in *Rolling Stone,* fraternity bozos buying his records at Target), mostly because the social role he was burdened to bear required that he remain inflexible about teenage ideals normal adults would never seriously consider. Koresh decided he was literally God. Cobain was told he was figuratively God. Taken on balance, which would make a man crazier?

4

It's hard to imagine any artist more shamed by his commercial success than Cobain, mostly because no one has ever made so much money by defining himself as anti-commercial. There's a famous story about how Cobain was outraged at Courtney Love's decision to purchase a Lexus automobile; he forced her to return it to the dealership so they could go back to driving a pre-*Nevermind* Volvo. After his suicide, that Lexus became wildly symbolic, a metaphor that confounds anyone who wasn't nourished by (or force-fed) punk rock idealism. I remember trying to explain this to a fellow newspaper journalist in 1998, a few days after the premiere of Nick Broomfield's documentary *Kurt and Courtney*. I have slowly come to understand why my attempt at explanation was so unfathomable.

"Who the fuck cares if she bought a Lexus?" the reporter asked me. "He could afford it. It's just a nice car. Why should his wife have to drive a shitty car?"

"But it wasn't just a nice car," I said. "It was a Lexus. A *Lexus*. That's a specific kind of nice car. Everyone knows what owning a Lexus means. To Cobain, a lavender limousine would have been preferable to a Lexus, because at least that would have been gratuitous and silly. The limousine is aware of its excess; a Lexus is at ease with it. A Lexus is a car for a serious rich person. There are no ironic Lexus drivers, or even post-ironic Lexus drivers."

"But Kurt Cobain wasn't ironically rich," the reporter responded. "He was literally rich."

"Yes, but he got rich by being the kind of person who self-identified with the underclass. Owning a Lexus made him feel hypocritical."

"Well, a rich person who self-identifies as being poor is certainly more hypocritical than a rich person whose wife drives a Lexus."

I must admit, even at the time of this conversation, I did not totally buy what I was arguing. The idea of Kurt forcing Courtney to return that car made me *like* Cobain more, but it also made him seem confused in an unknowingly solipsistic way. It's like when Oprah Winfrey creates a game show where the whole goal is to give money away to sycophantic strangers: It's an impossible act to criticize, because (of course) charity is wonderful. Yet there's something perverse about high-profile public altruism; it always feels like the individual is trying to purchase "good person" status with money they could never spend on themselves, anyway. Oprah is doing something good, but not necessarily for the motive of goodness. And the motive matters. The situation with Cobain and the Lexus was both similar and different: He was trying to retain "real person" status by *not* spending the money he was convinced he did not deserve. But that makes no sense. A "real" real person lets his dippy wife buy a Lexus when he has the GNP of Mexico in his checking account. No one in suburban Seattle was going to see Cobain behind the wheel of a used Volvo and forget that he could buy a better car; he merely looked like a millionaire trying to convince people that he still wanted to be the kind of guy who refused to buy a Lexus. Which is very, very different than simply not wanting one. Which he obviously realized, which is why he felt so awful.

In Utero sounds like what it is: Guilt Rock.

4A The most mind-bending episode in the history of the ABC program *Lost* is the finale of its third season, mostly because it's the first time the show deviated from its pattern of using the narrative device of the flashback (which provided clarity as to who individual characters truly are) and started to employ flash-forwards (which usually serve to make the motives and machinations of the plot all the more twisted). The third season ends with the story's overt protagonist and failed savior, Dr. Jack Shephard (Matthew Fox), desperate and paranoid at the airport, pleading with his love interest Kate (Evangeline Lilly) about how they must return to the mystical island from which they escaped. Jack is racked with remorse and culpability over what has transpired on the island; he has become alienated from everyone in his life, addicted to drugs, and suicidal. He cannot move beyond the singular experience that has come to define everything about his identity. And how do we know this? Well, partially because this is what he says. But also because—earlier in the same episode—Jack drives around Los Angeles aimlessly, wearing sunglasses and listening to "Scentless Apprentice" a decade after its release.

In Utero sounds like what it is: Guilt Rock.

4B In between *Nevermind* and *In Utero*, Nirvana released a B-side collection titled *Incesticide* that contained Cobain's finest first-person narrative ("Sliver"), a great Vaselines cover ("Molly's Lips"), two semi-okay originals ("Dive" and "Aneurysm"), something called "Aero Zeppelin" (which doesn't sound like Aerosmith or Led Zeppelin),

34

and a bunch of other songs I never listen to. The most interesting aspect of the record is the unorthodox liner notes, written by Cobain and printed in a thick, zine-like font. In later pressings of the record, Geffen discontinued these notes, which was both a wise and tragic decision. They open with Cobain telling a protracted story about how he was able to have an old album by the Raincoats mailed to him from London, and how this experience made him "happier than playing in front of thousands of people each night, rock-god idolization from fans, music industry plankton kissing my ass, and the millions of dollars I made last year." He goes on to talk about how his wife has been persecuted for choosing "not to function the way the white corporate man insists" and how she is preyed upon by an "army of devoted traitor women." He tells a few people to fuck off for thinking he's "naïve and stupid" (not sure who he means here), compares his band to Cheap Trick and the Knack, and poses a request to his fans: "If any of you in any way hate homosexuals, people of a different color, or women, please do this one favor for us—leave us the fuck alone! Don't come to our shows and don't buy our records."

There is, certainly, a lot of obvious weirdness to this letter, most notably (a) it's hard to imagine too many Nirvana completists self-identifying themselves as women-hating racist homophobes, regardless of how true that designation might have been, and (b) it doesn't make a whole lot of sense to tell people not to buy your album by including that message *inside* a shrink-wrapped CD. Kurt did not seem to have a very good grip on the return policies at most mainstream music outlets. But hey, it was December of 1992. Who could cast such stones? Nineteen ninety-two was the absolute apex of the PC era: The sexy goofs in Sonic Youth were writing entertaining songs about Anita Hill while lots of ponytailed boys in English 301 were trying to get laid by demanding the elimination of schoolyard dodgeball (granted, these events may not have been *directly* connected, but I think you know what I mean). Writing liner notes about how people needed to give more respect to your overbearing wife was simply what "enlightened" artists were doing at the time. Nobody should hold this against him. But there is at least one line from his manifesto that still strikes me as meaningful: "I don't feel the least bit guilty for commercially exploiting a completely exhausted Rock youth Culture because, at this point in rock history, Punk Rock (while still sacred to some) is, to me, dead and gone."

So tell me this: In the scope of your lifetime, how many people have you known who said they didn't feel guilty about something *you never accused them of doing*? And—if and when this happened—how often did the expression of their nonguilt only serve to prove the complete opposite of what they literally said?

This record came out three months before Nirvana began recording *In Utero*. This is not a coincidence.

5 How good was Nirvana? Generally, we accept that they were the best commercial rock band from a specific era of rock . . . but were they *great*? In 1998, VH1 surveyed a shitload of unnamed musicians and industry insiders and asked them to rank the one hundred greatest rock artists of all time. The top five were the Beatles, the Stones, Hendrix, Zeppelin, and Dylan. Nirvana placed forty-second, but they were the only "modern" band on the entire list ("modern" meaning that their entire body of work was produced within the same decade as the poll). If this same poll were conducted today, I suspect Nirvana would still hang in the top fifty, but they would certainly not rank any better and might even drop a few spots. The release of the 2004 Nirvana box set *With the Lights Out* somewhat validated the criticism Nirvana skeptics had been levying for years—the group simply did not produce enough material to warrant canonization.

This, however, seems wrong to me. I look at canonized rock bands the same way I look at canonized U.S. presidents. Even if America lasts ten thousand years, the list of our greatest presidents will never change; it will always include Washington and Lincoln and Jefferson.[2] They created the specific criteria for how we classify "greatness" in a president. To say a president is "great" is to argue that he (or she) is exhibiting leadership and judgment that's reminiscent of George Washington, which means that no new president can ever be as great as the person he (or she) is rewarded for emulating. Franklin Roosevelt is now included on the list of canonized presidents, but he cannot be on the same level as Lincoln; his greatness emerged from showing Lincolnian resolve during a period of twentieth-century crisis.

In the same way, the canon of rock 'n' roll is already set in concrete. Nirvana can't be as great as the Beatles or the Stones, and neither can anyone else; the greatness of any modern act is measured against what the Beatles and the Stones have come to represent as entities. But the reason I still think Nirvana warrants inclusion among the greatest bands of all time is because they established a new kind of band. They were the first rock group of the media age that was (a) regularly defined as the biggest band in the free world, while (b) using their espoused hatred of that designation as the principal means for their on-going success. Every band that becomes megasuccessful ultimately feels trapped by that adulation; the sensation of self-hatred is common among artists. What made Nirvana different was how that overt self-hatred

---

2. When Arthur Schlesinger Sr. pioneered the "presidential greatness poll" in 1948, the top five were Lincoln, Washington, Franklin D. Roosevelt, Woodrow Wilson, and Jefferson. Only Wilson appears to be seriously fading, probably because his support for the World War I–era Sedition Act now seems outrageous; in this analogy, Woodrow is like the Doors and the Sedition Act is Oliver Stone.

defined the totality of their being. It was their principal aesthetic. They always seemed like a group that was producing popular culture against their will. This notion is something they invented accidentally, so all future bands that mine this worldview can only hope to replicate what Nirvana already popularized. As such, they are in the canon (on the JV team, but still).

2A *In Utero* opens with Dave Grohl tapping his sticks together three times before the rest of the band strikes a dissonant, awkward chord, which—now, and maybe even then—seems like a band taunting all the people who wanted to like this record for nonmusical reasons. And there were *a lot* of people like that; regardless of Cobain's alleged obsession with the pop world thinking his album would be terrible, just about everyone who bought it immediately liked it (or at least claimed that they did). The mainstream reviews were positive: four stars in *Rolling Stone,* eight out of ten in *NME,* an "A" from Robert Christgau at *The Village Voice,* and a ranking of third in *Spin*'s 1993 albums of the year list (behind Liz Phair and Dr. Dre). It was platinum by Thanksgiving. More interestingly, the prerelease rumors about how difficult *In Utero* was supposedly going to sound had the opposite impact—people felt smart for enjoying a "difficult" record and were reticent to complain about its abrasive nature. A similar thing happened to Radiohead when they put out *Kid A* in 2000: The album's prerelease coverage so vociferously insisted that anti-intellectual audiences would not understand *Kid A* that people were terrified to admit being bored by *any* of it.

Within the critical circles I inhabit (and certainly within the critical circles I do not), it has become common to hear people argue that *In Utero* is superior to *Nevermind* and that the pop-metal sheen on songs like "On a Plain" and "Lithium" made the earlier effort seem craven and clinical. *Nevermind* was cool to kids who were not. This is a pretty ridiculous criticism, but—somewhat sadly—that ridiculous critic was the straw man Cobain was most concerned about. And that concern is not sad because of how it affected the album, because the album still turned out pretty good. It's sad because it illustrates Cobain's darkest, most depressing artistic weakness: He could not stop himself from caring about people who would only appreciate his work if he were a mainstream failure, just like they were. And that was never going to happen, because true genius is commercially uncontainable.

By and large, *Nevermind* and *In Utero* are not as different as Cobain had hoped: The songwriting is pretty similar ("Smells Like Teen Spirit" and "Rape Me" are essentially identical, both sounding like Boston's "More Than a Feeling"). The meaningful difference is that on *Nevermind*, the talent is top loaded and assertively present (the "talent" in this case being the melody and the drumming). On *In Utero*, the talent is still there, but it's buried under three meters of abstract credibility. All things considered, Albini actually did a wonderful job[3] of keeping the song structures as dynamic as they deserved, especially since (a) he always takes his cues from whatever the band claims to want, and (b) the band actively wanted to make a record that sounded awful to their preexisting fan base, or at least to anyone who thought the drums on *Dr. Feelgood* sounded boss. The recording process took six days. (In an interview with *Perfecting Sound Forever* author Greg Milner, Albini asserted, "If your record takes more than five or six days

---

3. For the especially serious listener, *In Utero*'s liner notes even included instructions on how to set one's equalizer for maximum effect: The bass should be at +2 and the treble should be at +5.

to make, it's bound to suck.") Compared to the theoretical raw-ness Cobain claimed to desire, *In Utero* merely sounds less reas-suring and less immediate than any musical product that's ever sold five million copies. Still, Albini became the fall guy for why *In Utero* seemed so self-absorbed with its own coolness, probably because—unlike 99 percent of record producers—he was actu-ally famous enough to publicly criticize. Gold Mountain Enter-tainment, the group that managed Nirvana, tried to blame Albini entirely.

"He is God, and he knows what's good," Danny Goldberg said sarcastically during the prerelease melee. Goldberg was the founder of Gold Mountain. "And if the artist doesn't like it, he is somehow selling out because they don't agree with his personal vision. Steve Albini takes the position that anything he thinks is good is good. He's David Koresh."

3A It is difficult for me to write objectively about Koresh. It's difficult because I cannot see any framework where he and his followers were not murdered by the U.S. government (or—in the absolute best-case scenario—driven to commit mass suicide). In 2000, I (along with two other *Akron Beacon Journal* reporters) spent a month rein-vestigating the 1970 national guard shootings on the campus of Kent State University, a chapter in American history that is uni-versally seen as a political tragedy. And it was. But I must admit that what happened at Waco seems worse. Kent State is tragic because four innocent people died while peacefully protesting an unpopular war. It was the result of underprepared national guardsmen responding extemporaneously (and poorly) in a situ-ation where they felt physically threatened. May 4, 1970, was the single worst day of a mostly horrible era. But what happened on April 19, 1993, was bigger. It wasn't four people who died—it was seventy-six. And those seventy-six were hiding in a bunker, cut off from the media, and threatening no one. There was nothing spontaneous about it; the federal government had been thinking about this for over a month. The Branch Davidians were essentially executed for being weirdos.

I realize Koresh was fucking crazy. I'm not denying it. *He was fucking crazy*. Though the child-molestation stuff has never been verified, I don't doubt it. The fact that he believed he had to sire twenty-four kids so that they could rule the world seems like a creative way for a psycho to meet girls. Anyone who reads every line of the Bible as non-metaphoric text has limited credibility. So I realize he was fucking crazy. But our government does not typically kill people for being crazy. In fact, the reason they killed Koresh was because a minority of the population in Waco thought he was sane. And I know I probably shouldn't write "They killed Koresh," because no one will ever know who started the fires inside the Waco compound (academic Kenneth Newport has written extensively about how he believes the fires were set by the Davidians themselves, since this behavior falls in line with their belief system). That will always be the central question to this debate, and it's significantly more than a minor detail. But in ways that are more meaningful, it almost doesn't matter at all.

The U.S. Treasury Department reviewed the Waco disaster in 1999. One of the reviewers was Henry Ruth Jr., who had served as a prosecutor in the Watergate trial. "At least part of the ATF's motivation," said Ruth, "even if it never rose to the surface of discussion, was to enforce the morals of our society. To enforce the psyche of right thinking by retaliating against these odd people." That, ultimately, was the crime committed by the Branch Davidians: oddness. And they weren't even that odd: One of the Davidians was Wayne Martin, one of the first African-Americans to graduate from Harvard Law School. A common misconception about the Davidians was that they were all separatist Texans, probably because the only voice ever associated with the cult is Koresh's drawl; the community was, in fact, remarkably international. Moreover, their unifying element does not strike me as unreasonable: They thought the world was ending. Which is not necessarily a ludicrous thing to believe—at some point, the world *is* going to end. I'm not sure why someone would assume that's going to happen sooner than later, but I also have no fucking idea why the government would care if a hundred Texans were betting short. The ATF claimed the Davidians were stockpiling guns, a claim that is both true and absurd; the reason the Davidians stockpiled weapons was because they made money by buying and selling them at gun shows, one of the few ways they could make money without holding jobs in the outside world. The idea that these self-interested Bible scholars were hoarding weapons in order to *attack the rest of America* only proves that no one in the government (or the media) tried to understand those people at all. Granted, some of the weapons were illegal. That's true. They did have some AK-47s in the mix. But perhaps they thought they needed a few assault rifles, because perhaps they thought the FBI would drive tanks into their homes and fire tear gas at their children while broadcasting the phrase "This is not an assault" over an intercom. Maybe they thought the government would shoot at them from helicopters and burn them alive. They were, after all, insane.

I'm not going to attempt to prove that the FBI actively ignited the fires at Waco or consciously vented the compound to accelerate the speed of the blaze. Those arguments can be better understood by watching the William Gazecki documentary *Waco: The Rules of Engagement,* the best resource for what (probably) happened that day. I'm actually going to go the other way on this; for the sake of argument, I will accept Joseph Biden's take on the

Waco holocaust: "David Koresh and the Branch Davidians set fire to themselves and committed suicide. The government did not do that." This is quite possibly false, but I will accept it. And I will accept it because if it is true, it changes nothing. If he destroyed himself and his followers, he did so because life convinced him that he was right about everything (and that this event was *supposed* to happen). He was being the person he had to be. And while that's a doomed perspective for anyone to embrace, it's certainly not uncommon: Koresh merely picked the wrong myths to believe unconditionally.

1A

A lot of my favorite bands habitually wrecked their shit. Paul Stanley smashed a guitar at the end of every Kiss concert (they were specifically modified to self-destruct on impact). Nikki Sixx of Mötley Crüe always smashed his bass, whipping it by the strap like a Jamaican farmer flogging a goat. When Guns N' Roses went on *Headbangers Ball,* they ended their segment by destroying the entire MTV set. This kind of thing was not uncommon and never unexpected. And because it happened during the 1980s, the meaning of such behavior was specific: It proved that your band was successful. Metal bands did not smash guitars as an extension of chaos or rebellion—they smashed them to prove they could easily buy more. It wasn't a punk move. It was an antipunk move. That's why I liked it.

The Clash smashed their instruments for political freedom, but also because it made for excellent photo opportunities. For years, the indie art rockers in . . . And You Will Know Us by the Trail of Dead destroyed their equipment at the conclusion of every single show, mostly to make people wonder how in the hell they were able to afford doing so without selling any records. When Nirvana was new, audiences were shocked when they destroyed their stuff—that was pretty much the only stuff they had. By the time they were touring in support of *In Utero,* people were equally shocked if they walked off the stage without Kurt diving into the drum kit like Walter Payton on third and goal. Near the end, it was widely known (or at least universally suspected) that Sub Pop founder Jonathan Poneman was mailing Cobain innumerable pawnshop guitars that he could break at his convenience, supposedly because Kurt was really attached to the Fender Mustang he had used during the recording of *In Utero.* He was still breaking things for the benefit of other people, but only things he did not want or need.

On a human-emptiness scale of one to ten (one being "emotionally complete," ten being "metaphysically devoid of feeling"), this is a fourteen.

2B "So many people would be expecting me to be writing about the last two years—about our experiences with drugs and having a new child and all the press coming down on us and the stuff like that. But I decided to just use experiences from books and other stories, without even dealing with my life." Cobain said these words in February of 1994, on a boat, smoking a cigarette. "There are little bits of my life [on *In Utero*]. Personal things. But for the most part, it's very unpersonal. Impersonal."

This is how it always goes: An artist gambles against society, using his own life as currency. He writes (in this case, songs) about his own experience, but in a manner that is malleable enough to be appreciated by the collective whole. When this is successful, the artist is validated. But if the artist grows too successful, the gears start grinding in reverse; people begin to see absolutely everything the artist says or does as a kind of public art that's open to interpretation. This makes the artist paranoid and creatively paralyzed. As a result, the artist decides to ignore his own experience completely, insisting that he's no longer the center of whatever he creates; instead, he will write about dead actresses who were sent to sanitariums or German novels about the olfactory sensation. His material will be "unpersonal." But this never works. The artist cannot stop himself from injecting his own experience into these subjects, because that is who the artist is—either you always write about yourself or you never do. It's not a process you select. So now the artist is trying not to write about himself (but doing so anyway), which means other people's interpretations of the work will now be *extra* inaccurate, because the artist has surrendered his agency. Any time you try to tell people what your work isn't supposed to mean, you only make things worse.

The lyrics from *In Utero* everyone recognized as consequential were the first two lines: "Teenage angst has paid off well / Now I'm bored and old." This was pretty straightforward and expository, and it was funny in the way Kurt was often funny (i.e., funny in a way that wouldn't make anyone laugh aloud). To me, the most compelling lines on the album are the ones that seem profound *because* they're inherently meaningless. On "Serve the Servants," Cobain moans, "I tried hard to have a father / But instead I had a dad." That complaint would seem just as valid if it were exactly reversed.[4] The album's closing lines—off "All Apologies," a song many uncreative critics would come to classify as "the real

---

4. There is, in fact, an episode of *M*A*S*H* where Major Winchester admits to Hawkeye Pierce how he privately envies the relationship Hawkeye has with his family patriarch, precisely because he only had a father while Pierce "had a dad." This may also explain why David Ogden Stiers did not become addicted to heroin.

suicide note"—are the repetition of the phrase "All in all is all we are." Here again, it's hard to see much difference if the sentiment is juxtaposed. It's kind of like how Vince Lombardi is famous for supposedly saying, "Winning isn't everything. It's the only thing." It feels insightful, but only because of what we know about the speaker—the words themselves are completely interchangeable. Sometimes I wonder if Cobain's transcendent depression was ultimately due to the combination of (a) having so many people caring about his words, despite the fact that (b) he really didn't have that much to say.

"There's nothing that hurts me more than being called a cult leader. If I'm wrong, people like me don't deserve to live." This is not Cobain speaking. This is David Koresh again, talking to ATF negotiator Jim Cavanaugh from inside the Waco compound. However, I think Kurt would have understood Koresh completely. "Look: I'm just an instrument, okay? I show them, out of a book, what God teaches. Then it's for them to decide."

But how do we tell the difference between an instrument and its sound? And—more importantly—what if we're uninterested in accepting that distinction?

6 I was down in Australia when the Waco debacle happened, and the Australians had a big contingency at the Branch Davidian compound, and I'm from Texas. So they were very curious. They were always asking me all about it: "Oh, this guy is so *weird*. This Koresh is so *weird*." And I was thinking: "Well, wait a minute: A frustrated rock musician with a messianic complex, armed to the teeth, and trying to fuck everything that moves. I don't know how to tell you this, but he sounds like every one of my friends from Austin."

— Bill Hicks, 1993

7 It is unfair to compare *In Utero* to Waco. It is unfair to compare Cobain to Koresh. I know that. They are not the same; just because two things happen at the same time doesn't mean they're connected. Babe Ruth's first home run and the premiere of *Birth of a Nation* both happened in 1915, but that doesn't dictate a relationship. If you stare long enough at anything, you will start to find similarities. The word *coincidence* exists in order to stop people from seeing meaning where none exists. So, sure, comparing Cobain and Koresh is a little unfair.

Although I'm not sure which one it's unfair to. I feel sorry for both of them. I can see it both ways. That's my problem.

5A Before he was a generational voice and flannel advocate, Cobain was a pretend roadie for the Melvins, a band who used to penalize festival audiences by crushing them with avalanches of tuneless, high-volume feedback. I experienced this at Ozzfest in 1998, inside the Akron Rubber Bowl, under a 102-degree sun; the sound of dying rabbits might not have been preferable, but it could not have been any worse. Still, it's easy to understand why someone like Cobain (or anyone else) would be drawn to the Melvins: They are more honest than virtually any band I can think of.

"I know what rock 'n' roll is about," Melvins guitarist King

Buzzo once said in an interview for Croatian television. "Most of it's a bunch of greedy, drug-taking monsters. Whoremongering drug addicts that are probably no good for anybody, generally speaking."

This is the mentality the young Cobain hoped to emulate. It was an aesthetic that ultimately proved impossible to adopt, simply because Nirvana got too big to make such contempt sincere. But Cobain still *wanted* to think this way about "mainstream rock," and he wanted his audience to think this way, too. He wanted to play music for people who had King Buzzo's worldview. He wanted to make Nirvana culture a hermetic culture; he wanted it to be insular and manageable and uncompromised. His strategy was to destroy a sector of his audience by making a record that a person who thought like King Buzzo would appreciate but a person who thought like Billy Corgan would find boring. And this was never going to work. It was never going to work because the sector of the audience Cobain hoped to alienate did not really care what *In Utero* sounded like. What Cobain failed to accept is that there is nothing that "sounds mainstream" to mainstream listeners. Music critics have an inflexible description of what mainstream music sounds like, but music consumers do not; to the consumer, the definition of *mainstream* is whatever everyone else is listening to. In 1993, "mainstream rock" was Nirvana, regardless of their style or intention. The sonic dimensions were a minor detail. Had *In Utero* sounded like *Stoner Witch,* it still would have gone multiplatinum.

Conversely, the Branch Davidians *were* able to construct a hermetic culture: In 1955, they were able to contract a smaller sect of hard-core cultists from the Seventh-Day Adventists, and Koresh splintered that population into an even smaller group of "Seven Seals" scholars during the 1980s. What Koresh did accept (but failed to fully grasp) was that there is something called *"living* mainstream," and that all mainstream livers are unyielding about what that concept is supposed to denote. Anyone who chooses to live in a manner that contradicts this concept is never going to get sympathy from anyone. This is not to say that average people will want you to die for having radical views, nor does it mean that living in a fucked-up compound with fifteen wives is merely "different" than living in a three-bedroom house in suburban Houston. But it *does* mean that if the government needlessly decides to attack your home with tanks, the rest of the world is going to assume you must have deserved it. If you openly admit that you're waiting for the world to end in fire, no one will take your side when somebody makes that happen. They will insist you should be happy about getting your wish. And maybe that's true; maybe what happened to the Branch Davidians on April 19 only proved their vision was always correct. They insulated their doomsday society enough to make it the totality of their world, and that world was, in fact, coming to an end.

So in this one way, I suppose, Cobain and Koresh are very different. The former failed at his attempt to separate his true followers from the rest of America, and he destroyed himself for that failure. The latter was destroyed by others for succeeding at the same goal.

It's fascinating and stupid to watch adults destroy things on purpose.

1B When Nirvana toured England in the fall of 1990, people told them not to demolish themselves. Melvins drummer Dale Crover was serving as the band's temporary percussionist (this was before Dave Grohl joined the band), and he made Nirvana sign a contract that barred any member of the band from jumping into his drum kit or smashing equipment onstage. Crover's argument, in short, was that destroying one's own set was fucking boring. The group complied.

When Nirvana made *In Utero* in spring of '93, everyone they knew told them not to demolish themselves. All they had to do was make a record. Any record would do. Whatever they produced would be exactly what the world wanted. But that was only true as long as nobody believed they cared; the reason America loved Nirvana was because they were convinced that Nirvana did not need their love. And that was not the case. Nirvana *did* need love, and that was Kurt Cobain's shame. So how do you make a record for people who want you to prove that you don't care how much they enjoy it? By making it sound "bad." You make it sound *a little great,* but you also make it sound a little bad. Because then everyone is happy, except for the alleged genius writing all the songs.

The world was ending. It was. It was ending in dissonance and it was ending in fire, and the vocals would be low in the mix. Besides, there is nothing worse than calling someone a cult leader. People like that don't deserve to live.

Q: Do you have any celebrity friends?

A: Not really. I've met a few semi-famous people, but nobody outstanding.

Q: Like who?

A: I met Delta Burke at a charity event. I met Jesse Eisenberg in Jamaica. I used to know a guy who looked like James Iha, but I suppose that doesn't count. I also met M. Night Shyamalan.

Q: What was that like?

A: Pretty interesting. He's actually a white guy from Canada.

Q: He is?

A: Yeah. That's the twist ending.

Tomorrow Rarely Knows

1 It was the 1990s and I was twenty, so we had arguments like this: What, ultimately, is more plausible—time travel, or the invention of a liquid metal with the capacity to think? You will not be surprised that *Terminator 2* was central to this dialogue. There were a lot of debates over this movie. The details of the narrative never made sense. Why, for example, did Edward Furlong tell Arnold that he should quip, *"Hasta la vista, baby,"* whenever he killed people? Wasn't this kid supposed to like *Use Your Illusion II* more than *Lōc-ed After Dark*? It was a problem. But not as much of a problem as the concept of humans (and machines) moving through time, even when compared to the likelihood of a pool of sentient mercury that could morph itself into a cop or a steel spike or a brick wall or an actor who would eventually disappoint watchers of *The X-Files*. My thesis at the time (and to this day) was that the impossibility of time travel is a cornerstone of reality: We cannot move forward or backward through time, even if the principles of general relativity and time dilation suggest that this is possible. Some say that time is like water that flows around us (like a stone in the river) and some say we flow *with* time (like a twig floating on the surface of the water). My sense of the world tells me otherwise. I believe that time is like a train, with men hanging out in front of the engine and off the back of the caboose; the man in front is laying down new tracks the moment before the train touches them and the man in the caboose is tearing up the rails the moment they are passed. There is no linear continuation: The past disappears, the future is unimagined, and the present is ephemeral. It cannot be traversed. So even though the prospect of liquid thinking metal is insane and idiotic, it's still more viable than time travel. I don't know if the thinking metal of tomorrow will have the potential to find employment as Linda Hamilton's assassin, but I do know that those liquid-metal killing machines will be locked into whatever moment they happen to inhabit.

It would be wonderful if someone proved me wrong about this. Wonderful. Wonderful, and sad.

2 I read H. G. Wells's *The Time Machine* in 1984. It became my favorite novel for the next two years, but solely for textual reasons: I saw no metaphorical meaning in the narrative. It was nothing except plot, because I was a fucking sixth grader. I reread *The Time Machine* as a thirty-six-year-old in 2008, and it was (predictably) a wholly different novel that now seemed fixated on archaic views about labor relations and class dynamics, narrated by a protagonist who is completely unlikable. This is a trend with much of Wells's sci-fi writing from this period; I reread *The Invisible Man* around the same time, a book that now seems maniacally preoccupied with illustrating how the invisible man was an asshole.

Part of the weirdness surrounding my reinvestigation of *The Time Machine* was because my paperback copy included a new afterword (written by Paul Youngquist) that described Wells as an egomaniac who attacked every person and entity he encountered throughout his entire lifetime, often contradicting whatever previous attack he had made only days before. He publicly responded to all perceived slights levied against him, constantly sparring with his nemesis Henry James and once sending an angry, scatological letter to George Orwell (written after Orwell had seemingly given him a compliment). He really hated Winston Churchill, too. H. G. Wells managed to write four million words of fiction and eight million words of journalism over the course of his lifetime, but modern audiences remember him exclusively for his first four sci-fi novels (and they don't remember him that fondly). He is not a canonical writer and maybe not even a great one. However, his influence remains massive. Like the tone of Keith Richards's guitar or Snidely Whiplash's mustache, Wells galvanized a universal cliché—and that is just about the rarest thing any artist can do.

The cliché that Wells popularized was not the fictional notion of time travel, because that had been around since the sixteenth century (the oldest instance is probably a 1733 Irish novel by Samuel Madden called *Memoirs of the Twentieth Century*). Mark Twain reversed the premise in 1889's *A Connecticut Yankee in King Arthur's Court*. There's even an 1892 novel called *Golf in the Year 2000* that (somewhat incredibly) predicts the advent of televised sports. But in all of those examples, time travel just sort of happens inexplicably—a person exists in one moment, and then they're transposed to another. The meaningful cliché Wells introduced was *the machine,* and that changed everything. Prior to the advent of Wells's imaginary instrument, traveling through time generally meant the central character was *lost* in time, which wasn't dramatically different from being lost geographically. But a machine gave the protagonist agency. The time traveler was now moving forward or backward on purpose; consequently, the time traveler now needed a motive for doing so. And that question, I suspect, is the core reason why narratives about time travel are almost always interesting, no matter how often the same basic story is retold and repackaged: If time travel *was* possible, why would we want to do it?

Now, I will concede that there's an inherent goofballedness

in debating the ethics of an action that is impossible. It probably isn't that different than trying to figure out if leprechauns have high cholesterol. But all philosophical questions are ultimately like this—by necessity, they deal with hypotheticals that are unfeasible. Real-world problems are inevitably too unique and too situational; people will always see any real-world problem through the prism of their own personal experience. The only massive ideas everyone can discuss rationally are big ideas that don't specifically apply to anyone, which is why a debate over the ethics of time travel is worthwhile: No one has any personal investment whatsoever. It's *only* theoretical. Which means no one has any reason to lie.

2A

Fictionalized motives for time travel generally operate like this: Characters go back in time to fix a mistake or change the conditions of the present (this is like *Back to the Future*). Characters go forward in time for personal gain (this is like the gambling subplot[1] of *Back to the*

---

1. This subplot refers to the actions of a character named Biff (Thomas F. Wilson) who steals a sports almanac from the future in order to gamble on predetermined sporting events in the present. There's a popular urban legend about this plot point involving the Florida Marlins baseball team: In the film, Biff supposedly bets on a Florida baseball team to win the World Series in 1997, which actually happened. The amazing part is that *Back to the Future Part II* was released in 1989, four years before the Florida Marlins even had a major league franchise. Unfortunately, this legend is completely false. The reference in the movie is actually a joke about the futility of the Chicago Cubs that somehow got intertwined with another reference to a (fictional) MLB opponent from Miami whose logo was a gator. I realize that by mentioning the inaccuracy of this urban legend, I will probably just perpetuate its erroneous existence. But that's generally how urban legends work.

Future Part II). Jack the Ripper used H. G. Wells's time machine to kill citizens of the seventies in *Time After Time,* but this was an isolated (and poorly acted) rampage. Obviously, there is always the issue of scientific inquiry with any movement through time, but that motive matters less; if a time traveler's purpose is simply to learn things that are unknown, it doesn't make moving through time any different than exploring Skull Island or going to Mars. My interest is in the explicit benefits of being transported to a different moment in existence—what that would mean morally and how the traveler's goals (whatever they may be) could be implemented successfully.

Here's a question I like to ask people when I'm ⅝ drunk: Let's say you had the ability to make a very brief phone call into your own past. You are (somehow) given the opportunity to phone yourself as a teenager; in short, you will be able to communicate with the fifteen-year-old version of you. However, you will only get to talk to your former self *for fifteen seconds.* As such, there's no way you will be able to explain who you are, where or when you're calling from, or what any of this lunacy is supposed to signify. You will only be able to give the younger version of yourself a fleeting, abstract message of unclear origin.

What would you say to yourself during these fifteen seconds?

From a sociological standpoint, what I find most interesting about this query is the way it inevitably splits between gender lines: Women usually advise themselves *not* to do something they now regret (i.e., "Don't sleep with Corey McDonald, no matter how much he pressures you"), while men almost always instruct themselves to do something they *failed* to attempt (i.e., "Punch Corey McDonald in the face, you gutless coward"). But from a more practical standpoint, the thing I've come to realize is that virtually no one has any idea how to utilize such an opportunity, even if it were possible. If you can't directly explain that you're talking from the future, any prescient message becomes worthless. All advice comes across like a drunk dialer reading a fortune cookie. One person answered my question by claiming he would tell the 1985 incarnation of himself to "Invest in Google." That sounds smart, but I can't imagine a phrase that would have been more useless to me as a teenager in 1985. I would have spent the entire evening wondering how it would be possible to invest money into the number 1 with one hundred zeros behind it.

It doesn't matter what you can do if you don't know why you're doing it.

2B I've now typed fifteen hundred words about time travel, which means I've reached the point where everything becomes a problem for everybody. This is the point where we need to address the philosophical dilemmas embedded in any casual discussions about time travel, real or imagined. And there are a lot of them. And I don't understand about 64 percent of them. And the 36 percent I do understand are pretty elementary to everyone, including the substantial chunk of consumers who are very high and watching Anna Faris movies while they read this. But here we go! I will start with the most unavoidable eight:

1. **If you change any detail about the past, you might accidentally destroy everything in present-day existence.** This is why every movie about time travel makes a big, obvious point about not bringing anything from the present back in time, often illustrated by forcing the fictionalized time traveler to travel nude. If you went back to 60,000 BC with a tool box and absentmindedly left the vise grip behind,

it's entirely possible that the world would technologically advance at an exponential rate and destroy itself by the sixteenth century.[2] Or so I'm told.

2. **If you went back in time to accomplish a specific goal (and you succeeded at this goal), there would be no reason for you to have traveled back in time in the first place.** Let's say you built a time machine in order to murder the proverbial "Baby Hitler" in 1889. Committing that murder would mean the Holocaust never happened. And that would mean you'd have no motive for going back in time in the first place, because the tyrannical Adolf Hitler—the one you despise—would not exist. In other words, any goal achieved through time travel would eliminate the necessity for the traveler to travel. In his fictional (and pathologically grotesque) oral history *Rant*, author Chuck Palahniuk refers to this impasse as the Godfather Paradox: "The idea that if one could travel backward in time, one could kill one's own ancestor, eliminating the possibility said time traveler would ever be born—and thus could never have lived to travel back and commit the murder." The solution to this paradox (according to Palahniuk) is the theory of splintered alternative realities, where all possible trajectories happen autonomously and simultaneously (sort of how Richard Linklater describes *The Wizard of Oz* to an uninterested cab driver in the opening sequence of *Slacker*). However, this solution is actually more insane than the original problem. The only modern narrative that handles the conundrum semi-successfully is Richard Kelly's *Donnie Darko,* where schizophrenic heartthrob Jake Gyllenhaal uses a portal to move back in time twelve days, thereby allowing himself to die in an accident

---

2. For whatever the reason, I've always assumed vise grips would be extremely liberating for Neanderthals.

he had previously avoided. By removing himself from the equation, he never meets his new girlfriend, which keeps her from dying in a car accident that was his fault. More important, his decision to die early stops his adolescence from becoming symbolized by the music of Tears for Fears.

3. **A loop in time eliminates the origin of things that already exist.** This is something called "the Bootstrap Paradox" (in reference to the Robert Heinlein story "By His Bootstraps"). It's probably best described by David Toomey, the author of a book called *The New Time Travelers* (a principal influence on season five of *Lost*). Toomey uses *Hamlet* as an example: Let's suppose Toomey finds a copy of *Hamlet* in a used-book store, builds a time machine, travels back to 1601, and gives the book to William Shakespeare. Shakespeare then copies the play in his own handwriting and claims he made it up. It's recopied and republished countless times for hundreds of years, eventually ending up in the bookstore where Toomey shops. So who wrote the play? Shakespeare didn't. Another example occurs near the end of *Back to the Future*: Michael J. Fox performs "Johnny B. Goode" at the school dance and the tune is transmitted over the telephone to Chuck Berry[3] (who presumably stole it). In this reality,

---

3. Semi-unrelated (but semi-interesting) footnote to this paradox: Before Fox plays "Johnny B. Goode" at the high school dance, he tells his audience, "This is an oldie . . . well, this is an oldie from where I come from." Chuck Berry recorded "Johnny B. Goode" in 1958. *Back to the Future* was made in 1985, so the gap is twenty-seven years. I'm writing this essay in 2009, which means the gap between 1985 and today is twenty-four years. That's almost the same amount of time. Yet nobody would ever refer to *Back to the Future* as an "oldie," even if he or she were born in the 1990s. What seems to be happening is a dramatic increase in cultural memory: As culture accelerates, the distance between historical events feels smaller. The gap between 2010 and 2000 will seem far smaller than the gap between 1980 and 1970, which already seemed far smaller than the gap between 1950 and 1940. This, I suppose, is society's own version of time travel (assuming the trend continues for eternity).

where does the song come from? Who deserves the song-writing royalties?

4. **You'd possibly kill everybody by sneezing.** Depending on how far you went back in time, there would be a significant risk of infecting the entire worldwide population with an illness that mankind has spent the last few centuries building immunity against. Unless, of course, you happened to contract smallpox immediately upon arrival—then *you'd* die.

5. **You already exist in the recent past.** This is the most glaring problem and the one everybody intuitively understands—if you went back to yesterday, you would still be there, standing next to yourself. The consequence of this existential condition is both straightforward and unexplainable. Moreover . . .

6. **Before you attempted to travel back in time, you'd already know if it worked.** Using the example from problem number 5, imagine that you built a time machine on Thursday. You decide to use the machine on Saturday in order to travel back to Friday afternoon. If this worked, you would already see yourself on Friday. But what would then happen if you and the Future You destroyed your time machine on Friday night? How would the Future You be around to assist with the destroying?

7. **Unless all of time is happening simultaneously within multiple realities, memories and artifacts would mysteriously change.** The members of Steely Dan (Donald Fagen and Walter Becker) met at Bard College in 1967, when Fagen overheard Becker playing guitar in a café. This meeting has been recounted many times in interviews, and the fact that they were both at Bard College (located in Annandale-on-Hudson) is central to songs like "My Old School," which was recorded in 1973. But what if Fagen built a time machine in 1980 and went back to find Becker in 1966, when he was still

a high school student in Manhattan? What would happen to their shared personal memories of that first meeting in Annandale? And if they had both immediately moved to Los Angeles upon Becker's graduation, how could the song "My Old School" exist (and what would it be about)?

8. **The past has happened, and it can only happen *the way it happened*.** This, I suppose, is debatable. But not by Bruce Willis. In Terry Gilliam's *Twelve Monkeys,* Willis goes back in time to confront an insane Brad Pitt before Pitt releases a virus that's destined to kill five billion people and drive the rest of society into hiding (as it turns out, Pitt is merely trying to release a bunch of giraffes from the Philadelphia Zoo, which is only slightly more confusing than the presence of Madeleine Stowe in this movie). What's distinctive about *Twelve Monkeys* is that the reason Willis is sent back in time is not to stop this catastrophe from happening, but merely to locate a primitive version of the virus so that scientists can combat the existing problem in the distant future (where the remnants of mankind have been to forced to take refuge underground). Willis can travel through time, but he can't change anything or save anyone. "How can I save you?" he rhetorically asks the white-clad dolts who question his sudden appearance in the year 1990. "This already happened. No one can save you." *Twelve Monkeys* makes a lot of references to the "Cassandra complex" (named for a Greek myth about a young woman's inability to convince others that her prophetic warnings are accurate), but it's mostly about predestination—in *Twelve Monkeys,* the assumption is that anyone who travels into the past will do exactly what history dictates. Nothing can be altered. What this implies is that everything about life (including the unforeseen future) is concrete and predetermined. There is no free will. So if you've seen *Twelve Monkeys* more than twice, you're probably a Calvinist.

These are just a handful of the (nonscientific) problems with going backward in time. As far as I can tell, there really aren't any causality problems with going forward in time—in terms of risk, jumping to the year 2077 isn't that different than moving to suburban Bangladesh or hiding in your basement for five decades. Time would still move forward on its regular trajectory, no differently than if you were temporarily (or permanently) dead. Your participation in life doesn't matter to time. This is part of the reason that futurists tend to believe traveling forward in time is more plausible than the alternative—it involves fewer problems. But regardless of the direction you move, the *central* problem is still there: Why do it? What's the *best* reason for exploding the parameters of reality?

With the possible exception of eating a dinosaur, I don't think there is one.

3 "Even back when I was writing really bad short stories in college," a (then) thirty-four-year-old Shane Carruth said in an interview with himself, "I always thought the time machine is the device that's missed most. Without even saying it out loud, that's the thing people want the most: The ability to take whatever it is that went wrong and fix it."

Carruth is the writer, director, producer, and costar of the 2004 independent film *Primer,* the finest movie about time travel I've ever seen. The reason *Primer* is the best (despite its scant seventy-eight-minute run time and $7,000 budget) is because it's the most realistic—which, I will grant, is a peculiar reason for advocating a piece of science fiction. But the plausibility of *Primer* is why it's so memorable. It's not that the time machine in *Primer* seems more authentic; it's that the time travelers themselves seem more believable. They talk and act (and *think*) like the kind of people who might accidentally figure out how to move through time, which is why it's the best depiction we have of the ethical quandaries that would emerge from such a discovery.

Here's the basic outline of *Primer*: It opens with four identically dressed computer engineers sitting around a table in a nondescript American community (*Primer* was shot around Dallas, but the setting is like the world of Neil LaBute's *In the Company of Men*—it's a city without character that could literally be anywhere). They speak a dense, clipped version of English that is filled with technical jargon; it's mostly indecipherable, but that somehow makes it better. They wear ties and white shirts all the time (even when they're removing a catalytic converter from a car to steal the palladium), and they have no interests outside of superconductivity and NCAA basketball. The two brightest engineers—Abe (David Sullivan) and Aaron (Carruth)—eventually realize they have assembled a box that can move objects backward through a thirteen-hundred-minute loop in time. Without telling anyone else, they build two larger versions of the (staunchly unglamorous) box that can transport them to the previous day.[4] Their initial motive is solely financial—they go back a day, drive to the local library, and buy stocks over the Internet that they know will increase in value over the next twenty-four hours. They try to do nothing else of consequence (at least at first). They just sit in a hotel room and wait. "I tried to isolate myself," Abe says when

---

4. This is too difficult to explain in a footnote, but one of Carruth's strengths as a fake science writer is how he deals with the *geography* of time travel, an issue most writers never even consider. Here, in short, is the problem: If you could instantly travel one hour back in time, you would (theoretically) rematerialize in the exact same place from which you left. That's how the machine works in the original *Time Machine*. However, the world would have rotated 15 degrees during that missing hour, so you would actually rematerialize in a totally different spot on the globe. *Primer* manages to work around this problem, although I honestly don't understand the solution as much as I see the dilemma.

describing his first journey into the past. "I closed the windows, I unplugged everything—the phone, the TV and clock radio. I didn't want to take the chance of seeing someone I knew, or of seeing something on the news . . . I mean, if we're dealing with causality, and I don't even know for sure . . . I took myself out of the equation."

If this sounds simple, I can assure you that it is not. *Primer* is hopelessly confusing and grows more and more byzantine as it unravels (I've watched it seven or eight times and I still don't know what happened). Characters begin to secretly use the time machine for personal reasons and they begin multiplying themselves across time. But because these symmetrical iterations are (inevitably) copies of other copies, the system starts to hemorrhage—Abe and Aaron find themselves bleeding from their ears and struggling with handwriting. When confusing events start to happen in the present, they can't tell if those events are the manifestations of decisions one of them will eventually make in the future. At one point, no one (not Abe, Aaron, or even the viewer) is able to understand what's going on. The story does not end in a clear disaster, but with a hazy, open-ended scenario that might be worse.

What's significant about the two dudes in *Primer* is how they initially disregard the ethical questions surrounding time travel; as pure scientists, they only consider the practical obstacles of the endeavor. Even when they decide to go back and change the past of another person, their only concern is how this can still work within the framework they're manipulating. They're geniuses, but they're ethical Helen Kellers. When they're traveling back for financial purposes, they discount their personal role in the success of the stocks they trade; since stocks increase in value whenever people buy them, they are retroactively inflating the value of whatever commodities they select (not by much, but enough to alter the future). When Abe and Aaron start traveling back in time to change their own pasts, they attempt to stoically ignore the horrifying reality they've created: Their sense of self—their very *definition* of self—is suddenly irrelevant. If you go back in time today and meet the person who will become you tomorrow, which of those two people is actually you? The short answer is, "Both." But once you realize that the short answer is "Both," the long answer becomes "Neither." If you exist in two places, you don't exist at all.

According to the director, *Primer* is a movie about the relationship between risk and trust. This is true. But it also makes a concrete point about the potential purpose of time travel—it's too important to use only for money, but too dangerous to use for anything else.

1A

I used to have a fantasy about reliving my entire life with my present-day mind. I once thought this fantasy was unique to me, but it turns out that this is very common; many people enjoy imagining what it would be like to reinhabit their past with the knowledge they've acquired through experience. I imagine the bizarre things I would have said to teachers in junior high. I think about women I would have pursued and stories I could have written better and about how interesting it would have been to be a genius four-year-old. At its nucleus, this is a fantasy about never having to learn anything. The defining line from Frank Herbert's *Dune* argues that the mystery of life "is not a question to be answered but a reality to be experienced." My fantasy offers the opposite. Nothing would be experienced. Nothing would feel new or unknown or jarring. It's a fantasy for people who want to solve life's mysteries without having to do the work.

I am one of those people.

The desire to move through time is electrifying and rational, but it's a desire of weakness. The real reason I want to travel through time is because I'm a defeatist person. The cynical egomaniac in Wells's original novel leaves the present because he has contempt for the humanity of his present world, but he never considers changing anything about his own role in that life (which would obviously be easier). Instead, he elects to bolt eight hundred thousand years into the future, blindly hoping that things will have improved for him. It's a bad plan. Charlton Heston's character in *Planet of the Apes*[5] tries something similar; he hates mankind, so he volunteers to explore space, only to crash back on a postapocalyptic earth where poorly dressed orangutans employ Robert's Rules of Order. This is a consistent theme in stories about traveling to the future: Things are always worse when you get there. And I suspect this is because the kind of writer who's intrigued by the notion of moving forward in time can't see beyond their own pessimism about being alive. People who want to travel through time are both (a) unhappy and (b) unwilling to compromise anything about who they are. They would rather change every element of society *except* themselves.

This is how I feel.

This is also why my long-standing desire to build a time machine is not just hopeless but devoid of merit. It has nothing to do with time. I don't think it ever does (for me, H. G. Wells, Shane Carruth, or anyone else). It takes a flexible mind to imagine how time travel might work, but only an inflexible spirit would actually want to do it. It's the desire of the depressed and lazy.

---

5. I realize *Planet of the Apes* isn't technically about time travel. Time moves at its normal rate while the humans are in suspended animation. But for the purposes of the fictional people involved, there is no difference: They leave from and return to the same geographic country. The only difference is the calendar.

On side two of the Beach Boys' *Pet Sounds,* Brian Wilson laments that he "just wasn't made for these times" ("these times" being 1966). He probably wasn't. But he also didn't want to be. I assume Wilson would have preferred dealing with the possibility of thinking liquid metal before he would accept the invisible, nonnegotiable shackles of the present tense. Which—sadly, and quite fortunately—is the only tense any of us will ever have.

Q: Are you surprised you fell so low in the draft?

A: Surprised? No. I'm surprised I was drafted at all.

Q: Do you feel like the negative pre-draft media coverage caused your stock to fall?

A: Absolutely. But I accept some of the blame for that. I mean, I came to the combine a little out of shape, and then I held a gun to another man's head on live television. I'm sure that didn't give scouts a lot of confidence.

What We Talk About
When We Talk About
Ralph Sampson

1 Inside the more unreasonable sectors of my brain's right hemisphere, Ralph Sampson is the best basketball player who ever lived. I am able to repress this notion, but the sensation remains. He had so much of everything: so much height, so much coordination, so much evolution of species. I would watch him play on Saturday afternoons in 1982; he never scored much and rebounded with indifference, yet he still looked better than any man who'd ever tried to perfect the sport he so casually toyed with. I was ten years old. Al McGuire was announcing those games for NBC, habitually comparing Sampson to an aircraft carrier. It was a valid analogy. But it wasn't Sampson's seven-foot-four frame that made him so astonishing; it was more that he seemed to have nothing in common with a man who was seven-foot-four. He was sinewy and deft and mobile; he played a finesse game, and I was too young to realize that this was a weakness. Sampson was better designed for basketball than any human who has ever lived: He possessed the maximum amount of dexterity within the longest possible skeletal structure.[1] In my

---

1. He also was blessed with good genes: His six-foot-eleven-inch son, Ralph III, is already having a nice career at the University of Minnesota.

imagination, he still seems unstoppable—an elegant extension of Darwinian engineering. He is more unstoppable than Michael Jordan; he's Jordanesque, but constructed like Jabbar. He's Jordan with a skyhook. But this is only in the abstract. Outside of abstraction, Ralph Sampson was the worst thing an athlete can be: Ralph Sampson was a bust. And though I know why that happened and I know why it's true, I struggle with what that means. It seems to exemplify the saddest thing about sports and culture, which means it's pretty much the saddest thing about life that doesn't involve death or secrets.

2 Here's the first thing we must establish and never forget: Ralph Sampson was better at his chosen craft than you are at whatever it is you pretend to do. In 1985, he made the NBA's all-NBA second team, which means—at worst—he was the tenth-best professional basketball player in America. Now, in 1985 Arvydas Sabonis was a healthy twenty-year-old playing center for the Soviet Union national team, and he was better than Sampson. Oscar Schmidt, a one-dimensional swingman from Brazil (and probably the best basketball player never to play in the NBA), was arguably in this class as well in '85, and Moses Malone (and maybe even Dominique Wilkins) was just as deserving of all-star status as Sampson at this point in history. But even if all this is accurate, Sampson was still the fourteenth-best individual in a world where fifty million kids regularly played basketball, living on a planet populated by four billion people. He was the NCAA player of the year three times, played in four NBA all-star games, and earned $17 million in less than a decade. His separation from the rest of society is beyond vast. But we are not working within the parameters of reality; we are working within the parameters of televised sport. And that's a critical difference. It essentially makes Ralph Sampson a tall, emotive, representational nonhuman slave.

And within these parameters, four thousand rebounds don't mean shit.

2A This is an essay about sports and life, and it will continue to be about sports after the following 382-word section. But before I return to the topic of Ralph Sampson, I need to mention Britney Spears.

Some might bristle at my use of the word *slave* in the previous section, partially because Sampson is black but mostly because that word exists in the same paragraph as "earned $17 million in less than a decade." Those are not slave wages. But Ralph was a different kind of slave; he was a cultural slave, and cultural slaves are compensated with colossal sacks of cash. But they're still paid less than they deserve, despite the fact that they produce nothing of consequence.

I do not know how much money Britney Spears earned last year. However, I do know that it's not enough for me to want her life, were I given the option to have it. Every day, random people use Britney's existence as currency; they talk about her public failures and her lack of talent as a way to fill the emptiness of their own normalcy. She—along with Lindsay Lohan and Paris Hilton and all those androids from *The Hills*—are the unifying entities within this meta era. In a splintered society, they are the means through which people devoid of creativity communicate with each other. They allow Americans to understand who they are and who they are not; they allow Americans to unilaterally agree on something they never needed to consciously consider. A person like Britney Spears surrenders her privacy and her integrity and the rights to her own persona, and in exchange we give her huge sums of money. But she still doesn't earn a fraction of what she warrants in a free-trade cultural economy. If Britney Spears were paid $1 every time a self-loathing stranger used her as a surrogate for his own failure, she would outearn Warren Buffett in three months. This is why entertainers (and athletes) make so much revenue but are still wildly underpaid: We use them for things that are worth more than money. It's a new kind of dehumanizing slavery—not as awful as the literal variety, but dehumanizing nonetheless. And this is what happened to Ralph Sampson, though I suspect he would disagree.

3 "I think, first of all, he was the victim of overstatement." This is Bill Fitch talking about Sampson in 1989, when the twenty-nine-year-old Ralph was having both his knees drained of fluid on a regular basis. Fitch was Sampson's coach when he was a Houston Rocket. They had gone to the NBA championship just three years before Fitch delivered this dark diagnosis; three years after Fitch's statement was printed, Sampson's career would end uneventfully in Spain. "He never had that one thing to go to in the pro game," Fitch continued. "He never had that one shot. Two weeks, three weeks after he came to us, you could see that. We had Elvin Hayes, who was an aging superstar. Elvin had that one shot. That turnaround. Ralph never had anything. People would say he wasn't trying, but that wasn't the case. If anything, he tried too hard. He just didn't have the bullets for the gun. And he needed a tank after what everyone had predicted for him."[2]

---

2. This quote, along with most that appear in this piece, originally ran in *Sports Illustrated,* the most consistent chronicler of athletes who disappoint us.

This, somehow, became the post-1985, pre-1990 consensus as to why Sampson was such a letdown: Suddenly, everyone seemed to agree that he had never been that good to begin with. Even McGuire, the TV analyst who advanced the "Sampson as aircraft carrier" mythos more than anyone, now viewed him differently. "He never got the wrinkles, the rub for the pro game," McGuire told journalist Leigh Montville. "He came from a good home in a place [Harrisonburg, Virginia] that is one of those towns where all the kids drive their cars around the square on Friday night beeping their horns. He went to Virginia, a gentleman's school. He never had to get tough. Plus, he never developed physically. He never developed those pop-out muscles. The pro game, if you're svelte, they push you around."

Similar attacks on Sampson's svelteness were less straightforward but still based around class and masculinity: He was sometimes criticized for wearing knit sweaters. In that aforementioned '86 championship series against a superior Celtics squad, Sampson made the mistake of throwing a punch at Boston guard Jerry Sichting, an act of toughness that made him look like a pussy. What kind of giant hits a six-foot-one white guy? When the Rockets landed Hakeem Olajuwon in the '84 draft, the strategy was to play the seven-foot Olajuwon and the seven-four Sampson at the same time, and it worked almost immediately—but it required the much taller Sampson to play power forward, often facing the basket from the wing. This seemed to validate everything critics had always disliked about Ralph. He was the professional incarnation of that oversized, mustachioed kid in middle school who won't join the team unless he gets to play point guard. Sampson didn't initiate contact. He aspired to elegance. It was like he refused to be the person he actually was. Which is curious, because that *is* the person Ralph Sampson actually was: He was a good, tall, soft player. People thought he was this amazing seven-four stud with the skills of someone six foot eight, but it was really the opposite—

he was just a better-than-average six-foot-eight small forward, trapped in a body that offered eight more inches than necessary. "I really would like to be a seven-foot-four guard," Sampson said as a college freshman, seemingly unaware that this would sound both arrogant and wrongheaded to everyone who understood basketball. He never claimed to be dominant. He never even implied that he wanted to dominate. That was what everybody else suggested. He was nothing more than a good pro with a world-class body. So this is the first part of the two-pronged explanation as to why Ralph Sampson busted: It was because *other people* were wrong about him. And this happens to athletes (and nonathletes) all the time. But it's the second part that's more complicated; the second part has to do with why certain minor athletic failures are totally unacceptable, even while other athletic failures are mildly desirable.

3A In the unwritten Wikipedia of world basketball history, Benny Anders is little more than a footnote. On his first day as a Houston Cougar freshman in 1982, Anders showed up at the gym wearing a T-shirt that said OUTLAW. He claimed this was his high school nickname in Louisiana, and he said he got it because he killed people. His era with the Cougars would end less than four years later, partially because he brought a handgun to practice. But I don't think Benny Anders ever shot anybody. He did not become a stick-up artist or a Mossad assassin or a Central American terrorist. He did not join the CIA, or even the CBA. He was not that type of outlaw. In fact, as of 2009, no one knows where Benny Anders is, what he's doing, or if he's alive. He was that type of outlaw.

It's virtually impossible to find clips of Benny Anders on You-

Tube, but that does not matter. They continue to exist in my mind. He was the greatest in-game dunker I've ever seen. Unlike his more heralded teammate Clyde Drexler, Anders did not hang poetically in midair; his dunks were fast and violent. Everything would happen at once: He'd cuff the rock, splay his legs, arch the spine, and *thwack*. It was a midair shark attack. His greatest jam happened against Louisville in the '83 Final Four, a contest many claim was the greatest dunking exhibition in NCAA history. Trailing the Cards by four points in the second half, the six-five sophomore stole the ball in the open court and crucified Charles Jones at the rim. It almost appeared as if Anders let Jones get into defensive position *on purpose* in order to humiliate him more effectively. He was that type of outlaw.

Houston proceeded to crush Louisville and face North Carolina State in the championship. That game was played closer to the ground and the undermatched Wolfpack pulled the upset. Anders was involved in the title game's final sequence—he tipped the ball away from NC State guard Dereck Whittenburg, who recovered the loose ball on one bounce and heaved a thirty-six-foot prayer that was memorably answered by teammate Lorenzo Charles. That April weekend was the pinnacle of Anders's career: By the time Houston returned to the NCAA finals twelve months later, he had been relegated to the deep end of the bench. Anders's main contribution in '84 was more aesthetic than athletic—Anders arrived in Seattle wearing a tuxedo with a pink bow tie. For reasons that remain unclear, a rival fan from Kentucky named John Gambill held up signs that read BENNY ANDERS FOR PRESIDENT. After Houston lost to Georgetown in Monday's final, Anders found Gambill and partied with him all night, driving around Seattle in a Jaguar. He was that type of outlaw.

So what does one make of this version of nostalgia? Anders was, by all technical accounts, a failure. He was devoid of humility (on a team filled with undisciplined personalities, he was the only player head coach Guy Lewis had to kick off the team). He started only one game in three years and never averaged more than six points a night. His espoused philosophy defined the context of no context: "Take it to the rack and stick it." For Benny, basketball never became more complicated than that: He came, he jammed, and he was gone. And now he's *really* gone. Benny Anders is off the grid. He is a Jheri-curled apparition. In a Final Four anniversary article for ESPN, writer Robert Weintraub reported various rumors about Anders's current whereabouts. Some claimed he was last seen in South America. Others said Chicago. Still others insisted he continues to play ball on the streets of Louisiana, eating glass as a three-hundred-pound not-so-small forward. Whatever he is, the specifics don't matter. Benny Anders is not coming back. But he doesn't need to. When you have unlimited potential and *an unwillingness to pursue that potential,* greatness doesn't need to be achieved; as fans, we only require glimpses of a theoretical reality that's more interesting than the one we're in.

On balance, Benny Anders's destruction of Charles Jones isn't better than the worst year of Ralph Sampson's life. It was one play in one game. But that dunk is enough to warrant a positive recollection twenty-five years after the fact. It does not matter that Anders accomplished nothing else. He will live forever, if only for all the things he never did. Ask any basketball fan who remembers who Benny Anders was, and he will almost certainly say great things about his ability. He is retrospectively beloved, expressly because he failed in totality. He's an example of blown potential, but people remain envious of the man he never became. He's like Syd Barrett after *The Madcap Laughs.* And that is very different than what happened to Sampson; he's an example of blown potential that makes average people feel better about themselves. He's like Mickey Rourke before *The Wrestler.*

3B So here is the question: Why did people feel good about Sampson's bust? Why was being "merely" a four-time all-star such a pleasurable catastrophe to fans who had no investment in his career? It doesn't make any sense—he wasn't a jerk, he wasn't terrible, and there was no social upside to his relative failures. It's not like people got a tax break when Sampson retired. Trying to understand why unrelated fans get personal joy from an athlete's brilliance is confusing enough, but at least it *feels* like a reasonable reaction to have; one could argue that it's akin to why people enjoy looking at beautiful art. But trying to understand why those same consumers might be equally happy about the opposite situation seems unfathomable and cruel; it's akin to looking at a bad painting and feeling happy that the artist failed. Although I suppose there are people who do that, too.

Whenever a high-profile player busts—Ryan Leaf,[3] Anna Kournikova,[4] Chris Washburn,[5] Brien Taylor,[6] whoever—there inevitably comes the question of Asking for It: Did the player who busted *deserve* to bust? Did they consciously put themselves in a position where a reasonable person might be justified in enjoying their collapse? The easiest example of Asking for It is Tony Man-

---

3. Before the 1998 NFL draft, it was common to get into arguments over who was going to be a better pro quarterback—Peyton Manning or Ryan Leaf. The latter ended his career with fourteen touchdowns and thirty-six interceptions.

4. Despite being among the five or ten most famous female tennis players of all time, this ultra-rich Russian sex cat never won a major singles tournament.

5. A cocaine casualty drafted third overall by the Golden State Warriors in 1986, the six-eleven Washburn averaged 3.1 points and 2.4 rebounds in the NBA.

6. Drafted first overall by the New York Yankees at nineteen and signed for (a then outrageous) $1.55 million, Taylor injured his pitching arm in a street brawl and never made it to the major league level.

darich, an offensive tackle for the Michigan State Spartans who openly begged people to despise him.

Before the 1989 NFL draft, Mandarich was considered the greatest offensive line prospect in the history of the college game. "In the 20 years I've been in this business," New York Giants player personnel director Tom Boisture told writer Peter King, "he's the best college football player I've ever seen." At a then-unthinkable 315 pounds, Mandarich ran the forty in 4.65 seconds. "Maybe the fastest offensive tackle in history," San Diego Chargers GM Steve Ortmayer said in the same article, "and just maybe the best." He was selected by the Green Bay Packers ahead of Barry Sanders, a decision that historians often use as an example of how comically wrong football scouts can be; in truth, not picking Mandarich would have been a wholly irrational act. There was not one football person in America who did not believe Mandarich would crush people in the NFL. They were all wrong. We were all wrong. As it turns out, Mandarich was a steroid creation and a technically inept pass blocker. He was an embarrassment with the Packers; defensive opponents openly mocked him. Everyone questioned his attitude. He would eventually become a serviceable lineman for the Indianapolis Colts, but even that was somewhat humiliating in light of how Mandarich had sold himself a decade before.

"I don't want to be a fat fuck like 90 percent of the NFL," he said before the Packers had even selected him. "I want to be a football player who looks like a body builder. I want to look like a defensive end. For self-esteem. If I look like a slob, I'll play like one . . . why can't I do what Arnold [Schwarzenegger] did? Bodybuilding. Movies. All of it. I want to be *Cyborg III*." These quotes come from an iconic 1989 *Sports Illustrated* issue[7] showcasing

---

7. Twenty years later, Mandarich gave another interview to *SI* where he apologized for all of his 1989 lies. It should be noted he was also promoting a book at the time.

Mandarich on the cover, shirtless and balding. Elsewhere in the interview he (a) fixates on hanging out with Axl Rose, (b) refuses to answer the telephone when the Packers call, (c) continually lies about taking steroids in an unconvincing manner, and (d) needlessly brags about stealing his girlfriend from a former teammate he described as "not real big, slow, a normal kind of guy." He once referred to the city of Green Bay as a village. Mandarich went out of his way to make people recognize and hate him, and for the worst possible motive—his obnoxiousness was a calculated, careerist move. Years later, he would admit this to the *Milwaukee Journal Sentinel*: "I wanted to create as much hype as I could for many different reasons—exposure, negotiation leverage, you name it. And it all worked, except the performance wasn't there when it was time to play football." Mandarich was a perfect storm of Asking for It. People enjoyed his failure because *he* was the specific person failing. It was personal, and one could even argue it was moral. And that makes it 180 degrees different from what happened with Sampson. The appreciation of Ralph's bust had nothing to do with anything he asked for; his problem was that people looked at him in a way that wasn't personal at all. He was *only* a symbol, and that's what makes it sadder.

1A Most of the time, Ralph Sampson was a fortress of solitude. Aloof and detached, he spent his collegiate years insulated by members of the Virginia Cavaliers football team who served as de facto bodyguards. When he did express emotion, it was delivered in awkward ways. The punch thrown at Sichting is the incident most people remember, but there were others. He once hit a Denver Nugget role player named Bill Hanzlik before flipping off the Denver crowd with both hands. When discussing a collegiate opponent from Georgia Tech named Lee Goza, Sampson dispassionately remarked, "If I had a gun, I would have shot him." However, his most revealing moments were more existential than angry: His final game at Virginia was a loss in the West Regional final of the NCAA tournament, a 63–62 defeat at the hands of NC State (the same team that would upset Benny Anders and the Houston Cougars one week later). In the game's closing seconds, the Cavaliers were unable to get the ball to Sampson; he didn't touch the rock until after the buzzer had already sounded. In an act of stoic frustration, Sampson flipped the ball nonchalantly toward the basket, underhand. It sailed straight through the twine, touching no rim—perfect, but pointless. It was an illustration of how easy the game came to him and of how hopeless his plight seemed to be. He never won an important game after high school. The most historically noteworthy contest in Sampson's college career was an unseen loss against an NAIA school no one had ever heard of (more on that later). His second-most noteworthy game came early in his senior year, when Virginia played Georgetown in December and Sampson faced seven-foot Hoya sophomore Patrick Ewing. Despite a gastric illness, the dehydrated Sampson outplayed Ewing as Virginia won by five. He was taller and more polished than Ewing— more civilized and nuanced and complete. He was better. But (once again) there was something allegorical about how these titans clashed, and (once again) it did not work in Ralph's favor. Sampson made things look easy. Ewing made things look hard. You could just tell that Ewing wanted it so fucking bad; you could see it in the sweat that poured off his nose and soaked his superfluous gray T-shirt. He was a gladiator. But how much did Sampson want it? No one really knew, and you certainly couldn't tell by watching him.

This is a ridiculous statement, but it's true: Sampson was too good. He was too big to be that skilled. His superiority seemed natural and therefore unearned. And while people don't necessarily hate that kind of greatness, they inevitably find it annoying. It plays into their insecurities about themselves and the inescapable unfairness of being human. Sampson's unobtrusive facade only made this phenomenon worse—his cool, quiet demeanor made him seem uninterested in his own aptitude. Unlike Mandarich, he did nothing to make anyone dislike him. But when you're naturally better than everyone else, and when that talent is so utterly obvious, being quiet doesn't translate as humble. It translates as boredom. He seemed like a bored genius.

This, ultimately, is what Sampson came to symbolize: supremacy coated in apathy. He looked like a player who was supposed to be the best, even if he wasn't; it did not matter how his team fared or how pedestrian his statistics were or if his final basket didn't come until after the final buzzer. It would still be self-evident that Sampson was better than everyone else on the floor. It was circular logic: He was better because he was better. He didn't need to prove anything. He didn't even need to try, and we didn't even need to question if that made sense. And the moment that stopped feeling true was the moment he collapsed into a black hole.

4 "I don't want to hear anybody say Ralph Sampson wasn't a great pro basketball player." This is the opinion of Terry Holland, Sampson's college coach at Virginia. "They actually invented the lottery in the NBA because of Ralph Sampson. He was a great pro basketball player until he injured his knee."

This is the positive retrospective spin on Ralph's legacy, advocated by Sampson himself: It can be argued that his inability to become a legend was mostly the fault of his knees. He had three surgeries over the course of his career and was essentially ruined after the first one. As is so often the case with athletic post players, his own supernatural prowess accelerated his erosion—there's certainly never been a seven-four player who jumped *higher* than Ralph Sampson. Most people don't remember that Sampson participated in the inaugural NBA Slam Dunk contest; had someone designed a contest to see who could dunk on the highest possible rim, he'd probably still be the world record holder. As a rookie, Sampson could have effortlessly jammed on a twelve-foot basket. He lived in the tropopause. And coming down from all that elevation pounded his gangly cartilage into mush. "He'd have been a Top 50 [all-time] player if not for his knees," said the sporadically rational Kenny Smith in 2006. "When it comes to Sampson, everybody seems to want to go for the easy negative instead of looking for the truth."

But what is the truth? Is the truth that Sampson could have posted ten excellent years with better knees? Sure (although—if we concede that those injuries were at least partially due to his combination of size and jumping ability—it stands to reason that a less injury-prone Ralph would have been a less physically gifted Ralph). But that seems less like the truth and more like the "easy positive." It doesn't explain anything about how he was perceived. Connie Hawkins lost most of his career to knee problems, but that makes everybody love him *more*. David Thompson had only five great years and Bill Walton had less than four, but they're both in the Hall of Fame. From a historical viewpoint, injuries tend to improve the way basketball players are remembered. It exaggerates their potential. But this didn't happen to Sampson. Without directly saying it, average people seem to *blame Ralph* for having bad knees. He needed to have a weakness, and it was reassuring to know that Sampson's body contained that weakness. He was hyped as invincible and inevitable, but he was just another guy.

5 Sampson could have gone straight into the NBA after high school. Everyone knew this. They said the same thing about the other great high school senior from the class of 1979, Sam Bowie.[8] But Sampson was a serious person who made serious decisions; he not only went to college but stayed all four years, despite the fact that he was projected as the league's top pick following every season he completed.[9] He won 96 percent of his games as a Cavalier, and his final season was designed as a worldwide showcase for Sampson's Samsonian sovereignty. Following that nationally televised mid-December clash with Georgetown, Virginia was scheduled to play two games in Japan before finishing the journey with a stopover in Hawaii to play the Chaminade Silverswords, an unknown school with an enrollment of nine hundred. Sampson—who'd been slightly ill against Georgetown but played anyway—became intestinally sick on the flight across the Pacific. He barely participated in the two games in Tokyo.[10] But by

---

8. Technically speaking, Bowie was a far greater bust than Sampson—he was injured for his entire career and is primarily remembered for being drafted one spot ahead of Michael Jordan in 1984. But people don't *hate* Bowie. He never seemed invincible to anyone.

9. In case you're curious, the three players selected first overall following Sampson's freshman, sophomore, and junior years were Joe Barry Carroll from Purdue, Mark Aguirre from DePaul, and James Worthy from North Carolina. It's possible that the seven-one Carroll would still have gone before Sampson in 1980, but Sampson was already viewed as having greater upside. Aguirre and Worthy were both smaller players and would have been less desirable commodities (although the Lakers would have faced an intriguing decision had Sampson applied to the draft in 1982—they already had Kareem Abdul-Jabbar on the roster).

10. Virginia still won both of these games. This is somewhat remarkable. The first game was against Hakeem Olajuwon (and Benny Anders!) and the rest of the Houston Cougars, a squad that would eventually play in that year's national championship. Sampson did not play a single minute in the win against Houston. Rick Carlisle must have had an awesome night.

the time they hit Hawaii, Sampson felt better. The world assumed this December 23 game was nothing more than an excuse for the Cavaliers to hit the beach before crushing a bunch of pineapple-gorged nags by 40. The world was wrong. Chaminade clogged the lane defensively, pushed the tempo on offense, and pulled the biggest upset in collegiate sports history,[11] defeating Virginia 77–72.

Within the scope of life, this should not have been a devastating loss for Sampson. It was a minor game played early in the season, he probably wasn't 100 percent health-wise, the game wasn't on TV, and only four thousand people were in the gym. Yet this is the night Sampson busted. We would not become collectively conscious of that rupture until 1988, but it happened in Hawaii in 1982. The Silverswords' center, Tony Randolph, was a six-six tweener from Virginia who had played against Sampson in high school and supposedly dated Ralph's sister. He was just a normal athlete who was slightly tall. But he was *a person*. And Sampson was not. Sampson was a monster who was going to change the language of his sport. He was beyond Goliath; he was the Goliath who was going to play point guard simply because he wanted to. He was David *as* Goliath. And you can't be both. You couldn't root for Sampson as an underdog, because that made no sense. He was favored against everybody. *He was the greatest.* But you also couldn't root for him as a colossus, because he refused to become the colossus purists wanted; instead of backing Tony Randolph into the lane and dunking everything he touched, Sampson wanted to be "a seven-foot-four guard." He was too pretty to

---

11. When Appalachian State beat Michigan in football early in 2007, many in the media (and even more in the blogosphere) argued that this was the biggest upset ever. In reality, it's not even close. App State was the defending 1-AA national champion, playing a Wolverine team that would go on to lose again the following week. Virginia was the best team in the country in 1983 and Chaminade was an NAIA school that had a basketball program for only the previous seven years.

be a soldier. Against the profoundly overmatched Chaminade, he took just nine shots and let his unbeatable team lose to a bunch of beach bum nobodies. *He was the greatest, but he wasn't that great.*

2B

I don't know why what happened to Ralph Sampson bothers me, but it does. I fully understand that the way people remember Sampson doesn't have any real impact on what he did (or did not) accomplish. He probably does not consider himself a bust, so why does it matter that other people do?

I don't know.

But it does.

It does, because I want to think about Ralph Sampson the way I thought about him thirty years ago, and I cannot. It does not matter how hard I try or by what means I rationalize the specific details of his career. He's busted to me. I am psychologically on his side, but I can't deny that he busted. His inability to become the greatest player of his generation has been so relentlessly recognized by the media that it's impossible for me to think about him in any context outside of that paradigm; this larger failure is now the *only* thing I think about when I think about Ralph Sampson. In 1986, he eliminated the L.A. Lakers from the playoffs by catching an inbounds pass and uncoiling a turnaround fourteen-footer in one motion, all within the span of a single second. This shot, technically, is the pinnacle of his basketball life. I am intellectually aware of this, as are most people who remember basketball from the eighties. But whenever that shot comes up in any conversation, it's now a depressing addendum that immediately returns to the larger, sadder narrative—it only serves to remind everyone that Sampson was *momentarily* great. And that's actually worse. Had he thrown his career away like Benny Anders, this entire essay would have been about how his failure was beautiful and interesting; as it is, it's about how being the MVP of the '85 all-star game is like being a brilliant pool player—sarcastic proof of a wasted life.

We used Ralph Sampson. I am using him right now, almost in the exact same manner I'm bemoaning. He is the post-playing piñata it's acceptable to smash. It's acceptable to fixate upon the things he did not do well enough, simply because all those personal catastrophes still leave him in a position of power. This is not an example of the media building someone up in order to knock him back down; this takedown was far less satisfying. Sampson busted big by succeeding mildly. That was the only role he ever played for anyone. There is no alternative universe where Ralph Sampson is a beloved symbol of excellence. There's no Philip K. Dick novel where he averages a career double-double and gets four rings. He could never be that guy. He was needed elsewhere, for other reasons. He was needed to remind people that their own self-imposed mediocrity is better than choking on transcendence.

My affinity for Ralph Sampson was a product of my age, but not in the usual way. It was not that I was too young to remember the outstanding players before him, and it was not because I was too young to see his flaws. It was that I was too young to envy a stranger for a life that wasn't mine. I did not subconsciously resent the fact that Sampson was born bigger and smoother than the rest of society. I had no idea that being six foot four is something a seven-foot-four man should not want. A ten-year-old boy doesn't want a hyper-dexterous giant to choke, just as a ten-year-old girl doesn't feel good when Britney Spears has a nervous breakdown on live TV. Only an adult can feel good about someone else's failure. I was not in a position to enslave Ralph Sampson, but other people were. And now, today, I can't erase those chains from my brain. I agree with the haters, against my will. They've enslaved me, too.

Q: Did you ever read that book of Sting's lyrics? I think it's just called *Lyrics* or something. Lou Reed published his lyrics as poetry, too. What do you think of that idea? Is that something you would consider?

A: Those books are balls. I hate them. I never give a shit about what a song is supposed to be about. I'm never amused by misheard lyrics, either. I tend to be more interested in people who hear lyrics correctly and still get them wrong. Like, are you familiar with the first song on Teenage Fanclub's *Bandwagonesque*? They open that record with this great song called "The Concept," and its first two lines are "She wears denim wherever she goes / Says she's gonna get some records by the Status Quo." When I initially heard that song, it never occurred to me that they were talking about the band Status Quo. 'Cause who the fuck listens to Status Quo? I always assumed that line meant this girl was buying records by "the status quo," which implied that she was buying all the records that scenesters felt an obligation to own. I thought she was buying records by Captain Beefheart and Gang of Four and Slick Rick. That's what I thought the term *bandwagonesque* referred to—jumping on the bandwagon of something that isn't even popular. Every time I learn the truth about something, I'm disappointed.

Through a Glass, Blindly

1 Standing at the window, I am inside my home. But windows are made of glass, so I see through other windows and I see into other homes. I see other people. They are baking bread and watching *Deadwood* and using a broom to get their cat off the air conditioner. They're doing nothing of interest, but it's interesting to me. It's interesting because they assume they are living unwatched. They would not want me (or anyone else) to watch them, despite the fact that they're doing nothing of consequence. Yet if these windows were TV screens—if these people had placed cameras in their apartments and broadcast their mundane lives on purpose—I would immediately lose interest. It would become dull and repetitive. So: These people don't want me watching them because they aren't aware that I'm there, and I wouldn't want to watch them if my watching was something they were aware of.

Everyone knows this, and everyone feels the same way. But does anyone understand why?

2 One of the minor tragedies of human memory is our inability to unwatch movies we'd love to see (again) for the first time. Even classic films that hold up over multiple viewings—and even those films that *require* multiple viewings—

can never deliver the knockout strangeness of that first time you see them, particularly if parts of the story are willfully designed to momentarily confuse the audience. When a film becomes famous and its theme becomes familiar, that pleasantly awkward feeling is lost even more. Sometimes I want to unknow things. An easy example is Alfred Hitchcock's *Vertigo*. By now, the theme of *Vertigo* is understood by all people interested in watching it, often before they see it for the first time: It's about every man's inherent obsession with attractive, psychologically damaged women. But for its first twenty minutes, *Vertigo* is about something else—it's about surveillance, and about how not knowing what's happening increases the phenomenon of attraction.

In *Vertigo*, Jimmy Stewart plays an ex-cop who's hired to follow a man's wife. As he watches her, the woman (Kim Novak) does a variety of strange, ostensibly meaningless things—she buys some flowers, stares at the portrait of a dead woman, and drives to a distant hotel for no clear reason. As the story unspools, we learn that she's possibly possessed by the spirit of a dead woman; later, we come to realize this is all a psychological con job (with Stewart as the mark). Because the plot is so complicated (and because the imagery is so beautiful), most people's memory of *Vertigo* focuses on the middle third of the movie—the psychology of the murder. But the reason *Vertigo* is effective is due to those opening twenty minutes. We watch Novak's mysterious behavior through Stewart's eyes, so we see her in the same way as he does. She makes all these (seemingly) bizarre decisions that are devoid of perspective, and it becomes far more compelling than logic would dictate. By surreptitiously watching the actions of a beautiful woman without the clarity of knowing her intentions, we stop caring about what those intentions are. Some might argue that Novak becomes interesting because the watcher can project whatever he desires onto her form, but that's not really what happens; what happens is that she becomes interesting simply because *it's interesting not to know things*. It's the unconscious, emotional manifestation of anti-intellectualism. We end up having the same response as Stewart's character: We fall in love with Kim Novak. That's why the absurdity of *Vertigo*'s premise[1] never becomes a problem—it doesn't feel unreasonable, because a person in love cannot be reasoned with. And we are that person. We are in love. Hitchcock's portrayal of surveillance is so effective that the audience never really recovers from the sensation; it carries the rest of the film.

So this, I suppose, is the first thing we can quantify: Observing someone without context amplifies the experience. The more we know, the less we are able to feel.

2A Ignorance is not bliss. That platitude is totally wrong. You will not be intellectually happier if you know fewer things. Learning should be a primary goal of living. But what if ignorance *feels* better—not psychologically, but physically? That would explain a lot of human incongruities.

There's a visceral, physiological charge that only comes from unknown pleasures. Think back to ordinary life situations where the outcome was unclear, and try to remember how you felt during those moments: You're introduced to someone you're immediately attracted to, but you don't know why. You attend a party where various guests dislike each other and everyone is drinking heavily. You're playing blackjack and the entire game rests on

---

1. It's hard to imagine a more convoluted way to commit a murder than what happens in *Vertigo*. Quite frankly, it would have been easier for the villain in this film to have simply killed every single person he's ever met.

whatever card is drawn next. You wake up, but you don't recognize where you are. Mentally, these situations are extremely stressful. But—almost inevitably—the physical sensation that accompanies that stress is positive and electrifying. You are more alert and more attuned to your surroundings. Endorphins are firing like revolutionary guerrillas. Adrenaline is being delivered by FedEx. Unknowing feels good to your body, even when it feels bad to your brain—and that dissonance brings you closer to the original state of being. It's how an animal feels. Take the wolf, for example: I suspect it's unbelievably stressful to be a wolf. The world would be an endlessly confusing place, because a wolf has limited cognitive potential and understands nothing beyond its instinct and its own experience. Yet the wolf is more engaged with the *experience of being alive*. A wolf isn't as "happy" as you, but a wolf feels better. His normal state of being is the way you feel during dynamic moments of bewilderment.

When you secretly watch the actions of a stranger, you're living like the wolf. You have no idea what could happen or what will happen. And while it's possible you enjoy that experience simply because you're nosy, it might also be because this makes you feel good for reasons unconnected to your curiosity. In reality, you probably don't want to know what's happening in someone else's life. You merely want to continue *not* knowing. And most of the time, that's exactly what happens.

2B When I lived in Fargo, I had a boring, curious apartment. It was a four-hundred-square-foot efficiency on the third floor of a three-story building. The only two windows were on the north wall, and they were both massive. By chance, the cable TV hookup was directly between these two windows. What this meant was that it was impossible to watch my thirteen-inch television without seeing directly into the opposing third-story efficiency apartment that was fifty feet to the north and identically designed. Everyone who visited my residence commented on this. Unless you had retinitis pigmentation (the source of nonmetaphorical tunnel vision), you could not avoid seeing what was happening in another apartment exactly like mine. This wasn't creepy, or at least it didn't feel like it at the time; it just felt like being unrich.

Because of this architectural circumstance, I had a nonverbal relationship with the twentysomething woman who lived in the apartment across the way. I never met her, but it was kind of like having an extremely mysterious roommate. For a while I thought she was schizophrenic, because it often looked like she was dancing with a houseplant; I later realized she owned a NordicTrack. I never witnessed anything sexual or scandalous. The lone intense moment happened while I was watching an episode of *My So-Called Life*: My neighbor was wearing a cocktail dress and cooking a (seemingly complex) meal. When her date finally arrived—a man whom I'd seen over there on multiple occasions in the past— they immediately had an argument, punctuated by her heaving a book at him from across the room. He left and she ate alone. Whenever she watched her own TV, I could see her peering into my apartment as well. I think she saw me throwing up one night, but that might have been a dream.

Now, as a writer, popular mythology would suggest that I should have taken these glimpses of my neighbor and created a fantasy world about what her life was like. I should have been stealing details from these fleeting voyeuristic moments and extrapolating them to their most absurd extreme. And I think that might have happened, had I seen her only once or twice or thrice. But this happened all the time. I accidentally saw her every day I watched television, which was every day I lived there. And the reason she never stopped being accidentally fascinating is because I *never* knew what was going on over there. I was clueless. The most commonly asked question within my internal monologue was always, *"Now* what is she doing?" To this day, I have no theory about what she did for a living or even what her regular hours were; I only know that she must have had the kind of job that required her to live in a place where the rent was $160 a month, because that's what I was paying, too. There is nothing she could have done that would have surprised me because I had no expectation as to how she was supposed to act. This is how it was, all the time. For two years, I watched a revolving door of nonevents that never stopped intriguing me. What's ironic is that this voyeurism coincided with the period of my life when I was most interested in MTV's *The Real World*. In fact, I can recall a handful of situations where I could glance into my neighbor's daily life while actively watching a show designed for that very purpose. As a critic, I have more things to say about the depiction of reality on MTV than about the depiction of reality in reality. But as a human, my boring neighbor felt infinitely more watchable, regardless of how little she did. So why was that? I think it was because I knew less. Even though MTV was actively trying to keep me interested, there were certain things I knew I would *always* see, because reality programming is constructed around predictable plot devices. There were also certain things I knew I'd *never* see, because certain types of footage would either be impossible to broadcast or broken as gossip before making it to the air (for example, we might eventually see a suicide on *The Real World,* but never a suicide we won't expect). The upside to knowledge is that it enriches every experience, but the downside is that it limits every experience. This is why I preferred watching the stranger across the way, even though she never did anything: There was always the possibility she might do *everything*.

2C *Vertigo* might be the best Hitchcock movie (or so Hitchcock himself sometimes implied), but *Rear Window* is my favorite (and for all the reasons one might expect). With the possible exception of *Goodfellas*, I can't think of another movie that's harder to stop watching whenever I stumble across it on broadcast television. There are a number of incredible things about this film, most notably the preposterous (yet still plausible) scenario of Grace Kelly needing a copy of *He's Just Not That Into You* until she becomes obsessed with a neighbor's murder, thereby prompting Jimmy Stewart to think, "Wow. Maybe I should consider marrying this smart, beautiful, ultra-nurturing woman— I had no idea she was into true crime!" The pacing, set design, and atmosphere could not be better. You can easily watch it twenty times. But the one thing *Rear Window* gets wrong is the quality most people remember most: the sensation of surveillance. The fact that wheelchair-bound Stewart becomes fixated on his neighbors makes sense; what doesn't compute is the way he engages with the content of his voyeurism.

The problem with *Rear Window* is that the things Stewart sees are too lucid. It does not feel like he's watching strangers; it feels like he is watching a collection of one-act plays. Miss Lonely-hearts (the pill-eating spinster) stages imaginary dinner dates in her kitchen and cries constantly. Miss Torso (the bombshell balle-rina) has cocktail parties and invites only men. A struggling musician sits at his piano and writes silly love songs, thinking out loud as he plinks out melodies. There is never anything confusing or non sequitur about how Stewart's neighbors behave. When he starts to suspect Raymond Burr has murdered his nagging wife, his logic is linear. "There *is* something to see over there," he tells Kelly. "I've seen it through that window. I've seen bickering and family quarrels and mysterious trips at night. Knives and saws and ropes. And now, since last evening, not a sign of the wife." A com-petitive game of *Clue* is less transparent than this story line. When Burr peers out of his window into the courtyard, it instantly trig-gers Stewart's suspicions. "That's no ordinary look," he tells his nurse. "That's the kind of look a man gives when he's afraid someone might be watching." That's a nice piece of dialogue, but not very convincing—what Stewart actually notices is "the kind of look" that only exists in Hitchcock movies.

Now, part of this can be explained by the way Hitchcock designed the people in his films (he was never as interested in characters as he was in character types, and all the people we see fit that description). But the fact that Stewart is ultimately correct about his murder theory is a problem; it makes for a much better plot, but it heightens the aesthetic distance. The only reason it's possible to piece this puzzle together is because the *only* things we see are inevitably connected, and that's not how window watch-ing works. *Rear Window* implies that voyeurism is enticing because we get to see the secret story of who people are—we peep at a handful of interwoven brushstrokes that add up to a portrait. The reality is that voyeurism's titillation comes from the utter chaos of noncontextual information. It's closer to a narrative that ignores all the conventional rules of storytelling; it's more Lynchian than Hitchcockian. If we could fully comprehend what was happening through a stranger's living room window, it would not be thrilling in the same way—it would feel more like reality TV. You'd think we'd care more, but we'd probably care less.

Surprisingly, a better depiction of window watching comes from Brian De Palma's 1984 effort *Body Double,* an attempt to rip off/pay homage to all the qualities Hitchcock perfected. *Body Double* is not half as good as *Rear Window,* but it's crazy perverse[2]

---

2. As evidence, Bret Easton Ellis made *Body Double* Patrick Bateman's favorite movie in *American Psycho*.

and incredibly fun to watch. It stars a guy strongly resembling Bill Maher (Craig Wasson) who gets tricked into living in the coolest apartment in Los Angeles. One of the apartment's advantages is a telescope that allows Wasson to watch his sexy next-door neighbor (Melanie Griffith), a woman who seductively dances and masturbates at the same time every night. Not surprisingly, this situation devolves into a grisly, complex fiasco. But what *Body Double* gets right is Wasson's reaction to the woman's nightly routine—he doesn't question it at all. It makes no sense, and—somehow—that seems more real. What makes her dancing so exciting is that there's no elucidation whatsoever. Wasson knows nothing, so everything feels good.

2D This is an idiotic situation to describe, but I will try nonetheless: During the same period I was living in my $160 Fargo apartment and watching my neighbor by accident, I spent a lot of my free time sitting in parked cars and being weird. My best friend had a vehicle we used for this specific purpose; we would park her car in a dark place and be weird together. One night we were doing this in the parking lot outside of the newspaper where we both worked. It was a little past eleven o'clock. We were listening to ELO. During the chorus of "Don't Bring Me Down," we noticed a bachelor friend of ours exiting the newspaper building; he had been working late on a concert review and was going home. He did not see us, so we decided to follow him.

Our friend got into his car and drove the ten minutes to his apartment. Our vehicle crept behind him, two lengths back. This was black ops. We were speaking in code. He arrived at his building. We parked across the street. Sitting in the car amidst the voice of Jeff Lynne, we continued to watch him through tinted windows. It took him twenty-five seconds to climb his stairwell (we couldn't see that part). The door of his second-floor flat finally opened and the overhead light came on. Our friend walked through his living room, shuffled through his mail, and then disappeared into the bathroom.

It was at this point that I came to a semi-sobering realization: We really had no fucking idea what we were going to see next. Both of us knew this man extremely well . . . but did we *really* know him? What if we didn't? I was already aware of his strangest interests (Nancy Drew novels, nonmelodic krautrock, department store mannequins, Tippi Hedren, etc.), but what if his private pursuits were even stranger than I imagined? What if we were about to see something we could not unsee? For the rest of our relationship, I would know secrets about this man that no one was supposed to know but him.

I mentioned this to my friend as she sat behind the wheel. She said she was having the same thought. "Maybe we should go," I said. "We probably should," she replied. But then our prey returned from the bathroom; instantaneously, the stakeout resumed. My coconspirator began taking notes on an envelope. We really knew how to be weird.

The two of us watched our friend walk over to his stereo. He thoughtlessly looked at the back of a few CD cases and then pushed the machine's *play* button, evidently content with whatever was in the disc tray. He sighed. He picked up a back issue of the *New Musical Express* and plopped into a chair that faced away from the window. It looked like he was reading about the band Ash, but I could not be positive. Maybe it was an article about Blur. I did not have binoculars or Jimmy Stewart's camera.

We continued to watch him read *NME* for twenty minutes, and then we drove home. It was a wonderful, memorable night. I still don't know why. What did I expect to learn? What was I afraid I might observe? There are no answers to these questions.

1A

The theory I am proposing, I suppose, is this: The reason voyeurism feels pleasurable is more physical than psychological. And this, I realize, is an easy hypothesis to torpedo; it takes a bad human trait and makes it seem both natural and amoral. It seems like an excuse for deviant behavior, which is the same reason people hate theories that suggest male infidelity is a product of sociobiology or that alcoholism is a congenital disease. But there *is* something unexplainable about spying on strangers that doesn't seem connected to what we actually see. On the surface, it seems like this should be similar to the human affinity for gossip, but it's not; we're never interested in gossip about people we've never heard of, and we're rarely interested in average gossip about average people. It's not interesting to hear that an old man was building a bookshelf at three AM last night, especially if I've never met the old man in question. But if I were to see this act through a neighbor's window, it would be different. I would watch him, and I would be transfixed. And I wouldn't imagine what books he was putting away, and I wouldn't speculate about why he was doing this construction so late in the evening, and I would not think I suddenly understood something about this person that's intimate or telling or complex. I would simply be seeing something I could not control and would never understand, and I'd be cognizant of a reality we all consciously realize but rarely accept—that almost all of the world happens without us. To look through the window of a meaningless stranger proves that we are likewise meaningless; the roles could just as easily be reversed with the same net effect. And that should disturb us, but it doesn't.

What are the things that make adults depressed? The master list is too comprehensive to quantify (plane crashes, unemployment, killer bees, impotence, Stringer Bell's murder, gambling addictions, crib death, the music of Bon Iver, et al.). But whenever people talk about their personal bouts of depression in the abstract, there are two obstructions I hear more than any other: The possibility that one's life is not important, and the mundane predictability of day-to-day existence. Talk to a depressed person (particularly one who's nearing midlife), and one (or both) of these problems will inevitably be described. Since the end of World War II, every generation of American children has been endlessly conditioned to believe that their lives are supposed to be *great*—a meaningful life is not just possible, but required. Part of the reason forward-thinking media networks like Twitter succeed is because people[3] want to believe that every immaterial thing they do is pertinent by default; it's interesting because it happened to *them,* which translates as interesting to *all.* At the same time,

---

3. This process becomes more interesting when the individual who's "tweeting" is an authentic person of interest. In February of 2009, Shaquille O'Neal sent a tweet on his "Real Shaq" account informing his (then) 257,000 followers that he was hanging out in a specific Phoenix shopping mall and would award two free Suns tickets to the first person who responded to his message in person. This was a jarring example of how the Internet is causing the celebrity phenomenon to fork: While most media personalities think the Internet destroys their sense of privacy, guys like Shaq actively use it to give themselves less separation from the rest of society. Shaq *wants* to be bothered by freaks. In general, it's continually amazing how obsessed early adopters of technology are with their own low-level activities. When Dennis Crowley was launching his phone application Foursquare in 2009, he argued, "What we wanted to do is turn life into a video game. You should be rewarded for going out more times than your friends, and hanging out with new people and going to new restaurants and going to new bars—just experiencing things that you wouldn't normally do." *Rewarded.* Crowley feels like technology should *reward* him . . . for eating at different restaurants!

we concede that a compelling life is supposed to be spontaneous and unpredictable—any artistic depiction of someone who does the same thing every day portrays that character as tragically imprisoned (January Jones on *Mad Men*, Ron Livingston in *Office Space*, the lyrics to "Eleanor Rigby," all novels set in affluent suburbs, pretty much every project Sam Mendes has ever conceived, etc.). If you know exactly what's going to happen tomorrow, the voltage of that experience is immediately mitigated. Yet most lives *are* the same, 95 percent of the time. And most lives *aren't* extrinsically meaningful, unless you're delusionally self-absorbed or authentically Born Again. So here's where we find the creeping melancholy of modernity: The one thing all people are supposed to inherently deserve—a daily subsistence that's both meaningful and unpredictable—tends to be an incredibly rare commodity. If it's not already there, we cannot manufacture it. But looking through another man's window helps. It diminishes our feeling of insignificance, because spying illustrates how all lives are equal ("We are the same"). It also feeds the hunger for spontaneity, because there is no sense of control or consistency ("This stranger's reality is beyond me"). No one thinks these thoughts consciously, but we feel them when we snoop. Seeing the secret lives of others removes the pressure of our own relative failure while reversing the predictability of our own static existence. It is more and less interesting at the same time. And our body understands this, even if we do not.

"We've become a race of Peeping Toms," Stewart's nurse remarks in *Rear Window* after rubbing him down with liniment. "What people oughta do is get outside their own house and look in for a change." Good advice, I suppose. But that won't make us feel any better, and it might make us feel worse.

Q: How did you deal with the response? Did it bother you, or was it kind of exciting?

A: At the time, we wanted to consciously anticipate the backlash and use it to our advantage. It seemed like the only way to stay viable. We were constantly trying to come up with an idea that would fail so horribly that everyone would decide it was too obvious to criticize or attack. For a while, we were going to make a live-action, shot-for-shot remake of the animated film *Heavy Metal*, but without using any CGI whatsoever. Matthew McConaughey was supposed to be the star. We were even going to use all the same songs off the soundtrack, except now they would be covered by Christian rock artists. We had convinced Jars of Clay to record "The Mob Rules," and I think dc Talk had been suggested for "Veteran of the Psychic Wars." Everyone sincerely believed that this was the one movie absolutely no one wanted. However, we couldn't agree on who the audience wasn't, so it became a marketing problem.

The Passion of the Garth

1 Half the energy I've spent writing (and reading) about music over the past fifteen years has been preoccupied with the same problem: "Is this thing I'm writing about *real*?" It wasn't something that always needed to be addressed directly, but it was always there. Is this artist genuine? Do his songs speak to an actual experience? Is the persona of this music's creator the same as who the creator is? What is the fidelity of these recorded sounds? Were the guitars actually synthesizers? Were the synthesizers actually guitars? What is the ultimate motive of the musician, and does that motive match the aspirations of his audience? These issues have formed the spinal cord of what music journalism inevitably is—the search for authenticity and the debate over how much authenticity matters. And certain conclusions finally seem apparent:

1. Nothing is completely authentic. Even the guys who kill themselves are partially acting.
2. Music that skews inauthentic is almost always more popular in the present tense. Music that skews toward authenticity has more potential to be popular over time, but also has a greater likelihood of being unheard completely.
3. In general, the best balance seems to come from artists who are (kind of) fake as people, but who make music that's (mostly) real. This would be people like Bob Dylan. The worst music comes from the opposite situation, such as

songs by TV on the Radio that aren't about wolves. If the singer is fake *and* the music is fake (Scott Weiland, Madonna, Bing Crosby), everything works out okay.

4. Normal people don't see any of this as a particularly pressing problem. They do not care. A few critics do, but that's about it.

5. The most telling moment for any celebrity is when he or she attempts to be inauthentic *on purpose*, and particularly when that attempt fails.

Like most Americans, I've lost interest in the first three conclusions. The fourth conclusion isn't interesting either, although the overwhelming truth of that sentiment makes it worth remembering. But the fifth point remains compelling. It speaks to the core confusion most humans have about who they truly are, and it illustrates why fame does not seem to make most famous people happy. When an artist successfully becomes somebody else, the result is defining and eternal: It's David Bowie morphing into Ziggy Stardust and becoming greater than either himself or the character. But when such a transformation fails, the original artist disappears into something else. He disappears into himself, and everybody gets sad and uncomfortable and inexplicably obsessed with all those authenticity issues they never cared about before.

This is what happened with Chris Gaines.

2 Rock writer Rob Sheffield once drunkenly argued that the supernatural success of nondescript country artist Garth Brooks was a social reaction to the temporary absence of Bruce Springsteen. This is the type of argument so simultaneously obvious and unseen that only someone as supernaturally brilliant as Rob Sheffield could possibly make it. There's a lot of evidence to support his theory: Springsteen essentially disappeared from America from 1988 to 1999. He even moved from New Jersey to L.A., casually claiming that building a new house in Jersey would be like Santa Claus building a new home at the North Pole. For roughly a decade, Springsteen stopped being Springsteen; he released a couple introspective albums, but he was not the man Americans knew. Garth filled that void by selling over a hundred million records. He created the Era of Garth. Brooks didn't always write his own material, but he made songs that satisfied all the same needs that Bruce's did, except with a little less sincerity and a better understanding of who his audience was. "Friends in Low Places" was as effective as pop music ever gets: It's a depressing song that makes you feel better. Singing along with that song was like drunkenly laughing at a rich person and knowing you were right. "Friends in Low Places" addressed class in the style of Pulp's "Common People," was as emotionally obtuse as Nazareth's "Hair of the Dog" and as pragmatic and mystical as BÖC's "(Don't Fear) The Reaper."[1] It's a song that makes me want to get drunk out of *spite*. Garth told stories about blue-collar people who felt good about what their bad life symbolized, which is the same reason *Born to Run* will never seem unimportant. Now, are the songs on *No Fences* as good as the material on *Nebraska*? No. But Garth understood an entire population of Americans he would never meet. I don't know if Garth Brooks could necessarily relate to the masses who loved his music, but they could relate to him. They fucking knew who he fucking was, because he made them feel like themselves.

And I think he felt weird about being able to do this.

And that's not unusual. And that's why certain things happened.

---

1. Gratuitous aside: I find that "(Don't Fear) The Reaper" significantly increases my fear of the Reaper. This song is a failure.

2A I don't have a lucid memory of what the world was like in 1999; it seems more distant to me than 1989, for whatever reason. I do know music was still selling like crazy, though: Total album sales in '99 were 940 million. What was playing on the radio still mattered, and most of it was mainstream alternative rock or Santana's *Supernatural*. There was a certain kind of semi-heavy, quasi-spiritual, midtempo track that could be three years old but still get endless airplay— Creed's "My Own Prison" was omnipresent at the bars and malls and Applebee's I was frequenting at the time. The most popular single in the world was "Livin' la Vida Loca," a song about how Pro Tools made Puerto Ricans gay. There were a lot of bands who selected random numerical names on purpose (Matchbox 20, Third Eye Blind, Seven Mary Three), and there were a lot of people trying to convince themselves that a double album by Nine Inch Nails wasn't ridiculous. Two disposable teens killed a bunch of beautiful people in suburban Colorado for reasons completely unrelated to Marilyn Manson, but traffic at Hot Topic improved nonetheless. Meanwhile, I was storing potable water and Oreo cookies in my hall closet; I was obsessed with Y2K, which negatively impacted my interest in things like TLC. At the time, TLC was advising me not to hang around with scrubs. This was kind of like their advice from 1994 about not chasing waterfalls. I never got that. Why not chase waterfalls? They're so easy to chase. It would have been far more sensible if deceased arsonist Lisa Left Eye had told me not to chase something dangerous, like wildebeests. "Don't go chasing wildebeests." It was that kind of millennium. People cared about shit, but not really.

It was into this hazy malaise that Chris Gaines emerged, widely noticed but generally unattacked (this being the pre-blog age). The big reveal/marketing initiative happened on *Saturday Night*

Live, a program that's always fun to read about but almost never fun to watch: Brooks hosted the November 13 show with alter-ego Gaines as the musical guest, as if they were two different, unrelated people. The fact that I was even watching this program clearly suggests (a) the SEC football game on ESPN must have been a blowout and (b) I had a drug problem. There was also a fake VH1 *Behind the Music* about Chris Gaines, although I never caught that; I think it might have aired during the Iron Bowl. But *anyway,* all initial logic suggested that this was just an unortho-dox way to promote *The Lamb,* the fictionalized biopic of Gaines's "life" that was supposed to hit theaters in early 2000 but never actually came into existence. At the time, most people made the same assumption as me. But Garth had his own unique perspec-tive: His concern over the transformation dwelled almost exclu-sively on its consumer viability.

"So the big question is this," Brooks said at the time. "If we don't have the traditional first week, that 'Garth Brooks week' that we've been so fortunate to have [in the past]—is [the new album] going to be deemed a failure? I'm hoping that Chris gets a chance, like all new artists, gets to come out and then hopefully word of mouth gets around and he starts to pick up and gain speed, and starts to actually live and breathe like artists do."

On the surface, this statement does not seem strange; it sounds like the normal kind of bullshit major recording stars offer up when they have to give twenty interviews in two days. But it *is* strange, and not just because Garth is talking about a different person and himself at the same time. It's strange because Brooks is obsessed with the one thing that he did not need to reinvent himself to achieve—mainstream commercial success. His motive for becoming a different person was to become the person he already was, minus the hat.

Even more than the album itself, the liner notes to *In the Life of Chris Gaines* (the fake Chris Gaines anthology) indicate a specificity of confusion that's too abnormal to be insignificant. The opening pages of the CD booklet show a photo of Gaines standing in an industrial kitchen, clad in black; its facing page is a biography of our nonexistent musician, presumably explaining what would have become the narrative thread for *The Lamb* (had it ever been produced). The biographical details[2] are explicit, charming, and stupid in the manner one might expect. But more curious is the emphasis Brooks placed on chronicling the chart success of Gaines's career: He notes that Gaines's first imaginary solo album spent "an extraordinary 224 weeks" in the Billboard Top 200 before winning a Grammy. His second imaginary album, the sexually "dark and angry" *Fornucopia,* debuted at number one and spent eighteen weeks at the top of the charts. His imaginary 1994 album *Apostle* spent eight imaginary weeks at number one "without any artist promotion." It's almost as if Brooks was honestly dreaming of a world where he did not exist, so he felt obligated to create a musician whose career would fill the commercial void left by the disappearances of *No Fences* and *Ropin' the Wind.*

In his imagination, Garth knocked himself out of the Billboard charts with himself.

---

2. It would be easy to get sidetracked by all the goofy details in his five-hundred-word biography, so here are my favorites: Gaines was allegedly born in 1967 in Australia, the son of an Olympic swimmer. For some reason, the bio also mentions that this woman medaled in the Commonwealth Games. He is said to have completed his GED in 1987, which I'm guessing was included for inspirational reasons. A lot of people he knew throughout his life died violently, and Gaines almost perished in a 1992 one-car accident that forced him to get plastic surgery on his face, shoulder, and hands. I still have no idea why a doctor would do plastic surgery on somebody's shoulder. I could understand reconstructive bone surgery, but not cosmetic work. Who looks at a musician's shoulder blades? It seems about as relevant as Chris Gaines getting Tommy John surgery.

2B *In the Life of Chris Gaines* ended up selling two million copies in two months, a relative failure in the musical economy of 1999.[3] It got as high as number two on the Billboard charts, but it never had a "Garth Brooks week," just as its creator feared. And while *feared* might be too strong a verb, it's not far off: Garth Brooks really, really cared about record sales. I can't think of any artist who ever cared about sales more. Which is not to say Brooks was obsessed with *money,* because that's totally different—the Rolling Stones care deeply about money, but they don't give a shit how it's acquired. If Kiss could make more money farming than playing in a band, Gene Simmons would immediately sign an endorsement contract with John Deere. Jimmy Page is probably counting his money *right now,* as you read this very sentence. The desire for wealth complicates artistic vocation, but it doesn't tell us much about the music. What Garth cared about more were statistics. Like a nongambling Pete Rose, Brooks was consumed by the magnitude of his own numbers: With career album sales over 128 million, he is currently the bestselling solo artist of all time. This was not happenstance: At Brooks's request, some outlets slashed the retail price of his late nineties albums to guarantee massive openingweek sales. "I believe in the Wal-Mart school of business," Brooks has said. "The less people pay, the more they enjoy it." After he released a double live album in 1997, Capitol Records put out a press release chronicling his dominance in random U.S. cities: A Media Play in Rockford, Illinois, sold three hundred albums when

---

3. Of course, retail sales of two million in 2009 would have made it one of the five biggest albums of the year. The ongoing deflation of sales figures makes it difficult to find a corollary for how *In the Life of Chris Gaines* would have performed in the present tense, assuming all the other factors were the same—I would estimate total sales of around 180,000 in the current climate. Maybe less.

the album went on sale at midnight. Tower Records in Sacramento sold four hundred copies in two hours. A Sam Goody in California sold out of the CD in two hours. Some outlet called Gallery of Sound in Edwardsville, Pennsylvania, sold a thousand copies on opening day. Brooks has received twenty-four Billboard Music Awards, an honor based solely on quantifiable unit moving. All his concerts sell out (in 2007, he played nine straight "comeback" shows in Kansas City's Sprint Center, selling 23,750 tickets on every single night). No other nineties artist comes close to his dominance. For ten years, Brooks was twice as popular as U2 and REM *combined*.

This is interesting for lots of reasons, but particularly for one: Since his semi-retirement in 2000, Brooks has inexplicably evaporated from the public consciousness. His highest-profile moment was covering Don McLean's "American Pie" at an inaugural ball for president-elect Obama in 2009. Modern country radio rarely plays his music, and he isn't yet viewed as part of the "classic country" contingent. None of his songs have become standards. I spent a weekend in Nashville and went to half the honky-tonks on Broad Street, and I didn't hear his music once. He already seems half as famous as Brad Paisley.

So why did this happen? How does someone this beloved not become a legend once he's absent? It wasn't like Brooks was a Lou Reed–level jerk, or even a Clint Black–level jerk. He was always magnanimous and respectful toward his principal influences (George Strait and George Jones) and once played five sold-out shows in L.A. for charity. Yet the minute he stepped out of the room, nobody cared. And I think the reason this happened is the same reason Brooks tried to become Gaines in '99: His persona was somehow real and fake at the same time. It was real in the sense that it was not contrived or imaginative—he was just the same normal guy he always was. It was fake in the sense that it was unnaturally straightforward—it's impossible for a normal

person to sell 128 million albums, or even to *want* to sell 128 million albums. And Brooks seemed to understand that. There was
eventually a three-pronged disconnect between (a) who Garth
thought he was, (b) who the audience thought Garth was, and (c)
how Garth assumed his audience *wanted* to think of him. So he
tried to connect those dots through Chris Gaines, and he failed.
But that aborted reinvention tells us more about Brooks than anything else he's ever done. It exposes the confusing truths that had
always been there, lurking unnoticed.

3 In the late 1960s, when three (or at least two) of the four
Beatles had started to lose interest in being "the Beatles,"
Paul McCartney gave an interview where he mentioned
how it would be fun to re-form the Beatles under a different name
and to wear masks on tour, thereby allowing the band to perform
without the responsibility of being who they were. Supposedly,
McCartney was shocked and disappointed when the journalist
informed him that everyone would immediately figure out who
they were the moment they started singing. The first time I read
this story was in the introduction to *The Bachman Books,* a collection of four Stephen King novels written under the pseudonym
Richard Bachman. King's intro is titled "Why I Was Bachman."

Because King directly mentions McCartney in his essay, one
assumes he must have related to Paul's desire, which would
explain why he wrote books with a fake name. But this is not
accurate. McCartney—seemingly unaware of how distinctive his
preexisting identity was—wanted to play music without hassle
and cultural meaning. He wanted an artistic life with less pressure, where the only thing that mattered was his own experience.
King—keenly aware of how his preexisting persona was impact-

ing his work's perception—wanted to see if his success was based on authentic skill or established celebrity (at one point in "Why I Was Bachman," he begrudgingly notes that the book *Thinner* sold 28,000 copies when published under the Bachman moniker but 280,000 when rereleased as a King title). He wanted an artistic life with *more* pressure, where the only thing that mattered was how audiences consumed the literal content.

Now, I'm certain Brooks did not make *In the Life of Chris Gaines* because he thought it would be easier; he probably did more promotion for this album than any other.[4] But is it possible that Gaines was his version of Bachman? The transformation wasn't masked and anonymous, but it provided an opportunity to test the actual parameters of his enormity. He was easily the biggest artist in the country-western idiom, but critics (of course) still questioned his realness; if he were able to sell eight million albums in the more judgmental, less forgiving world of rock, all those prior criticisms would be moot. Realness would no longer matter—the sound of his voice would transcend everything. If he could sell records as Chris Gaines, it would mean he could sell records as anybody. It would prove he was great (or at least that he had established a certain kind of greatness). But this is the problem with finding oneself through the numerical calculation of one's commercial achievement: It only makes sense the first time it happens. After that, it keeps perpetuating itself, over and over and over again. It starts to seem like it isn't based on anything. So maybe the only way to make it feel real is to do something that *doesn't* succeed, just to demonstrate that the work itself actually played a role in whatever made you good in the first place.

---

4. Of course, it's entirely possible Brooks *enjoyed* promoting things. Some people are like that.

2C In 2008, hyper-Christian DirecTV advocate Beyoncé Knowles released *I Am . . . Sasha Fierce*. This record is principally remembered for the song "Single Ladies (Put a Ring on It)," arguably the first song overtly marketed toward urban bachelorette parties. The original hook of the album, however, was the concept of Knowles becoming "Sasha Fierce," a character *Entertainment Weekly* described as her "sensual, aggressive alter-ego." During an appearance on *Oprah,* Beyoncé described Sasha Fierce in the same way; in fact, I believe she used the same exact words. The whole time she spoke with Winfrey, Beyoncé appeared to be working off a script, once misspeaking in a manner that made it obvious she'd rehearsed the entire conversation. I don't know who came up with the Sasha Fierce concept, but I'm pretty sure it wasn't God. Beyoncé claims Ms. Fierce was invented during the making of "Crazy in Love" in 2003, but the whole thing seemed so unnatural and out of character that the only explanation can be strategy. Somewhere along the line, somebody important came to the conclusion that there is a segment of Knowles's audience who likes to imagine that Beyoncé's secret personality is erotic and confrontational and street. Someone concluded that making this personality into a product would expand the brand (and maybe it did). But as an artistic creation, Sasha Fierce did not work. It only excites those who desperately want to be fooled. When Sasha covered Alanis Morissette's "You Oughta Know" in concert, it was far more entertaining than provocative. It did not make her personality more complex; mostly, it reminded people that Beyoncé doesn't really have any personality at all. She loves Christ, she loves her husband, she sings reasonably well, and she's beautiful. That's the whole package. Becoming a different person only served to make that all the more obvious, because it seemed like she was trying to *guess* what a cool person might act like.

It was the same for Garth. His self-portrait of Chris Gaines—a sullen, post-*Nevermind* alt rocker who aspired to compete against bands like Cake and Marcy Playground—resembles an attempt at sarcasm by the FBI's witness protection program. His decision to grow a soul patch pretty much said it all: In the ten-thousand-year history of facial hair, no one has ever looked nonidiotic with a soul patch. In fact, the zenith of the soul patch's legacy was Matt Dillon in *Singles;* Dillon grew a soul patch specifically *because* he was portraying an alt rock d-bag. Gaines's hair is likewise confused; it's styled in that severe, midlength manner all the hair metal dudes adopted after grunge convinced them to record their version of *Superunknown.* He's dressed completely in black from the neck down, except when he wears a black-and-white leotard. But still. He does not look like a rock 'n' roll machine. He looks like somebody who should be trying to assassinate Castro for Gerald Ford. And unlike Sasha Fierce, I suspect the look for Chris Gaines was totally Garth's vision—an amalgamation of all the signifiers of modern rock, tied together by his desire to be liked by both (a) the kind of person who typically disliked him and (b) the kind of person who would like him no matter what he did. As it turns out, there were exactly two million consumers in that second category. But it was the jerks in that first category who mattered more, and they knew he was guessing all along. This, oddly, is the one musical situation where authenticity *does* matter: If you want to adopt an unnatural persona, that persona needs to be an extension of the person you secretly feel like. You have to be "authentically pretending." You have to be the only person who could have become the character you embody. This is why Ziggy Stardust never seemed like a Halloween costume. It's also why Chris Gaines felt like marketing, even if that hadn't been the intention. He was crazy, but he wasn't *singularly* crazy. He wasn't crazy enough.

4 What will always remain unclear, of course, is what would have happened if Chris Gaines had made a song that people legitimately loved. *In the Life of Chris Gaines* technically gave Brooks the biggest pop single of his career ("Lost in You," which was evidently supposed to sound a little like an upbeat incarnation of Tracy Chapman's "Fast Car"), but virtually no one remembers that this track even exists. Brooks wrote none of the material on *In the Life of Chris Gaines*; the majority of it was penned by two ex-members of the Christian rock group White Heat. It was produced by Don Was, a Grammy award winner who's best known for being the white dude with dreadlocks who produced the worst Stones albums of all time, walked the dinosaur, and generally talks like he's full of shit. Several of the songs were tied to the nonexistent movie *The Lamb*: "Maybe" was pegged as a tribute to Gaines's fictional dead friend Tommy, supposedly a huge Fab Four fan (the melody falls somewhere between late-era Beatles and lazy-era Oasis, and one of the lyrics is "Even though the bird has flown"). What's disappointing about *In the Life of Chris Gaines* is that it's supposed to be a creative overview of Gaines's entire fake life, but the songs all sound like they come from the same period (the "earliest" track, something called "My Love Tells Me So," does not resemble anything that could have been popular in 1985, even in a Coke commercial). The goal of every song on *In the Life of Chris Gaines* was to become the male equivalent of Sheryl Crowe's "All I Wanna Do"—an accessible single that nobody would necessarily love but that most people would offhandedly like (and that could thereby inhabit AOR stations and drive album sales for ten to eighteen months). What he wanted was a quiet smash, and he did not get it.

But let's assume that he did.

Let's pretend some song off *In the Life of Chris Gaines* resonated with rock audiences the way "The Thunder Rolls" had resonated with country listeners. Let's say his new success mirrored his old success. Let's say he guessed right. What would have happened? It's a difficult reality to imagine, especially since Brooks no longer talks about this period of his career. When cross-dressing gutter punk David Johansen turned himself into Buster Poindexter and became a hundred times more famous than he was as a member of the "important" New York Dolls, the initial assumption was that the new alter ego was the person he actually wanted to be. As it turns out, the only part Johansen liked was the money (he would eventually tell National Public Radio that the 1987 song "Hot Hot Hot" had become the bane of his existence). But I think Garth would have felt differently. I don't think he would have ever completely returned to himself. If large numbers of consumers had wanted a new Chris Gaines record every two or three years, he would have kept making them; if they had adored Gaines more than Garth, he would not have felt sad. He might have preferred it—it would have made more sense to him. Authenticity was never really the catalyst here, for him or anyone else. Despite all the weirdness and craven promotion, *In the Life of Chris Gaines* was not an indulgent vanity project. It was the opposite. A vanity project is something you do for yourself. *In the Life of Chris Gaines* was done exclusively for other people, which is why no one noticed.

Q: What was the worst thing you ever did to one of your romantic rivals?

A: That's easy. I was dating this guy who was living with another woman. This was in Tulsa. Technically, I guess he was cheating on her with me. But she was a bitch. She was this superrich whore who lied to him constantly. So one night I'm over at this dude's apartment, and we're drinking tequila and fighting about whether or not he was ever gonna break up with this bitch. It's a bad fight—I'm crying, he's crying, somebody threw a lamp at the TV, all that jazz. And sure enough, the bitch comes home. We hear her car pull into the driveway—she drove this green convertible Jaguar. It was a beautiful—probably the nicest car I ever saw up close. But I'm drunk and I'm sobbing and he starts screaming at me to get the fuck out, so I jump over the balcony just before she opens the front door. I escape. So now I'm limping back to my truck, and I see her Jag. And I'm furious. And I feel really sick, cause we've been drinking tequila for five hours. And the top is down on her convertible, so I decide to vomit into the front seat. I walk over to the car, stick two fingers down my throat, and start throwing up into the front seat of her Jag, and it's projectile vomit. It's like Godzilla's radioactive breath—I can actually *aim* the vomit stream. So I aimed straight into the vents of her air conditioner. That's probably the worst thing I ever did to another person.

Q: Did you ever see the man again?

A: Yeah, a little bit. That woman ended up committing suicide. But not because of the air conditioner vomit, as far as the state of Oklahoma is concerned.

Going Nowhere and Getting There Never

1A I once drove a car across the country. This, obviously, is not a remarkable feat. Lots of people drive cars across the country. But I'm not mentioning it because the drive was amazing; I'm mentioning it because it was not. It took three weeks and was financed by a rock magazine, and not much happened along the way. But two years after that trip, a roomful of people from California with exceptionally comfortable office chairs contemplated making a movie out of my driving experience, and they wanted to do this *because* the trip was unremarkable. They openly admitted this. Our ensuing two-hour conversation evolved into a mystifying, nonlucrative abortion. Enthusiastic strangers with European eyeglasses kept asking me to imagine how this film would look. I assumed it would look like the video for Tom Cochrane's "Life Is a Highway," partially because of the song's lyrical content but mostly because I look Canadian. That was not the answer they were anticipating. I got the impression they were hoping I would say it would be like a combination of *Trainspotting* and *Dazed and Confused*, although maybe they were just trying to figure out if I was holding drugs. They also wanted me to sign a 715-page contract that would give them control over my "life rights," which included the option of making me an ancillary character in *You, Me and Dupree*. (The contract also required that my character execute an albino horse with razor wire on camera, which did not seem central to the original story. My character was also supposed to be "one-third gay," but we couldn't agree on what that classification required.)

This theoretical Road Movie would not have been interesting and does not exist, although those two points are not necessarily related. I have no doubt that the film would have followed the conventional Road Movie trajectory, which has remained intact since before *The Wizard of Oz*. The trajectory is as follows:

1. A character experiences abstract loss and attempts an exodus from normal life.
2. The character reinvents his or her self-identity while moving from place to place.
3. Along the way, the character encounters iconic individuals who illustrate authenticity and desolation.
4. Upon the recognition of seemingly self-evident realizations, the character desires to return to the point of origin.

I assume the Road Movie I did not become involved with would have been predominantly built on the most elementary of Road Movie clichés: Where you're going doesn't matter as much as how you get there. But that philosophy raises at least three questions, some of which are equally cliché but all of which are hard to answer: What *is* a Road Movie, really? Why do so many directors (from so many different eras) long to make them? And what makes traveling by car any more inherently interesting—or even all that different—than staying in one place?

1B

Everyone concedes that America is obsessed with cars, and everyone is correct. The car is, more than anything else, the definitive American instrument. Its symbolism seems infinite—it simultaneously denotes personal independence, social class, sexual maturity, blue-collar masculinity, manifest destiny, and ZZ Top. It's the first major purchase most people make; with the exception of New York, there aren't any major American cities designed for people who don't possess one. Cars kill binge-drinking teenagers and sustain local economies; they make our government dependent on the Muslim world and look awesome on wall calendars. It almost feels idiotic to make a series of points about the import of cars, simply because it's hard to imagine anyone taking an adversarial position. Cars are as important to the people who hate them as they are to the people who love them. We all know this. And that's what makes it so easy to avoid thinking about what they mean.

Americans are obsessed with automobiles, but the obsession is rarely intellectual. It's almost always emotional (the car as a metaphor, the car as a memory, the car as a Beach Boys song, etc.). It's hard to think of a machine in which form and function are so intimately intertwined, but consumers internally separate those qualities without even trying. Cars are so central to the experience of American modernity that we no longer consider the most basic questions about what they are and what they do. These questions include:

1. Why do cars look the way they look?
2. What is a reasonable expectation for what a car can do?
3. How do the answers to those questions influence how we feel about them?

I don't know much about cars. I can operate them, but not particularly well. I no longer own one, and if I did, I certainly couldn't fix it. I understand how engine size is calculated (and I realize that bigger engines generate greater power), but I don't understand the process of internal combustion. I know that a catalytic converter fights pollution, but I have no idea how. I've only watched one NASCAR race from flag to flag and I can't remember who won. When I see any collection of cars on the road, they strike me as more similar than different. It's almost like I don't *want* to understand cars, because I would rather have them remain consequential in the abstract; I immediately accept whatever I am told about the nature of the automobile. But a handful of people do not. A handful of people see potential where I see sameness. And it's amazing how difficult life inevitably becomes for any man who asks simple questions about what the car is supposed to be. It's almost like cars are the one thing no American is ever supposed to wonder about.

2A The defining domestic road narrative is Jack Kerouac's 1957 novel *On the Road*, a novel that readers either take much too seriously (at least in the opinion of dead author Truman Capote, who didn't even classify the prose as writing) or not seriously enough (if you happen to be nondead author John Leland, who just published a book titled *Why Kerouac Matters*). A film adaptation of *On the Road* has been percolating for years; still hopelessly scheduled for 2011, the movie is slated to be produced by Francis Ford Coppola and directed by Walter Salles, a Brazilian-born filmmaker already known for crafting semi-epic, semi-boring road pictures (most notably 2004's *The Motorcycle Diaries,* but also 1996's *Foreign Land*

and 1998's *Central Station*). It was my intention to interview Salles for this piece, but he was working in South America and unwilling to chat. He did, however, e-mail me a two-thousand-word essay[1] he wrote for a Greek film festival, which is akin to getting an extremely long answer to a question that was never technically asked.

The essay is (rather straightforwardly) titled "About Road Movies." Salles suggests that all of this starts with Homer's *The Odyssey* and reflects a specific kind of human discovery. Here are a few of his core thoughts, mostly unedited:

> The early road movies were about the discovery of a new geography or about the expansion of frontiers, like Westerns in North American cinema. They were films about a national identity in construction. In more recent decades, road movies started to accomplish a different task: they began to register national identities in transformation.

This first point addresses something almost everyone who talks about Road Movies feels obligated to reference: The idea of moving west across the country is such a deeply American tradition that virtually all Road Movies borrow from this motif. This is even true when a movie consciously adopts the opposing philosophy. In 1969's *Easy Rider*, Peter Fonda and Dennis Hopper start in California and travel east. They're part of the counterculture, so they move in the opposite direction of manifest destiny. When Jack Nicholson's character says things like "This used to be a hell of a good country! I don't know what's happened to it," he is essentially suggesting the discovery of America in reverse.

---

1. When I initially received this essay from Salles, it had not been published anywhere. However, it ended up running in the November 11, 2007, issue of *The New York Times Magazine*.

In terms of architecture, road movies cannot be circumscribed to the traditional three-act structure that defines the screenplays of so many mainstream films. Road movies are rarely guided by external conflicts; the conflict that afflicts its characters is basically an internal one . . . I have the impression that the most interesting road movies are the ones in which the identity crises of its main characters mirror the identity crisis of the culture these characters originate from, or are going through.

Salles's second point is interesting because—though true—it often represents the easiest criticism of any movie focused on characters who seem obsessed with movement for the sake of movement alone. For example, there's really no conflict in *Smokey and the Bandit* (it's actually easier to understand the plot by listening to the three-minute Jerry Reed song "East Bound and Down" than by watching the movie itself). However, *Smokey and the Bandit* becomes more compelling if viewed from the perspective of Burt Reynolds as the idealized embodiment of how a masculine, semi-blue-collar Southern male would think about the world in 1977 (i.e., not taking it seriously and not giving a shit about anything it contains, including the things he knows he *should* give a shit about, such as Sally Field's pugnacious optimism).

Because of the necessity of accompanying the internal transformation of its characters, road movies are not about what can be verbalized, but about what can be felt. About the invisible that complements the visible. In this sense, road movies contrast dramatically with the present mainstream films, in which new actions are created every five minutes to grab the attention of the spectator. In road movies, a moment of silence is generally more important than the most dramatic action.

Salles's third point is more debatable. It speaks to the divide between people who claim they like "films" and those who willfully insist they prefer "movies." The deeper question becomes this: Are flickering images more interesting when something is happening, or are they more interesting when nothing is happening? In the case of Vincent Gallo's sublimely gratuitous *The Brown Bunny,* the latter argument feels more accurate; what makes that film hypnotizing is its ability to replicate the focused boredom of long-form highway driving. But this is usually the exception.

There are cataclysmic, melodramatic deaths at the end of 1967's *Bonnie and Clyde* and 1991's *Thelma and Louise.* My assumption is that Salles thinks those traumatic events were less important than the (mostly) unspoken agreement of the characters' decision to die together. Yet that's not how it feels when the movies are actively consumed, which indicates one of two things: Either Salles's description of Road Movies is imperfect, or those two examples aren't Road Movies at all. Maybe they're just movies that happen to have roads in them.

3A

"Going from Point A to Point B is kind of the obvious criteria here." This is Gus Van Sant, speaking via telephone. He is speaking very cautiously; the questions I've asked him are so vague and abstract that he suspects I'm trying to trick him into saying something he doesn't believe. "In a movie like *Gerry*[2], the characters are looking for a road, which really isn't the same thing as a Road Movie. All of this probably comes from our own history—wagon trains and lit-

---

2. This is a movie about two dudes who get lost in the desert.

eral trains and exploring the west. But by the time we got to the 1960s, it didn't really matter which direction you were going. Ken Kesey had business on the East Coast, so that required a reversal."

The reason I am interviewing Van Sant is two-pronged, although it appears neither of my prongs is particularly sharp. The first reason is that I had fallen under the impression that he'd agreed to direct an upcoming version of *The Electric Kool-Aid Acid Test*, Tom Wolfe's nonfiction account of the aforementioned Kesey's LSD-fueled 1968 bus trip across the United States. As it turns out, Van Sant hasn't even signed on to this project (he said he was still in the midst of negotiating the deal and writing the script). My second reason for calling is that I closely associate Van Sant with the Road Movie genre, as association that (in retrospect) is totally specious. A lot of his films feel like Road Movies in my memory, but they weren't when I rewatched them. As Van Sant noted, *Gerry* doesn't even have a road. *My Own Private Idaho*[3] starts on a highway and ends in Rome (where all roads are said to lead), but everything in the middle seems detached from movement. In *Drugstore Cowboy,*[4] the characters stay in motion and actively take a road trip, but it's still not a Road Movie.

That said, there *is* something about Van Sant's work that (perhaps inadvertently) inhabits the relationship between travel and life experience. His interest in *The Electric Kool-Aid Acid Test* is not surprising: Besides holding a career-long cinematic interest in drug use, Van Sant claims to have crossed the country by car at least twenty times in his life and still drives from his home in Oregon to Los Angeles on a regular basis.

"I don't know if I've ever shot a physical landscape through the window of a moving car, but I've always thought the idea of road

---

3. This is a movie about two gay dudes who talk like they're characters in *Othello*.

4. This is a movie about taking pills and not having sex.

stories on film was the central metaphor of a beginning, a middle, and an end," he says, slightly challenging Salles's notion that Road Movies don't operate like traditional three-act plays. "The trip creates a natural progression through the middle of a film. I think a story like *On the Road,* for example, will actually be more effective as a film than as a book. Going from Point A to Point B is not what really holds a novel together. But movement can hold a movie together."

In the hope of finding clarity, I ask Van Sant what he thinks a Road Movie is. Somewhat predictably, his response makes things more confusing (and also seems to contradict something he already said about one of his own films).

"Well, if *Duel* isn't a road movie, then such a thing as Road Movies don't exist," he says. "But does there even have to be a road at all? Is *2001: A Space Odyssey* a road movie? I think that you could argue that it was."

This, I suppose, is true. You could argue that *2001* was a Road Movie, just as you could argue that *My Dinner with Andre* is a Road Movie Of The Mind. But that kind of definition leads nowhere. The more telling detail is Van Sant's mention of *Duel,* Steven Spielberg's 1971 made-for-TV movie about an unassuming man—a person literally named "David Mann"—in a Plymouth Valiant who falls into an inexplicable personal war with a flammable tank truck, driven by a faceless stranger who longs to kill him. *Duel* eliminates the idea of a road trip as some sort of spiritual quest. Instead, it exclusively ties its story to the most fundamental elements of the genre: vehicles, people, and the nonmetaphorical physicality of the earth itself.

2B Part of what makes the evolution of the automobile so complex is that—much like America itself—cars are (relatively) new. People had ideas for horseless carriages by the end of the 1700s, but the social import of the car didn't really start until Henry Ford popularized mass production with the Model T in 1914. We're dealing with a timeline that's less than a century, and mobile technology takes time. From a historical perspective, we're still figuring out what cars are supposed to be—I mean, boats have existed for forty thousand years, but nobody managed to consistently sail anywhere distant until the Middle Ages.[5] If you look at a Model T and a Lexus LS, there are far more similarities than differences.

Aesthetically, the force behind the auto's evolution has always been streamlining. The first car designed to fight wind resistance was the Tatra T77, a Czech vehicle introduced in 1934. (Czechoslovakia remains somewhat underrated as a nation of industrial innovators—in the thirties, they were more militarily prepared for the Nazis than either France or England.) The science of aerodynamics is purely practical: It increases velocity and decreases fuel consumption. But the collateral consequence was a shift in associated perception. The degree to which a car is streamlined is directly proportional to how "futuristic" it looks to consumers. This was never more evident than with John Z. DeLorean's DMC-12, a vehicle so forward-thinking that it will always be best known as a cinematic time machine for Michael J. Fox.

---

5. This, I will grant, is hard to quantify. Some say the Vikings were the first civilization who figured out how to sail into the wind, and that's central to long-distance sea travel. But "distant" is a relative term; two thousand years ago, people thought the earth was much smaller than it is. The world seemed smaller still fifteen thousand years ago. Did early sailors travel shorter distances because they simply thought there was nowhere else to go?

DeLorean is the type of historical figure who seems more charming in retrospect than he did at the height of his powers; over time, his abrasive playboy indulgences have become glamorous idiosyncrasies. When he expired in 2005, his obituary in *The Guardian* openly called him a con man and proclaimed, "Almost everyone who had business dealings with car-maker John DeLorean, who has died aged 80, suffered either money losses in the millions, public vilification for the vanished cash, or both . . . DeLorean remained unscathed: even if he did lose a fortune, he had not been entitled to it in the first place." He was, by all accounts, as much a criminal as a carmaker. But those illicit traits are what make him so interesting—they were necessary qualities for any man with the kind of goals DeLorean had. His motive was to break the stranglehold that Ford, General Motors, and Chrysler had on the U.S. car economy, and he was willing to sell hard narcotics to make that happen.

Born in Detroit to an alcoholic Ford factory employee, DeLorean first came into prominence by engineering the Pontiac GTO for General Motors in the 1960s. The definitive "muscle car," GTOs were powerful automobiles that *looked* powerful, even to the casual observer. The body expressed something about the owner. Years later, DeLorean would take that notion further with the DMC-12, a car that became known simply as the DeLorean. Constructed out of unpainted stainless steel and featuring distinctive "gull wing" doors that opened vertically, the original DeLorean prototype—now over thirty years old—still appears weird and otherworldly. But the DMC-12 was a failure, and for many of the same reasons DeLorean lost his empire: It was ahead of its time, but not in a good way.

In order to make the DMC-12, DeLorean needed $175 million. He got $12 million from private investors (most notably Johnny Carson and Sammy Davis Jr.) and $156 million from the British government (in exchange for locating his factory in Northern Ireland). He risked very little of his own capital and tried to shift the paradigms of both car design and car production. The only problem was that people did not really *want* the DMC-12. It cost $26,000 in 1981 dollars, which—in the heart of a recession—was already $8,000 more than a Corvette. Everyone seemed to agree that the DMC-12 looked interesting, but it was a gratuitous kind of interesting; it was so cutting-edge that it felt gimmicky. DeLorean sold only three thousand DMC-12s in its first year of existence. When Britain threatened to close the factory in fall of 1982, DeLorean desperately needed $17 million to keep himself in business. His solution? Cocaine smuggling (or—more accurately—fronting the seed money for a group of Colombian smugglers and taking a cut of the final profit). Mr. DeLorean fully realized he was getting into some serious shit: Before his meeting with the coke associates, he wrote a letter to his attorney and instructed him not to open the sealed envelope unless he never returned.

DeLorean was eventually seized in a motel room near LAX with 15 pounds of cocaine. He was negotiating the purchase of an additional 205 pounds; unfortunately, he was negotiating with undercover agents from the FBI. In time, DeLorean would be found not guilty of these charges on the basis of entrapment (his lawyer argued that the crime was "fictitious" and only existed because of the government's involvement). But the damage was already done. DeLorean's company was destroyed and he was publicly humiliated. He became a born-again Christian, divorced his wife, and filed for bankruptcy in 1999. All that remains of his legacy are the six thousand DMC-12s still in existence, mechanical detritus that makes the 1980s seem even more ridiculous than they were.

3B In a 1983 *Rolling Stone* article, DeLorean theorized that the auto lobby persuaded the U.S. government to destroy him (he also speculated that it might have been a conspiracy by the British government, or even the Irish Republican Army). This is a consistent theme among automotive mavericks—any innovation with the potential to alter the industry inevitably collapses under mysterious circumstances. The most famous example is Preston Tucker, the human face of unjust failure.

Tucker is an example of how media shapes memory: By now, the 1988 Jeff Bridges biopic of his life (*Tucker: The Man and His Dream*) is better known than either the actual man or the actual dream. The main detail most people remember about Tucker's car design is its third headlight (a cyclops-like eye near the middle of the front fender that moved in concert with the steering wheel), but the entire apparatus was radically modern—shaped like a shallow teardrop, the "Tucker Torpedo" boasted an impossibly low drag coefficient of .27 (and just in case you don't have a degree in fluid dynamics, a drag coefficient is measurement of wind resistance—a square block of wood, for example, has a drag coefficient of roughly 1.05). Tucker's intentions were as modern as his product: He was trying to build a safe, middle-class car in an era when automakers didn't consider personal safety or social class. Predictably, he was doomed by the altruism of his ambition; just about everyone now concedes that Tucker's company was sabotaged by the Big Three auto cartel, although the details remain confusing.[6]

---

6. Here are the rudimentary facts behind his demise: Tucker was financing his operation with a curious (although not necessarily illegal) financial system—essentially, he was selling accessories for the Tucker Sedan before the car

So what is the lesson here? Is it that resistance is futile? Is it that the relationship between truth and power doesn't exist in Detroit? Maybe. But the case of Preston Tucker might also suggest this: When reflected in the rearview mirror, we love the image of the auto iconoclast. We make movies about him, and we recall him fondly and sympathetically. From a retrospective position, failure almost seems to validate the value of his ideas—I mean, why would the government destroy a man unless that man was right? At least anecdotally, history is almost always kind to people who try to change what the car is. But people don't live inside their history; people live in the present tense. And the present abhors innovation, particularly when those innovations require people to think differently about things they feel like they intuitively understand. And Americans feel like they understand cars *completely*.

1C Every fight is unique, but wars are always the same. There are only six types of narrative conflict, and they're usually described like this: Man vs. Himself, Man vs. Man, Man vs. Society, Man vs. Nature, Man vs. Machine, and Man vs. God. In his essay, Salles writes that Road Movies are generally internal conflicts, so he'd probably see *Duel* as Man vs. Himself; if consumed devoid of subtext, the screen-

---

itself existed. This made him look like a con man, particularly when Mr. Harry Aubrey Toulmin, the chairman of Tucker's own company, contacted the Securities and Exchange Commission and suggested that these business practices were corrupt. Even worse, Toulmin implied the vehicle itself would probably never run. Tucker was indicted for fraud on June 10, 1949. His factory closed the same day. Though Tucker was eventually cleared of any criminal wrongdoing, he lost everything. It's now widely accepted that Michigan senator Homer Ferguson, acting on behalf of Detroit's existing auto giants, engineered the dismantling of Tucker's program.

play for *Duel* seems like an obvious Man vs. Man scenario. But those would both be attempts at simplifying what a Road Movie is about, and I don't think it's that simple. To me, Road Movies often adhere to this equation:

$$(Man + Machine) - (God\ vs.\ Society) + Nature/Himself$$

What this means is that Road Movies often focus on amoral humans, inside cars, racing against the structure of society and the limitations of the natural world, filtered through the perception of the character's life experience. For some reason, this was especially common in 1971. Along with *Duel,* that year also saw the release of *Vanishing Point* and *Two-Lane Blacktop,* companion films that romanticize driving to a degree that now seems vaguely absurd.

Made with a budget of $1.3 million, *Vanishing Point* is about a 1970 Dodge Challenger, driven by "Kowalski," a stoic portrayed by a man named Barry Newman who spends a lot of time looking like Elliott Gould and acting like Dustin Hoffman (the director originally wanted the role to go to Gene Hackman). In order to win a meaningless bet with a Benzedrine dealer, Kowalski tries to drive his white Challenger from Boulder, Colorado, to San Francisco in fifteen hours (normally, such a trip takes about twenty hours). As the trip ensues, the Challenger evolves into a sort of memory machine that allows Kowalski to mentally replay past episodes from his life. That's pretty much the whole movie. *Two-Lane Blacktop* was made more cheaply (an estimated $850,000) and managed to be even more plotless: Two drag-racing slackabouts (musicians James Taylor and Dennis Wilson) get into a cross-country Route 66 road race against a drifter in a GTO (the always crazy Warren Oates). This turns into a three-way sexual competition for an extremely annoying hippie (Laurie Bird). The story is generally incomprehensible, partially because untrained actors Taylor and Wilson tend to oscillate between acting unnaturally stiff and supernaturally high.

Still, there are two things that make *Vanishing Point* and *Two-Lane Blacktop* compelling, regardless of how underwritten they feel in the present tense. The first is that both films are auto-centric in every possible context. The audience is constantly shown images inside the rearview mirror or over the top of the hood. The sound of the vehicle engines is extremely high in the audio mix. You get used to seeing people gripping a steering wheel while cocking their skull slightly to one side. "I'm gonna make the car the star," claimed *Vanishing Point* director Richard Sarafian, but that's not really what happens; in both movies, *the process of driving* is the star. The other (more obvious) link between *Vanishing Point* and *Two-Lane Blacktop* is how they conclude. In the former, Kowalski drives his Dodge into a pair of bulldozers and explodes. Man and Car die together, and there's no explanation as to why. *Two-Lane Blacktop* ends even more abruptly; while racing in Tennessee, the movie's sound drops out and the celluloid film itself burns up.

If you like either or both of these movies, you almost certainly find both of these endings "existential." If you dislike these movies, you probably find these finales meaningless (which is another way of saying "existential in a bad way"). The only reason I like them is because *Vanishing Point* and *Two-Lane Blacktop* seem to solve the Road Movie Equation I mentioned a few paragraphs earlier. It's no longer a question of "versus." Now the equation reads more like this:

$$(\text{Man} + \text{Machine}) - (\text{God} < \text{Society}) + \text{Nature}/\text{Himself}$$

What this boils down to is that there are two idioms of Road Movies, and the only thing that truly connects them is the presence of asphalt. Films in the vein of *Vanishing Point* are external, aggressive, mechanically oriented abstractions where the characters remain static (this genus also includes movies like *Cannonball Run, The Road Warrior,* and *The Fast and the Furious*). In contrast, movies like Wong Kar-Wai's terrible *My Blueberry Nights,* the overrated *Two for the Road,* or the terrible and overrated *Little Miss Sunshine* are supposed to be meandering, personal, and transformative. In short, you are either (a) going nowhere fast or (b) going somewhere slow. The fact that we all unconsciously understand those philosophies is why Road Movies succeed.

But sometimes it's why they fail. The themes we all understand are not always true.

One of the best Road Movies from recent years is Kelly Reichardt's *Old Joy,* a minimalist indie project set in the Pacific Northwest. The movie is about two old friends (Will Oldham and Daniel London) who have grown apart over time. In an unconscious attempt to salvage the friendship, they decide to take a road trip together. Now, were this a conventional Road Movie, that experience would foster rediscovery—the two friends would address their differences and bind a new friendship. But this does not happen. They do not argue, evolve, or even recall why they originally liked each other. It's a slow, hyper-personal movie that offers no transformation whatsoever. The characters have nothing profound to say to each other, and they both understand that this diffidence is disenchanting. But because they are in a car together, *they can still talk.* When two people are sitting in a car, they don't have to look at each other. They don't have to be interesting or funny or even themselves, because they're not there for entertainment; they are there to get somewhere else. That's what makes movement more interesting than staying in place: Road trips exist outside of reality. Cars are not just memory machines. Cars are avoidance machines. And we will always watch anything that keeps us from being here, regardless of where that is (or isn't).

"The Best Response"

The best response to being caught in an illicit homosexual relationship after spending much of your political career pushing antigay legislation and campaigning on a family values platform.

"I will concede that I am more confused than the average person. I've spent my entire life denying who I truly was. But my motive for that denial was political, even before I was a politician. I always believed that I could serve the greater good by advancing myself into a position of power, and— in order to make that a reality—the compromise I made was to attack the social mores that were extensions of everything I feared about myself. I felt extremely guilty for doing this, and I felt as though I deserved to be punished. My religious upbringing dictated retribution. So by publicly criticizing the gay community, I felt like I was silently punishing myself. Now, I was totally aware that this was hypocritical, and that hypocrisy consumed me. It was all I ever thought about. It became so pervasive within my consciousness that I found myself acting upon my own suppressed desires. I became romantically involved with someone of my own gender, completely aware that this could destroy me politically. That was part of the attraction. Sadly, I enjoyed feeling self-destructive. When that relationship became more intense, I began to accept that I was gay. And that's why I kept pushing for laws that hurt the gay community. Political duplicity was the only way I could confront my own personal demons. I deeply apologize for hurting other people, but the only person I was trying to hurt was myself.

"Also, I am an alcoholic."

The best response to allegations that you used steroids throughout your playing career, particularly if those allegations are true and verifiable.

"I did experiment with steroids. I am not denying that. But the fact of the matter is that I only took them for a short while, simply because my body did not respond the way I anticipated. They did not help me the way they helped other athletes. Look: I'm a very competitive person. I will do anything to win, because that's what my character dictates and what my fans demand. I'm like Michael Jordan. I'm like Tiger Woods. So, yes, I did try steroids. That was what virtually everyone I knew was doing. It didn't feel like cheating. It felt like *not* using steroids was *not trying* to win. But they didn't work for me the way they worked for the others. I felt more susceptible to injury and less in control of my emotions. It deadened my sex drive and gave me acne, and I've always been a narcissistic guy. I saw no dramatic improvement in my on-field performance, so I quit using them. I'm ashamed to admit that I would have kept taking them if they had helped, but they didn't. So if I am on trial for competitive immorality, I plead guilty. I'm dangerously cutthroat. But if the larger question is whether or not my career statistical achievements are less valid because I used stanozolol and testosterone cypionate, I can honestly say they are not. History may judge me as a vain person who was willing to cheat to win, but my actual attempts at cheating didn't work. I'm the same natural athlete everyone always imagined."

The best response to having the film you directed go $200 million over budget while single-handedly bankrupting the movie studio.

"Critics will say I lost control of this project, but that's not accurate. The reason my film became so sprawling and costly is because—for the first time in my life—I was *completely* in control of the creative process. The film inside my brain was literally being transferred onto the celluloid, image by image by image. It was almost akin to a scientific breakthrough. This has never happened before, to anyone. In the past, movies were merely an interpretation of what someone intellectually conceived, inevitably falling short of the ultimate intention. But this was different. This was the perfect transfer of theory to reality, and that did not come without a cost. I realize the constraints of capitalism have inflicted a degree of collateral damage at the studio, and that disappoints me. There were a lot of fine people working there, and I hate that this endeavor has caused them to lose their jobs. It's awful. But on balance, $200 million seems like a small price to pay for this kind of aesthetic advance. Even if all the reviews are negative and it does no business whatsoever at the box office, this will have to be remembered as the first truly successful film."

The best response to not remembering the name of someone you've met several times before.

"This might seem weird, but you really, really remind me of the best friend I've ever had. My friend's name was Jamie. You look the same, you act the same, you have the same mannerisms, and you exhibit the same depth of humanity. When I see you, I see Jamie.[1]

---

1. Note: This does not work if the person whose name you can't recall happens to be named Jamie.

But ten years ago, Jamie died in a boating accident. That accident still feels like it happened yesterday. I've never gotten over it. And because of that, all I can think about whenever I see you is this dead friend of mine. It blocks out everything else in my consciousness, including your first name. I always want to call you Jamie. It's the only name my brain will accept.

"Also, I am an alcoholic."

The best response to being arrested for carrying an unlicensed handgun into a nightclub and accidentally shooting yourself in the leg, thereby jeopardizing your pro football career.

"First of all, you people probably don't know anyone who's been shot. I, however, know *lots* of people who've been shot. In fact, I know lots of people who claim they want to shoot me, and some of these people are technically my friends. So that's why I carry a gun. Second, you people probably trust the government, and you probably trust it because your personal experience with law enforcement has been positive. I've had the opposite experience all my life. I'm afraid of the government. I'm afraid of the world, and you can't give me one valid reason why I shouldn't be. So that's why I did not apply for a gun license. Third, I shot myself in the leg, which is both painful and humiliating. What else do I need to go through in order to satiate your desire to see me chastised? The penalty for carrying an unlicensed weapon is insane. How can carrying an unlicensed firearm be worse than firing a licensed one? I broke the law, but the law I broke *is a bad law*. Would you be satisfied if the penalty for unlawful gun possession was getting shot in the leg? Because that already fucking happened!"

The best response to a police officer who's just asked the question "Have you been drinking tonight?"

"That's a great question, and I totally understand why you're asking it. I can see where you're coming from, sir. I realize my behavior seems a little erratic. I smell vaguely of alcohol, I'm in a motor vehicle, and it's three o'clock in the morning. It's a unique circumstance. But I'm not intoxicated. I'm *distraught*. I'm a hyper-emotional person who can't accept the inherent unfairness of the universe. Have you ever read Arthur Schopenhauer? You know, that dead German pessimist? He once said that the vanity of existence is revealed in the form that existence assumes: in the infiniteness of time and space contrasted with the finiteness of the individual in both; in the fleeting present as the sole form in which actuality exists; in the contingency and relativity of all things; in continual becoming without being; in continual desire without satisfaction; in the continual frustration of striving of which life consists. Crazy, right? I don't really get what he's saying. But I do know this, officer: That's how I feel *all the time*. And to make matters worse, I'm an insomniac. I haven't slept more than two hours in any given night since I was sixteen. That's why I'm awake right now, wandering the roadways of quasi-reality, living my wretched, vampiric existence. I suppose you could say I was suicidal, but too depressed to kill myself. And then, when I saw the rolling blue lights of your squad car in my rearview mirror, I realized that nothing I could say or do would reflect positively on my condition. The game was over. I've lost. Why fight it? I pulled over to the side of the road, depressed the parking brake, turned off my vehicle, and imbibed one full shot of Bombay gin, which I happen to keep in the glove box of my car, precisely for this type of situation. That is the alcohol you smell. In fact, it's still coating the inside of my mouth. Which also means that if you give me a Breathalyzer right now, the remnants of the alcohol will still be there, so I'll fail the test, even though I'm not intoxicated. So—to answer your original question—*yes*. I have been drinking. I've had exactly one drink tonight, thirty seconds ago, in response to the hopelessness of existence. Do I still need a lawyer?"

The best response to the final jury on *Survivor*, assuming you've made it through the entire game by lying, breaking promises, and relying on other players who were more physically talented than you.

"This game is an imaginary universe we have created, as both players and fans. The idea of people being dropped onto an island with no food and forced to compete in weird contests and asked to conduct secret votes has no relationship with the rest of the world. But this is what we choose. We willfully look into the cameras and speak the fabricated language of this game show—we use words and phrases like *alliance* and *immunity* and *going to tribal* as if they have the same meanings outside of this TV program. Basically, we are living inside a fabricated society that we all appreciate. We became contestants on this show because we liked the idea of a mediated reality that would not intersect with who we are in the mundane game of real life; we preferred the high-definition world we saw on CBS, where the morals and values were specific to the experience of the game. This being the case, it's your responsibility as a member of the jury to uphold the ideals that originally made you want to watch this television show. And what values are those? Well, think about the first season of *Survivor* from 2000—the year it was *really* popular, even among people who didn't care. The final vote came down to a decision between two people—a naked gay guy who lied to everybody, and a female wilderness guide who won almost all of the individual challenges. In real life, the naked gay guy would not have survived on a deserted island. But the naked gay guy won the game. He got the votes. You see, those first voters made a critical distinction: They decided that the ability to succeed at *Survivor* without natural skills was more impressive than succeeding by one's own aptitude and work ethic. They decided that the ability to drag everyone down to the middle required more strategy than transcending the group alone. They invented what success at *Survivor* was supposed to signify. *So this is the game we must play*. You may not like the idea of rewarding someone for being deceitful and opportunistic, and you may not like the symbolism that such a practice expresses to audiences watching at home. But if you like this TV show—and since you're here right now, you obviously do—you have no option but to uphold the precedent that made *Survivor* the experience that it is. If you don't, you'll disrupt the framework of the show. You *must* vote for the person who seems to deserve it less, because that person ultimately deserves it more. And if you don't agree with that concept, you're killing *Survivor* itself, which means your own personal participation will eventually become unimportant. So if you want this experience to be meaningful, vote against your conscience.

"Also, I am an alcoholic."

Football

1 As I type this sentence, I'm watching the Michigan Wolverines play the Minnesota Golden Gophers in football. Michigan is bad this year and the Gophers are better than expected, but Michigan is winning easily. They're winning by running the same play over and over and over again. Very often, it seems to be the only effective play they have. It has certain similarities to the single-wing offenses from the 1950s, but the application is new and different. It's called the read option, and it looks like this.

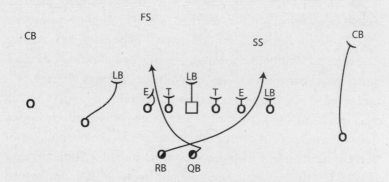

As of this moment in 2008, the read option is by far the most pervasive offensive play in college football and an increasingly popular gadget play in pro football, especially for the Miami Dolphins (who run it by moving quarterback Chad Pennington to

147

wide receiver and using running back Ronnie Brown at QB, a formation commonly called the Wildcat). If somebody makes a movie about American life a hundred years from now and wants to show a fictionalized image of what football looked like, this is the play they should try to cinematically replicate.[1] Every week of autumn, I watch between nine and fifteen hours of football; depending on who's playing, I probably see this play eighty to a hundred and fifty times a weekend. Michigan has just run it three times in succession. This play defines the relationship between football and modernity; it's What Interesting Football Teams Are Doing Now. And it's helped me rethink the relationship between football and conservatism, a premise I had long conceded but never adequately questioned.

2 *Okay* . . . Let me begin by recognizing that you—the reader of this book—might not know much about football. In fact, you might *hate* football, and you might be annoyed that it's even included in this collection. I'm guessing at least fifty potential buyers flipped through the pages of this book inside a store, noticed there was a diagram of a football play on page 147, and decided not to buy it. This is a problem I have always had to manage: Roughly 60 percent of the people who read my books have a near-expert understanding of sports, but the remaining 40 percent have no interest whatsoever. As such, I will understand if you skip to the next essay, which is about ABBA. **But before**

---

1. The spread offense was so culturally pervasive in 2008 that it briefly became a plot point in season three of *Friday Night Lights,* undoubtedly the first time a prime-time TV show felt the need to respond to what was happening in major college football.

you give up, let me abridge the essence of the previous paragraph: The aforementioned "read option" is an extremely simple play. The main fellow for the offense (this would be the quarterback, whom you might remember as a popular guy from high school who dated lots of girls with bleached hair) receives the ball deep in the backfield and "reads" the weakside defensive end ("read" is the football term for "looks at and considers," while "weakside" refers to whatever side of the field has fewer offensive players). If the defensive player attacks upfield, the quarterback keeps the ball and runs it himself, essentially attacking where the defensive end used to be (and where a running lane now exists). If the defensive end "stays home" (which is the football term for "remains cautious and orthodox"), there's usually no running lane for the quarterback, so the QB hands the ball to the running back moving in the opposite direction (which is generally the strong side). Basically, the read option is just the quarterback making a choice based on the circumstance—he either runs the ball himself in one direction, or he hands the ball off in the opposing direction.

Now, why should this matter to you (or anyone)? Here is the simplest answer: Twenty-five years ago, the read option didn't exist. Coaches would have given a dozen reasons why it couldn't be used. Ten years ago, it was a play of mild desperation, most often used by teams who couldn't compete physically. But now almost everyone uses it. It's the vortex of an offensive scheme that has become dominant. But ten years from now—or even less, probably—this play will have disappeared completely. In 2018, no one will run it, because every team will be running something else. It will have been replaced with new thinking. And this is football's interesting contradiction: It feels like a conservative game. It appeals to a conservative mind-set and a reactionary media and it promotes conservative values. But in tangible practicality, football is the most progressive game we have—it constantly innovates, it immediately embraces every new technology,[2] and almost all the important thinking about the game is liberal. If football was a politician, it would be some kind of reverse libertarian: staunchly conservative on social issues, but freethinking on anything related to policy. So the current upsurge of the read option is symbolic of something unrelated to the practice of football; it's symbolic of the *nature* of football and how that idea is misinterpreted because of its iconography.

So there you go.

If you'd still rather get to the shit about ABBA, you should go there now.

3 The single most radical aspect of football is something most casual (and even most serious) fans take for granted: Football *added* the forward pass. It was an extraneous addition to the original game, implemented long after the sport had gained national attention. There is no corollary for this in any other meaningful spectator sport. The DH rule in baseball and the three-point line in hoops are negligible when compared to the impact of passing; it would be like golf suddenly allowing tackling on the putting green. By now, watching football on television is mostly the act of watching passing—in 2008, the NFL's worst passing team (the Oakland Raiders) still gained more yards through the air than all but five teams gained rushing. At

---

2. I feel like the addition of radios inside the helmets of NFL quarterbacks has been an overlooked innovation in how football embraces change. The Cleveland Browns invented QB radios in 1956, but they were banned until 1994. This legislation, along with the use of instant replay for officials, shows how football is unusually willing to let technology dictate performance. More conservative sports (like baseball or soccer) would fight such modernization tooth and nail.

the NCAA level in '08, seven of the starting quarterbacks in the Big 12 Conference completed 65 percent of all the passes they attempted, a rate of success that made running the ball seem almost wasteful. Passing is what drives the sport and passing is what sells the sport. But passing only exists because of violence.

Imagine football at the turn of the twentieth century, before passing was part of the game: How would it look? The entire game is contained in the middle of the field, away from the side- lines. There's almost no benefit in aligning defensive players away from the ball, because there's no way for the offense to take advantage of their tight proximity. Instead of ten yards for a first down, teams only need five. As a result, every single play is like a goal-line surge during a driving blizzard—the best strategy is to simply pound the ball straight ahead. And because this is the nineteenth century (which means equipment is essentially non- existent), football is a laughably violent undertaking. It's nothing but a series of collisions, sporadically interrupted by one or two touchdowns and a whole lot of punting. In 1905, eighteen college kids die from playing football. President Theodore Roosevelt sees a photograph of Swarthmore lineman Bob Maxwell walking off the field after a game against Penn, and he's so utterly pummeled and disgusting that Roosevelt (despite being a fan) decides that football needs to be outlawed. This becomes a hot-button issue for a year. Finally, Roosevelt decides that football can continue to exist, but only if some of the rules are changed. One change increases the distance needed for a first down. Another legalizes passing, which has been going on illegally (but often unpenal- ized) for decades. Essentially, Roosevelt decriminalizes the pass- ing game. And this decriminalization actually makes the rules of football easier to comprehend: Previously, it had been unclear how referees were expected to enforce a penalty for forward pass- ing—there wasn't a rule *against* passing, much as there isn't any rule against making your slotback invisible. How do you legislate against something no one had previously imagined? When an illegal forward pass was used by Yale against Princeton in 1876, the ref allegedly decided to allow the play to stand after flipping a coin. Action had evolved faster than thought.

Interestingly, Roosevelt's rule changes did not significantly alter the violent nature of college football; by 1909, the number of nationwide deaths from football had risen to thirty-three. But these changes totally reinvented the intellectual potential for football. It was like taking the act of punching someone in the face and shaping it into boxing. Suddenly, there were multiple dimensions to offense—the ball could rapidly be advanced on both its X and Y axis. The field was technically the same size, but it was vaster. You could avoid the brutality of trench warfare by flying over it. It liberalized the sport without eliminating its conservative underpinnings: Soldiers were still getting their skulls hammered in the kill zone, but there was now a progressive, humanitarian way to approach the offensive game plan. Size mattered less (Knute Rockne's 1913 Notre Dame squad was able to famously slay a much bigger Army juggernaut by out-passing them), but it was still a game where blocking and tackling *appeared* to be the quintessence of what it was about. It was at this point that football philosophy forked: There were now two *types* of football coaches, as diametrically opposed (and as profoundly connected) as Goldwater and McGovern.

By portraying itself as the former while operating as the latter, football became the most successful enterprise in American sports history.

4 As of this morning, I am one of only forty million Americans who receive the NFL Network in their living room. This is less than the number of Americans who get BBC America, the Golf Channel, or VH1 Classic. The NFL Network has only existed for five years. However, I can tell it's going to succeed. I can tell by the sheer amount of time I end up watching it during the day, even when the network is doing nothing except repeating and promoting the same information I didn't need to know yesterday. Because of the NFL Network, I've been convinced to consume information about issues I previously saw as ridiculous. I (now) watch the NFL draft combine every spring. I am (now) acutely aware of what's happening in the off-season owners' meetings. One night in July, I watched the Seattle Seahawks work on a seven-on-seven passing drill for forty minutes. I wouldn't classify any of these things as phenomena I care about, but they are things I still watch, particularly when they compete against other pre-recorded TV shows that don't feel like news, despite the fact that the Seahawks' seven-on-seven passing drill isn't "news" any more than *Panda Nursery*.

What the NFL has realized is that they have no better marketing tool than the game itself. Every other sport tries to fool us. Baseball sells itself as some kind of timeless, historical pastime that acts as the bridge to a better era of American life, an argument that now seems beyond preposterous. The NBA tries to create synergy with *anything* that might engage youth culture (hip-hop, fuzzy primordial competition, nostalgia for the 1980s, the word "amazing," Hurricane Katrina, etc.). NASCAR connects itself to red state contrarianism. Soccer aligns itself with forward-thinking globalists who enjoy fandom more than sports. But football only uses football. They are the product they sell. Unlike David Stern's failed vision for the NBA, the NFL Network does not try to expand its empire by pushing the sport toward nonchalant audiences with transitory interest; it never tries to trick anybody into watching something they don't already like. Instead, the NFL Network's goal is to enliven its base. It solely tries to (a) make football essential to people, and (b) make football *more* essential to those who are already invested. The casual fan does not matter. In essence, the NFL Network works exactly like FOX News: It stays on message and invents talking points for its core constituency to absorb. If Donovan McNabb is temporarily benched for Kevin Kolb during week ten of the season, that decision is turned into a collection of questions for football people to ponder until Sunday. How will McNabb react? Will he be traded to Washington? Has Eagles coach Andy Reid lost control of his offense? How will this impact your fantasy team? These are the ideas football fans are supposed to talk about during the run-up to week eleven, and the NFL Network ensures that those debates will be part of the public discourse. It does not matter that McNabb did not lose his job or if the Eagles are out of playoff contention. By inventing and galvanizing the message, the NFL Network (and by extension the NFL) can always deliver the precise product people want. They construct how I think about pro football.

This is the genius of the NFL, and it is how they came to power long before they had their own network: The league can always make people think they're having the specific experience they desire, even if they're actually experiencing the opposite. Pete Rozelle—the greatest sports commissioner in world history— did this better than anyone. He convinced America that football was conservative. During the 1970s, he tried to stop NFL players from having long locks and facial hair, and he mostly succeeded (and even when he failed—as with the Jets' Joe Namath and the miscreants on the Raiders—those failures worked to the league's advantage by appealing to the antiauthority minority). He created a seamless relationship with NFL Films, an organization that specialized in cinematically lionizing the most old-school elements of the game (blood, mud, the frozen breath of Fran Tarkenton, Jack Lambert's missing teeth, etc.). He fostered the idea of the Dallas Cowboys as "America's team," led by a devout Catholic quarterback who had served in Vietnam. He made football replace baseball in every meaningful, nationalistic way. And he did this while simultaneously convincing all the league's owners to adopt revenue sharing, arguably the most successful form of socialism in U.S. history. The reason the NFL is so dominant is because the NFL is basically Marxist. This was Rozelle's greatest coup, and everybody knows it. But you'd never guess that from watching the NFL Network. Marxism is not a talking point.

And that's smart, too. The mechanics of distraction are not to be seen.

For the past fifteen years, the face of Old World pro football has been Brett Favre. He was the most beloved sports media figure I'd ever witnessed. The adoration was inescapable. Favre has always been among my favorite players, but even I had a hard time listening to broadcasters rave about his transcendent grit.[3] The rhetoric never evolved: "He just loves to play the game. He just loves to throw the old pigskin around the old backyard. He just wears Wrangler jeans and forgets to shave. Sure, he throws a few picks now and then, but that's just because he's a gunslinger. That's just Brett being Brett." He was so straightforward and authentic that analysts were unable to discuss Brett Favre without using the word *just* somewhere in the sentence. He was the human incarnation of how the NFL hopes to portray itself—as a collection of unpretentious throwbacks who still manage to thrive inside a civilized, nonwarrior society. He directly appealed

---

3. I feel an obligation to note that it wasn't really Favre's fault that announcers were in love with him. But *it kind of was,* because Favre perpetuated it, too. He openly played to their girlish worship.

to the self-righteous, reactionary mentality of the American sports media. Favre is football, or at least he seems to be. And the operative word here is *seems*. He *seems* essential, but he isn't. The men who truly dictate the reality of modern football are not like Brett Favre; the men who dictate the reality of modern football are generally classified as nuts.

2A This is another message for non–football followers who are nonetheless reading this essay out of literary obligation, mild interest, or sheer boredom: You might consider skipping most of the next section. Just skim down to the last paragraph in 3A and continue on from there. Thanks.

3A Right now, the most interesting coach in America is Mike Leach[4] of Texas Tech, a former lawyer who's obsessed with pirates and UFOs and

---

4. In late December of 2009, Leach was fired by Texas Tech for locking a player with a mild concussion in an empty equipment room for over an hour. This situation was complicated by several factors, most notably (a) the player in question, Adam James, was the son of ESPN personality Craig James, and (b) had Texas Tech not fired Leach, they would have owed him an additional $800,000 as of December 31. This controversy was further exacerbated by Leach's eccentric behavior, his refusal to apologize, the December 3, 2009, departure of Kansas football coach Mark Mangino over player abuse issues, and allegations that Craig James used the PR firm Spaeth Communications to attack Leach. Spaeth Communications is the same group that engineered the "Swift Boat" allegations against John Kerry during the 2004 presidential election. Leach finished his career at Texas Tech with a record of 84–43.

grizzly bears. He never played football at the college level and
barely played in high school. But his offensive attack at Texas Tech
is annually the best in the country, and it seems to be the best
no matter who his players happen to be. The Red Raiders play
football the way eleven-year-old boys play Xbox: They throw on
almost every down, they only punt when the situation is desperate, and they'll call the same play over and over and over again.
The Texas Tech linemen use unnaturally wide line splits and the
quarterback lines up in the shotgun, even when the offense is
inside the five-yard line. If you describe the Red Raiders' style
of play to any traditional football follower without mentioning
the team's name, they reflexively scoff. But Texas Tech hammers
people. Over the past five years they've outscored opponents by
an average score of 39.4 to 24.8 while outgaining them by over
nine thousand yards, despite the fact that Tech is forced to recruit
second-tier high school players who are overlooked by Texas and
Oklahoma. Everywhere Leach has gone, he's had success—as an
assistant at the University of Kentucky, he found ways to turn
an ungifted quarterback (Tim Couch) into a Heisman candidate
who passed for 8,400 yards and was drafted first overall by the
Cleveland Browns. In a single season assisting at Oklahoma, he
designed the offense that would ultimately win a national championship. So how did he do it? What is the secret to his brilliance?

"There's two ways to make it more complex for the defense,"
Leach told journalist Michael Lewis, writing for *The New York
Times Magazine*. "One is to have a whole bunch of different plays,
but that's no good because then the offense experiences as much
complexity as the defense. Another is a small number of plays
run out of lots of different formations. That way, you don't have
to teach a guy a new thing to do. You just have to teach him new
places to stand."

It's easy to overlook the significance of this kind of quote,
mostly because it seems obvious and casual and reductionist. But

it's none of those things. It's an almost perfect description of how thinking slightly differently can have an exponential consequence, particularly when applied to an activity that's assumed to be inflexible. There is this inherent myth about football that suggests offensive success comes in one of two ways: You can run a handful of plays with extreme precision, or you can run a multitude of different plays in the hope of keeping defenses confused. The Green Bay Packers of the Lombardi era embraced the former philosophy (they rarely used more than fifteen different plays in the course of any game, but the fifteen they ran were disciplined and flawless), as did the straightforward running attack of USC during the 1970s and early '80s.[5] Two modern coaches (Steve Spurrier and Urban Meyer) have both found success at the talent-rich University of Florida, seemingly by never running the same play twice. But the inverted thinking of Mike Leach allows Texas Tech to do both: If Texas Tech focuses on only fifteen different plays—but runs them all out of twenty different formations—they're instantly drawing from a pool of three hundred options, all of which could still be executed with the repetitive exactitude of the Packers' power sweep. It wasn't that Leach out-thought everybody else; it was merely that he thought *differently*. Instead of working within the assumed parameters of football, he decided to expand what those parameters were. For a while, that made him seem like a crazy person. But this is how football always evolves: Progressive ideas are introduced by weirdos and mocked by the world, and then everybody else adopts and refines those ideas ten years later. To wit:

- Bill Walsh, the architect of the San Francisco 49ers dynasty, who built the West Coast offense on an interesting combina-

---

5. As a senior in 1981, USC's Marcus Allen rushed for 2,432 yards in twelve games. This is both astounding and understandable when you watch tape of the Trojans from that season—it often seems like half of the offensive plays were simple toss sweeps over the right tackle (the so-called "Student Body Right").

tion of mathematics and psychology: He realized that any time a team rushed for four yards on the ground, the play was viewed as a success. However, any time a team completed a pass that gained four yards, the defense assumed they had made a successful stop. Walsh understood that the two situations were identical. By viewing the passing game as a variant of the running game, he changed everything about how football is played.

- Sam Wyche, the principal innovator of the no-huddle offense: Wyche was known for having curious ideas about everything, but his theory of a chaotic attack (that ignored the pre-snap huddle in order to generate matchup problems and tire defenses) is now common. In 1989, Wyche's Cincinnati Bengals played the Buffalo Bills in a play-off game. Members of the Bills defense constantly feigned injury in order to stop the Bengals from rushing to the line of scrimmage. Prior to the game, Bills coach Marv Levy had openly questioned the moral credibility of Wyche's approach. The following season, Levy stole the Bengals' no-huddle offense and went on to play in four straight Super Bowls.

- Darrel "Mouse" Davis, the passing guru who popularized the Run and Shoot offense: Nobody really runs the Run and Shoot anymore (it didn't really work whenever a team was inside the twenty), but almost every pass-first coach has stolen some of its principles. One of these principles was allowing wide receivers to make adjustments to their pass routes while they were running them, so-called "choice routes"[6] that are especially popular with present-day slot

---

6. This is especially significant within the context of football's traditional relationship with hierarchical control: Since the 1970s, much of football's fascist reputation had to do with the way offensive plays are dictated by the coaching staff, often from a press box a hundred feet above the field of play. The actual athletes sometimes seem like pawns. But choice routes gave autonomy to receivers.

receivers like Wes Welker and Anthony Gonzalez. The one-RB, four-WR offensive set Davis invented at Portland State in the late 1970s is standard today, even though it seemed otherworldly and unstoppable at the time: In 1980, Portland State beat Delaware State 105–0 and Cal Poly Pomona 93–7. Mouse may have been a genius, but he was something of a prick.

- Mike Martz, a lunatic whom no one seems to respect[7] but who consistently creates innovation by ignoring conventional thinking. Sometimes, this hurts him (while coaching the St. Louis Rams, Martz seemed briefly obsessed with the possibility of onside kicking when the Rams were ahead). But sometimes his strange mind leads him to interesting places: Fundamentally, it was always believed that receivers should run in straight lines and make their downfield cuts at hard angles. Martz considered the possibility of WRs running curved pass patterns, a subtle change that helped make the Rams impossible to contain during the late nineties.

- Dick LeBeau: In 1984, as a coordinator in Cincinnati, he borrowed basketball philosophies to develop the "zone blitz"—the concept of attacking the opposing QB with linebackers and defensive backs while dropping hulking defensive linemen into pass coverage. In '84, the idea of using a 270-pound defensive end in the secondary seemed about as practical as using a sledgehammer to fix a clock radio. But by the turn of the century, the zone blitz was everywhere.

- Gus Malzahn, the unheralded offensive coordinator at the University of Tulsa[8] who took Wyche's hurry-up offense

---

7. ESPN commentator Tom Jackson once called Martz "The worst kind of idiot—an idiot who thinks he's a genius."

8. Malzahn is now at Auburn.

to its illogical extreme: The goal of Malzahn's approach is to play at full speed at all times, lengthening the game and wearing out opponents mentally and physically. As a high school coach at tiny Shiloh Christian in Arkansas, he once won a play-off game by a score of 70 to 64. In that contest, his quarterback passed for 672 yards. Tulsa averaged 47.2 points per game in 2008.

- Steve Humphries, a bored high school coach in Piedmont, California, who came up with the A-11 offense: The A-11 exploited a loophole in the rulebook allowing every player on the field to become an eligible pass receiver during kicking situations. The A-11 also employs two quarterbacks simultaneously, making every snap a gadget play. Because of its reliance on a bad rule, the A-11 is being outlawed by the National Federation of High Schools—but elements of the scheme will still be adopted by every coordinator who takes the time to study it. Even more radical are mathematical minds like Kevin Kelley of Pulaski Academy in Arkansas, a high school coach who went 13–1 and won the Arkansas 5A title in 2007 by never punting the football all season, even when his team was pinned inside its own ten-yard line. All of Kelley's in-game decisions are considered from a risk-reward standpoint, exclusively viewed through statistical probability; he has concluded that the upside of working with an extra play on every set of downs is greater than the risk of surrendering thirty-five yards of field possession on every change of possession. His numeric strategy is also applied to kickoffs—Pulaski onside kicks about 75 percent of the time. Despite their success, just about everyone who watches Pulaski Academy play still thinks they're joking. "You can just tell people are in the stands thinking, 'You're an idiot,'" Kelley said after winning the championship.

I could list these types of guys ad nauseam. I could include everyone from Sid Gillman[9] to Emory Bellard[10] to Don Coryell.[11] But the size of the list doesn't matter; what matters is how these men were all criticized in the same way. Whenever an innovation fails to result in a title, its unorthodoxy takes the hit; every time a football coach tries something unorthodox, he is blasted for not playing "the right way." But all that "not playing the right way" means is that a coach is ignoring the eternal lie of football: the myth that everything done in the past is better than anything that could be invented in the present. As a result, the public arm of football—the conservative arm—bashes innovation immediately, even while adopting the principles it attacks.[12] The innovators are ridiculed. And that kind of reaction is reassuring to fans, because it makes us feel like football is still the same game we always want to remember. It has a continuity of purpose. It symbolizes the same

---

9. Gillman introduced the idea of the vertical passing game in the 1950s and '60s.

10. Bellard popularized the wishbone option at the University of Texas in 1967, having taken the idea from Charles "Spud" Carson, a junior high coach in Fort Worth, Texas.

11. Coryell is the father of the modern pro passing game, particularly with the San Diego Chargers in the early 1980s. He also changed the way people looked at collegiate talent: He won 104 games with the San Diego State Aztecs by almost exclusively recruiting from junior colleges.

12. Easy example: In the annual *New York Times Magazine* "The Year in Ideas" issue for 2008, there was a brief examination of the Wildcat formation and the spread offense. The piece concludes with a dismissive quote from Aaron Schatz, a contributor to *Pro Football Prospectus*. "Wildcat got crazy," said Schatz. "It's a silly fad, like leg warmers or parachute pants." Time may prove Schatz correct, but his condescension ignores some irrefutable results. The year before Miami started using the Wildcat, they were 1–15; the next season, the Dolphins went 11–5 and won the AFC East. In 2007, Ole Miss went 3–9, so they fired their head coach and hired Wildcat innovator Houston Nutt; with almost identical talent, Ole Miss won nine games in 2008 and were the only school to defeat the University of Florida all season. Ole Miss ultimately beat Leach's Texas Tech in the 2009 Cotton Bowl.

ideals and appeals to the same kind of person. It feels conservative, but it acts liberal. Everything changes, but not really.

1A As I continue to watch Michigan's quarterback run the read option against the Gophers, I now find myself wondering if this play is authentically simple or quietly complex. The read option is a combination of three rudimentary elements of football: spreading the field, running a back off tackle, and the quarterback keeper. It would be an easy play to teach and a safe play to run, even for junior high kids. But it's still *new*. It didn't really exist in the 1970s and '80s, and when I first saw it employed in the late '90s, it seemed like an idiotic innovation. It seemed like a way to get your quarterback killed without taking advantage of your tailback. I had always believed teams could not succeed by running the ball out of the shotgun formation. I thought it would never happen. But I was wrong. And I suspect the reason I was wrong was not because I didn't understand what was happening on this specific play; I suspect it was because I felt like I already understood football. I had played football and written about football and watched it exhaustively for twenty years, so I thought I knew certain inalienable truths about the game. And I was wrong. What I knew were the *assumed* truths, which are not the same thing. I had brainwashed myself. I was unwilling to admit that my traditional, conservative football values were imaginary and symbolic. They belonged to a game I wasn't actually watching but was still trying to see.

Over time, I realized this had happened with almost every aspect of my life.

3B When we think of football, we think of Woody Hayes, or at least we think of men like Woody Hayes, even if we don't know who Woody Hayes is. Hayes coached Ohio State for twenty-eight years, won five national championships, never asked for a pay raise, and ended his career in disgrace by punching an opposing player in the Gator Bowl. "Show me a gracious loser," he would say, "and I will show you a busboy." People who write books about Woody Hayes give them titles like *War as They Knew It* and note his hatred for popular culture (Hayes was memorably outraged by a reference to lesbianism in Paul Newman's hockey film *Slap Shot*). His quarterbacks never passed,[13] his linebackers always went to class, and every kid who loved him lived in a state of perpetual fear. It felt normal. *That's what football is.* These are the types of images we want to associate with the essence of the game. Bill Parcells used to refer to wideout Terry Glenn as "she" during press conferences. That's what football is. Barry Sanders running to daylight. Earl Campbell running to darkness. Settling for a field goal late in the first half. Playing for field position when the weather is inclement. Blocking sleds. Salt tablets. Richard Nixon's favorite sport. That's what football is, always—and if we stopped believing that, it would seem to matter less.

But that isn't what football is.

It isn't. It changes more often than any sport we have. Football was Nixon's favorite sport, but it was Hunter S. Thompson's favorite, too. Football coaches will try *anything*. They're gonzo. In the 1970s, teams only used a 3-4 defense[14] if their defensive

---

13. Although some of them did become addicted to gambling and cocaine.

14. This refers to a defensive alignment that has three linemen and four linebackers. And if you didn't know that already, I am pretty fucking impressed you're still hanging with this. It should also be noted that certain NFL teams have succeeded wildly with the 3-4 defense even when it was unpopular, particu-

personnel was flawed. During the early eighties, that assumption changed; the new objective was to cover the field with as many linebackers as possible. Suddenly, nobody was playing a 4-3 except Dallas. But then the '85 Bears hammered people with their 46[15] defense, so every coordinator decided he had to create his own bastardized version of the 46. As a result, the only teams that still played 3-4 were the ones with defensive flaws, exactly how things had been originally. Every innovation is seen as a positive innovation, even if it has a negative result. Throughout the 1980s, the hot trend in the NFL was barefoot place kickers. A few guys even punted barefoot. It retrospect, this was probably the strangest fad in football history (it was the sports equivalent of peg-rolling your Guess jeans, which was going on at about the same time). There is absolutely no reason that kicking a football without a shoe could be better than the alternative, particularly when one is outdoors in the dead of winter. But this is what people did. Someone tried it, so it must be worth trying. When my friends and I played four-on-four football at recess, we would remove our moon boots and kick the Nerf pigskin with raw toes, even when the ground was blanketed by nineteen inches of snow. We thought we were being tough. We were actually being liberal.

---

larly in the AFC; Miami won championships with the 3-4 during the mid-1970s and Pittsburgh has used a 3-4 attack for more than twenty years.

15. Unlike the 4-3 or the 3-4, the name of the 46 defense does not indicate the number of linemen and linebackers who are on the field. The reason Bears defensive coordinator Buddy Ryan called this formation the 46 was because its effectiveness hinged on the play of Chicago strong safety Doug Plank, whose jersey number was 46.

2B "In those days football seemed the almost perfect sport and it seemed unlikely we could ever get enough of it," David Halberstam wrote in 1974, alluding to the NFL games he had watched with Gay Talese during the LBJ administration. "What we really rooted for was the game itself." Interestingly, the title of the magazine essay this comes from is "Sunday, Boring Sunday: A Farewell to Pro Football." Halberstam was bemoaning (what he considered to be) the sad decline of pro football during the seventies, a supposition that now seems totally wrong in every possible way.[16] A more prescient statement comes from something Halberstam wrote in 2006, again reminiscing about watching Johnny Unitas and Frank Gifford on black-and-white TV sets over twenty-five-cent beers: "Nobody needed to sell the NFL to us. We could see how good it was."

I am thirty-seven years old. I now like football more than I ever have, or at least as much as I ever have since those wonderful days in fourth grade when I'd take off my moon boot to kick barefoot in the snow. I never thought this would happen. Never. I always assumed that my interest in football would wane over time, just as it has for everything else I was obsessed with as a kid. For a few scant years, this did seem to happen—my interest in pro sports decreased during the height of my college experience, and I missed one Super Bowl completely.[17] But since entering the

---

16. Even Halberstam would ultimately concede that his '74 piece did not hold up over time: In 2001, he wrote a much more affectionate essay called "How I Fell in Love with the NFL."

17. It was the year the Redskins played the Bills, and I was at a party. How I was at a party on a Sunday night in Grand Forks, North Dakota, that somehow *wasn't* a Super Bowl party is pretty hard for me to fathom, but this was around the same time I started drinking "proactively."

workforce in the summer of '94, my obsession with football has risen every single autumn. I love watching it and I love thinking about it. And I want to understand why that happened. I assume it is one of three explanations or—more likely—a combination of all three: Either (a) the game itself keeps improving, (b) the media impacts me more than I'm willing to admit, or (c) this is just what happens to men as they grow older. I suppose I don't care. I'm just glad to have something in my life that is so easy enjoy this much. All I have to do is sit on my couch and watch. It is the easiest kind of pleasure.

My wife is awesome, but she hates football (as wives are wont to do). Every game seems the same to her. I will be watching a contest between Kent State and Eastern Michigan on a random Thursday night, and she will say, "Go ahead and watch that game. I will just sit here and read this magazine featuring a plus-sized black female TV personality from Chicago." Two days later, Georgia will be playing LSU for the SEC championship. Now she will want to rent *Scenes from a Marriage*. "You want to watch football again?" she will ask. "Didn't you already watch football on Thursday?" *Every game seems the same to her*. And I can't explain the difference, even though the differences feel so obvious. And I don't want to explain the difference, because I always want to watch Kent State and Eastern Michigan, too. They are as different to me as they are similar to her.

I don't know what I see when I watch football. It must be something insane, because I should not enjoy it as much as I do. I must be seeing something so personal and so universal that understanding this question would tell me everything I need to know about who I am, and maybe I don't want that to happen. But perhaps it's simply this: Football allows the intellectual part of my brain to evolve, but it allows the emotional part to remain unchanged. It has a liberal cerebellum and a reactionary heart. And this is all I want from everything, all the time, always.

Q: As a woman, did that offend you?

A: What do you mean? Why would it offend me more as a woman?

Q: I don't know. It just seems like this issue has a rather obvious feminist component. Doesn't being a woman change how you think about things?

A: Personally, I was more offended because of my Irish heritage.

Q: Really? How so?

A: End of interview.

ABBA 1, World 0

1 Sometimes it's hard to tell if things that happened in your life only happened to you or if they happened to everyone. Every formative incident feels normal to the child who experiences it, so sometimes it takes twenty-five or thirty years to realize a particular event was singularly bizarre. For example, it took me a long time to recognize that being institutionally taught to dislike disco in my second-grade social studies class was deeply weird—unless, of course, this was a totally normal thing that happened to *everybody* in America who was born in 1972 and attended a public elementary school. I still can't tell.

Once or twice a month (and usually on a Friday), my social studies class would not read from our textbooks. Instead, we were given a publication called the *Weekly Reader,* which was like a newspaper for four-foot illiterates. It concisely covered the entire spectrum of current events, most notably the eruption of Mount St. Helens, the ongoing success of NASA, and whatever was supposedly happening in women's sports and national politics. For some reason, one of the exposés tackled by the *Weekly Reader* in autumn of 1980 was the rising unpopularity of disco, punctuated by "Disco Demolition Night" at Chicago's Comiskey Park during the summer of '79 (news cycles were slower in those days). Disco Demolition Night was a promotional event where a bunch of intoxicated baseball fans blew up Village People albums with dynamite in center field. Things, as they say, did not go smoothly. Thirty-nine people were arrested in the subsequent riot, which

169

actually seems like an amazingly low number considering the stupidity of the original idea. There was an allusion to this in the *Weekly Reader* (or at least in the fake *Weekly Reader* I've created in my memory), and it went on to explain how disco was this insidious, unserious social force. This story was evidently written to convince me and all my eight-year-old friends to continue playing kickball instead of frequenting discothèques. Along with the article was a photograph of four people with comical pants and uncommitted expressions. They were described as "The Disco Group ABBA": They were beards and teeth and natural breasts and whiteness. I suppose my feelings about them would be best described as "mixed," inasmuch as I wasn't sure if they made me bored or hungry for cookies. Part of me still wonders if this actually happened. Maybe it took place during that academic year I was involved with the Dharma Initiative.

But now—obviously—I am older. I have my own beard and my own comical pants, and I am sitting at a computer listening to "The Winner Takes It All" for the two hundredth or three hundredth or seven hundredth time, and I find myself continually shocked by how profoundly *adult* this song is. The chords are sonically limitless. The lyrics refer to judicial proceedings and express uncomfortably specific details about the end of love: I can think of no other pop song that examines the self-aware guilt one feels when talking to a person who has humanely obliterated your heart.

I don't wanna talk
If it makes you feel sad
And I understand
You've come to shake my hand
I apologize
If it makes you feel bad
Seeing me so tense
No self-confidence

The message of "The Winner Takes It All" is straightforward: It argues that the concept of relationships ending on mutual terms is an emotional fallacy. One person is inevitably okay and the other is inevitably devastated. There is a loser who metaphorically stays and a winner who literally leaves, and the individual leaving takes everything with them. Like virtually all of ABBA's music, "The Winner Takes It All" was written by the two male members of the group, Björn Ulvaeus and Benny Andersson. The vocals were sung by Agnetha Faltskog (she was the blond one), who divorced Ulvaeus in 1979 after moving out of their home on Christmas night in '78. "The Winner Takes It All" was released as a single in 1980. Ulvaeus has claimed that the song is not an autobiographical depiction of his failed marriage to Faltskog, but that's hard to believe when one considers the original title of the song was "The Story of My Life."

When thinking about ABBA, this is the song to think about.

2 "When the eighties were over," Scandinavian ABBA historian Carl Magnus Palm wrote in 2001, "it was clear that none of the former ABBA members had any relevance whatsoever in the international pop landscape." This statement isn't false, but it's wrong. I suppose it's true if you use the word *relevance* like most people who regularly write about music, but it's false if you think about how the world actually operates. As a rule, people who classify art as "irrelevant" are trying to position themselves above the entity; it's a way of pretending they're more in step with contemporary culture than the artist himself, which is mostly a way of saying they can't find a tangible reason for disliking what something intends to embody. Moreover, the whole argument is self-defeating: If you classify something as

"irrelevant," you're (obviously) using it as a unit of comparison against whatever *is* "relevant," so it (obviously) *does* have meaning and merit. Truly irrelevant art wouldn't even be part of the conversation.

Since at least 1979, AC/DC has been allegedly irrelevant. When the Knack and Nick Lowe were hot, Angus Young seemed oversexed and stupid. AC/DC was irrelevant in 1984 because they lacked the visual impact of less-heavy metal acts like Dokken, and they were irrelevant in 1989 because they weren't releasing power ballads about teen suicide. They were irrelevant in 1991 because of grunge. They were irrelevant in 1997 because they weren't involved with the mainstreaming of alternative culture. They were irrelevant in 2001 because they weren't implementing elements of hip-hop into their metal. When they played Madison Square Garden in 2008, the always likeable *New York Times* critic Jon Caramanica opened his review like this: "All the recent talk of how AC/DC is due for critical reappraisal? Ignore it." As far as I can tell, AC/DC has been irrelevant for the vast majority of their career. And this has played to their advantage. Judging the value of any band against the ephemeral tastes of the hyper–present tense always misinterprets its actual significance. Moreover, any act lauded as "especially relevant" (and any critic[1] preoccupied with hunting whomever that's supposed to be) is almost guaranteed to have a limited career, simply because so much of their alleged value is tied to an ephemeral modernity they only embody by chance. The reason AC/DC will leave

---

1. In March of '09, this is what Darryl Sterdan of the *Toronto Sun* wrote about U2: "After more than a quarter-century of virtually uninterrupted tenure as The Most Important Band in the World, it would appear Bono, The Edge, Larry Mullen Jr. and Adam Clayton have reached the ultimate plateau in a band's life—the magical place where fame meets irrelevance." What this "irrelevance" means is that U2 is still a major act that Darryl Sterdan has to write about, because that's his job—but he's run out of obvious things to say about their iconography.

a larger, deeper footprint than virtually all of their competition is because they've never been relevant *or* irrelevant; they make music outside of those parameters. This quality is rare. It's also a hard truth for creative personalities to accept. There's a scene in the 2004 Metallica documentary *Some Kind of Monster* where guitarist Kirk Hammett is upset over the band's unwillingness to let him play a conventional rock guitar solo on their new record. Hammett argues, "Can I say something that I think is bullshit? This whole fucking [notion that including a guitar solo] dates the whole thing? That's so bullshit. Because if we *don't* play a guitar solo in one of these songs, that dates it *to this period*. And that cements it to a trend that's happening in music right now." When this exchange occurs during the film, everyone in the audience giggles. It seems like Nigel Tufnel logic. But Hammett intuitively understood something the other guys in Metallica didn't want to accept: The mere recognition of an extrinsic reality damages the intrinsic merits of one's own reality. In other words, it's a mistake to (consciously) do what everyone else is doing, just as it's a mistake to (consciously) do the opposite.

According to the aforementioned C. Magnus Palm, the members of ABBA were irrelevant at the end of the eighties, presumably because they were (a) not creating singles that were on the pop charts, or (b) not overtly influencing the work of people who were (like Madonna and Paula Abdul). That's one way to look at it. But a better way is to view ABBA in 1989 like AC/DC in '99—they were neither germane nor extraneous. They were not attempting to replicate or refute anything else that was happening in pop; they were living in ABBA World, where ABBA Music is the only sound that exists.

3 It's difficult to say anything new or insightful about ABBA, mostly because they've already absorbed every possible criticism and accolade that a musical act can entertain. They first became famous after winning the televised Eurovision Song Contest, which is sort of an Old World precursor to *American Idol*; it took them three tries, but they finally won in '74. Across Europe, that TV appearance raised their profile but immediately shackled them with a credibility deficit that was solely a product of the medium (thirty years later, Adam Lambert would relate). Still, the group had a natural narrative and a romantic appeal (two strange men writing songs for their beautiful girlfriends to sing), and all the songs were immediately accessible and ridiculously well crafted. Initial U.S. reviews were almost entirely positive—the *Los Angeles Times* called their debut "compelling and fascinating." By 1975, ABBA was the most popular band in the Western world, eventually having at least one number one single in fifteen different countries. And this, somewhat predictably, was roughly the same time dismissing ABBA became the only acceptable stance for anyone serious about culture. The core complaint (from the most predictable sources) was that ABBA records sounded like collections of commercial jingles. In retrospect, this criticism is as misdirected as it is uninspired: By erroneously tying "Waterloo" to advertising, it somehow implied that ABBA were capitalist stooges who wanted to sell something beyond the music itself (in truth, it was the TV commercials who wanted to affect people as easily as ABBA, not the other way around). Much like the Carpenters, ABBA became representative of a musical aesthetic so distant from the edge of rock that clever people weren't even willing to expend energy hating them. The Sex Pistols openly despised Led Zeppelin and Pink Floyd, but they punished ABBA by paradoxically stealing their material—after hearing ABBA's "S.O.S." on

the radio, Pistols bassist Glen Matlock copied the riff for the song titled (not coincidentally) "Pretty Vacant." As is so often the case in mainstream pop, the fact that ABBA made simple songs that were not political or antiestablishment positioned them as vapid. ABBA's dissolution in 1983 was scarcely noticed by the American media (not even the *Weekly Reader* cared), and any reasonable person could have concluded that their legacy was already carved into Swedish limestone. But (of course) it wasn't. The core audience for ABBA did not waiver throughout the next decade; the popularity of their most memorable singles (particularly "Dancing Queen") expanded despite minor FM radio exposure. When the compilation *Gold* came out in 1993, every college girl who dressed goofy played it whenever she pretended to be drunk. In 1994, Janeane Garofalo's character in *Reality Bites* needed ABBA to define her quirk, while *Priscilla, Queen of the Desert* needed ABBA to invent gay Australians. The first artist listed in the 1995 *Spin Alternative Record Guide* was the traditionally unalternative ABBA; that same year, MTV's Kurt Loder gave an interview to *Playboy* and mentioned he "missed ABBA a lot." By the end of the twentieth century, it was far more contrarian to hate ABBA than to love them.

Now, who was "right" among these factions (the original ABBA supporters, their antagonistic detractors, or the modern revisionists) is not important to me. I have no interest in convincing anyone they need to download *Voulez-Vous* posthaste, because I am post-taste. But what *is* compelling is how this polarizing trajectory occurred. The pattern is certainly not unique to ABBA; it's not unusual to see artists who are (a) initially appreciated before (b) falling out of favor, and then (c) returning to prominence after the fact. But it's more pronounced here: The highs were crazier and the lows were grosser. What makes this arc even more noteworthy is that the group itself did not seem actively involved with any of these machinations (the members will retrospectively talk about how they were perceived by the media and by fans, but they scarcely seem to care). They appear uninvolved with the rest of the world; throughout the 1990s, Faltskog did not even own a home stereo. And this natural disconnect is the central reason ABBA has succeeded over time—and it's something I noticed through other people before I realized it on my own.

My first clue, I think, was hearing people talk about *Muriel's Wedding* in 1994. I don't think I saw *Muriel's Wedding* until 1997. It did not seem like a movie I would enjoy.[2] But whenever I heard people talking about how great it was, they inevitably used a very specific phrase when describing the soundtrack: "It's all ABBA music." They did not say, "All the music is by ABBA," or "It's nothing but ABBA songs." They would always say, "It's all ABBA music." And what I came to realize is that these moviegoers were unknowingly making a critical distinction that explains why this group is so resilient and timeless. They weren't just saying, "It's all ABBA music." They were saying, "It's all ABBA Music." The M requires capitalization. And this is because—more than any other group of the post-Beatles era—ABBA is a genre unto itself. It's a brand of music that's sometimes recognizable in different songs and sometimes glimpsed through other artists, and everyone naturally grasps the qualities that come with it; you sometimes hear elements of it in department stores or druggy foreign films or New Age religious services. But only ABBA could make ABBA Music *in totality*. They are the only group who completely understands what they do, including the things they do wrong. So if that is what you like, there is only one place to really get it. The rest of culture does not matter. The Grateful Dead were kind of like this as well, but not as singularly as ABBA; while it's easy to

2. The film is a black comedy about a nonglamorous woman (Toni Collette) who dreams of getting married and is obsessed with ABBA. Like most films involving ABBA, it's set in Australia.

think of artists who deliver a comparable sonic experience to the
Dead, the closest equivalent to ABBA Music—probably the Bee
Gees—doesn't come close at all.

The harder question, of course, is "What qualities does ABBA
Music possess?" Its musical traits have been outlined ad nauseam
elsewhere: Their records feature a wall of sound where overdub-
bing makes every detail bigger and brighter than it should be.
The hooks are mammoth and the lyrics are unspecific. The songs
are made for dancing in a very big room. Now, these traits can
be found elsewhere (they're just as present in ABBA replicants
like Ace of Base, albeit recorded less artfully due to advances in
technology). What makes ABBA different is time and geography;
operating out of Stockholm in the seventies, they were (a) singing
in a second language, and (b) living with real ideological distance
from the trend-conscious worlds of New York and L.A. and London. They had an intense Tin Pan Alley professionalism (if Björn
and Benny felt like writing an uptempo T. Rex song, they'd just sit
down and knock off "Watch Out" in three hours), but they were
also laissez-faire Scandinavian hippies who didn't have to worry
about crime or sexual mores or health care. It was impossible to
tell if they were progressives or reactionaries.[3] ABBA wanted
to reach audiences in America, but they lacked a framework for
what that entailed. Their best option was to make one up. They
tried to create a simulacrum for how the American pop ethos

---

3. In the 2002 documentary *The Winner Takes It All: The ABBA Story*, Benny
Andersson casually describes his divorce from bandmate Anni-Frid Lyngstad
(after twelve years of marriage) like this: "It's no big deal here. You get divorced,
your wife marries somebody else and they get kids and you get new kids with
your family and we can all join together. It's not like you never see each other
again. It doesn't work like that in Sweden." Not being Swedish, it's hard for me
to tell how accurate this sentiment is, but it does stay consistent with how ABBA
never let the end of their dual relationships negatively affect the band's onstage
interaction.

appeared to objective Swedish outsiders. This is where we get the weirdness of ABBA: the *Star Trek* outfits, the histrionic onstage super-vamping, and the curious decision to consistently make Swedish women sing English narratives with Spanish[4] themes. What ABBA built was a previously nonexistent pop universe: It was a serious attempt to embody U.S. culture, attempted by European citizens who weren't remotely interested in being American. Consequently, it was always a little off. Sometimes it was too much. But it was *successful*. And *everyone* knew it. And that success became part of the sound. The fact that every human on earth (including their most vehement detractors) was keenly aware of ABBA's magnitude changed how the songs came across. It validated the obtuseness and bewildered the inflexible. "ABBA was so mainstream," Barry Walters would eventually write in *The Village Voice*, "you had to be slightly on the outside to actually take them to heart." ABBA had figured something out about America that we could effortlessly hear but only partially comprehend. This was the supernatural element of ABBA Music—flawless, shiny, otherworldly songs that evoke both mild confusion and instantaneous acceptance.

It was never, and therefore always, relevant.

4   There's no reason for me to tell you to listen to more ABBA. There are lots of other people more qualified (and perhaps more motivated) to do that than me: salt-and-pepper soccer moms, the members of Erasure, people who watch *Mamma Mia!* on JetBlue flights, dudes who shop at Crate and Bar-

---

4. "Fernando," "Chiquitita," "Put on Your White Sombrero," "Hasta Mañana," etc.

rel, Vladimir Putin,[5] etc. I don't think ABBA is a band you can really change anyone's opinion about, anyway. It's kind of like trying to convince someone that Coca-Cola is delicious—if they don't agree with you immediately, they probably never will.

That said, I also can't think of any other band who needs my public support less. This, I suppose, is my essential point: ABBA succeeds because the rest of the world isn't necessary. They operate within their own actuality. In 2002, ABBA was offered $1 billion to reunite. That's a *billion*, with a B. That's $250 million apiece. If someone reads this book in the year 2110, that will still be a lot of money. But they turned it down. "We had to think about it," Björn told *The Guardian*, "because one could build hospitals with that much money . . . [But] we don't want to go through the stress of disappointing people evening after evening." This is crazy for lots of reasons. The first is that I'm sure the main explanation as to why this didn't happen was because Agnetha (the blond one) did not want to do it (she now lives as a semi-recluse and never enjoyed fame, even while she was pursuing it). The second reason is that it would be funny to wake up from a skiing accident in a hospital named after ABBA. The third is that I cannot imagine ABBA fans being disappointed by even the lamest of cash-grabbing reunions (ABBA fans are not exactly authenticity hard-liners). The fourth is that—regardless of how awesome or unawesome these concerts might have been—any tour

---

5. The Russian prime minister has denied that he paid the ABBA tribute band Björn Again to perform for him and eight other people at a Russian lake resort in 2009. This is such a strange thing to deny that it obviously must have happened. According to Björn Again member Jennifer Robb (who portrays Anni-Frid) in the UK online newspaper *The Daily Telegraph*: "The prime minister didn't stand but he and his wife, or whoever it was, were jigging about on the sofa and singing the words to 'Honey Honey.' All his officials were singing away and doing a finger-pointing dance. They really got into it, even though there were only nine of them. At the end, the prime minister shouted 'bravo, bravo' and gave us great applause."

where a band is promised $1 billion would be doomed to financial failure (the total revenue from *every single North American concert* in the year 2002 was only $1.8 billion). The fifth is that ABBA is probably the biggest group I can think of that *nobody* ever talks about seeing live. (When is the last time you heard some old codger reminisce about how mind-blowing it was to hear "Hey Hey Helen" back at the Cow Palace?) I could go on and on with this list. But why? The reunion didn't happen, and it won't happen. Unlike just about every other act from their era, ABBA doesn't need the money or want the attention (or *want* the money and *need* the attention). They don't have to worry about the future of their music, because other people will make sure it never disappears. It doesn't matter if the critical consensus surrounding their import changes, because no one who likes ABBA Music cares if it's supposed to be good or bad. They'll never have to reunite and pretend to be in love. They'll never have to convince anyone of anything. They'll never have to leave Sweden. They'll never have to read this essay (or any essay like it); in ABBA World, this kind of discussion doesn't even subsist. They are so much themselves that they're beyond the rest of us. ABBA won, and the winner takes it all.

Q: Is that how you explain your sense of morality?

A: Christ, man. I can't answer that. Who knows? It's so confusing now. The world has shifted. Like, I now have all these friends who have kids. All my friends have kids now. Last year, one of them told me that he was sleeping with his kid's babysitter. He was actually having sex with this sixteen-year-old babysitter. I was like, "Dude. That's so fucked up. That's so inappropriate. You're her employer."

"Ha ha," he said. "Ha ha."

1 Sometimes writing is difficult. Sometimes writing is like pounding a brick wall with a ball-peen hammer in the hope that the barricade will evolve into a revolving door. Sometimes writing is like talking to a stranger who's exactly like yourself in every possible way, only to realize that this stranger is boring as shit. In better moments, writing is the opposite of difficult—it's as if your fingers meander arbitrarily in crosswise patterns and (suddenly) you find yourself reading something you didn't realize you already knew. Most of the time, the process falls somewhere in between. But there's one kind of writing that's *always* easy: Picking out something obviously stupid and reiterating how stupid it obviously is. This is the lowest form of criticism, easily accomplished by anyone. And for most of my life, I have tried to avoid this. In fact, I've spent an inordinate amount of time searching for the underrated value in ostensibly stupid things. I understand Turtle's motivation and I would have watched *Medellin* in the theater. I read *Mary Worth* every day for a decade. I've seen Korn in concert three times and liked them once. I went to *The Day After Tomorrow* on opening night. I own a very expensive robot that doesn't do anything. I am open to the possibility that everything has metaphorical merit, and I see no point in sardonically attacking the most predictable failures within any culture. I always prefer to do the opposite, even if my argument becomes insane by necessity.

But sometimes I can't.

Sometimes I experience something so profoundly idiotic—and so deeply universal—that I cannot find any contrarian perspective, even for the sole purpose of playful contrarianism. These are not the things that are stupid for what they are; these are the things that are stupid for what they supposedly reflect about human nature. These are things that make me feel completely alone in the world, because I cannot fathom how the overwhelming majority of people ignores them entirely. These are not real problems (like climate change or African genocide), because those issues are complex and multifaceted; they're also not intangible personal hypocrisies (like insincerity or greed), because those qualities are biological and understandable. These are things that exist only because *they exist*. We accept them, we give them a social meaning, and they become part of how we live. Yet these are the things that truly illustrate how ridiculous mankind can be. These are the things that prove just how confused people are (and will always be), and these are the things that are so stupid that they make me feel nothing. Not sadness. Not anger. Not guilt. Nothing.

These are the stupidest things our society has ever manufactured.

And—at least to me—there is one stupid idea that towers above all others. In practice, its impact is minor; in theory, it's the most fucked-up media construction spawned by the twentieth century. And I've felt this way for (almost) my entire life.

I can't think of anything philosophically stupider than laugh tracks.

2 Perhaps this seems like a shallow complaint to you. Perhaps you think that railing against canned laughter is like complaining that nuclear detonations are bad for the local bunny population. I don't care. Go read a vampire novel. To me, laugh tracks are as stupid as we get. And, yes, I realize this phenomenon is being phased out by modernity. That's good. There will be a day in the future when this essay will make no sense, because canned laughter will be as extinct as TV theme songs. It will only be used as a way to inform audiences that they're supposed to be watching a fake TV show from the 1970s. But— right now, today—canned laughter is still a central component of escapist television. The most popular sitcom on TV, *Two and a Half Men*, still uses a laugh track, as does the (slightly) more credible *How I Met Your Mother* and the (significantly) less credible *The Big Bang Theory*. Forced laughter is also central to the three live action syndicated shows that are broadcast more than any other, *Friends, Home Improvement,* and *Seinfeld. Cheers* will be repeated forever, as will the unseen people guffawing at its barroom banter. And I will always notice this, and it will never become reassuring or nostalgic or quaint. It will always seem stupid, because canned laughter represents the worst qualities of insecure people.

Now, I realize these qualities can be seen everywhere in life and within lots of complicated contexts. Insecurity is part of being alive. But it's never less complicated than this. It's never less complicated than a machine that tries to make you feel like you're already enjoying something, simply because people you'll never meet were convinced to laugh at something else entirely.

2A I am not the first writer who's been perversely fascinated with fake laughter. Ron Rosenbaum[1] wrote a story for *Esquire* in the 1970s titled "Inside the Canned Laughter War" that chronicled attempts by Ralph Waldo Emerson III[2] to sell American TV networks on a new laughter device that was intended to usurp the original "Laff Box" designed by Charlie Douglass for the early fifties program *The Hank McCune Show*. Rosenbaum's piece is apolitical, mainly memorable for mentioning that the voices heard on modern laugh tracks were often the same original voices recorded by Douglas during pre-ancient radio shows like *Burns and Allen*, which would mean that the sound we hear on laugh tracks is the sound of dead people laughing. As far as I can tell, this has never been proven. But it must be at least *partially* true; there must be at least a few people recorded for laugh tracks who are now dead, even if their laughter was recorded yesterday. People die all the time. If you watch any episode of *Seinfeld*, you can be 100 percent confidant that *somebody* chuckling in the background is six feet underground. I assume this makes Larry David ecstatic.

During the height of the Laff Box Era (the 1970s), lots of TV critics railed against the use of canned laughter, so much so that TV shows began making a concerted effort to always mention that they were taped in front of a live audience (although even those live tapings were almost always mechanically sweetened). At the time, the primary criticism was that laugh tracks were being used to mask bad writing—in *Annie Hall*, Woody Allen's self-styled

---

1. Rosenbaum would later write a controversial nonfiction book titled *Explaining Hitler*, which was controversial for suggesting that Hitler was (possibly) an un-evil infant.

2. Yes, they were related.

character chastises a colleague working in the TV industry for adding counterfeit hilarity to a terrible program ("Do you realize how immoral this all is?"). Less concrete aesthetes argued that the Laff Box obliterated the viewer's suspension of disbelief, although it's hard to imagine how realistically invested audiences were ever supposed to feel about *Mork and Mindy*. I concede that both of these condemnations were accurate. But those things never bothered me. Laugh tracks never detracted from bad writing, and they never stopped me from thinking the cast of *Taxi* weren't legitimate taxi drivers. Those issues are minor. What bothers me is the underlying suggestion that what you are experiencing is different than whatever your mind tells you is actually happening. Moreover, laugh tracks want you to accept that this constructed reality can become the way you feel, or at least the way you behave. It's a concept grounded in the darkest of perspectives: A laugh track assumes that you are not confident enough to sit quietly, even if your supposed peer group is (a) completely invisible and (b) theoretically dead.

1A I lived in eastern Germany for four months of 2008. There were a million weird things about living there, but there was one that I didn't anticipate: Germans don't fake-laugh. If someone in Germany is laughing, it's because he or she physically can't help themselves; they are laughing because they're authentically amused. Nobody there ever laughs because of *politeness*. Nobody laughs out of *obligation*. And what this made me recognize is how much American laughter is purely conditioned. Most of our laughing—I would say at least 51 percent—has no relation to humor or to how we actually feel.

You really, really notice this in German grocery stores. When paying for food in Leipzig, I was struck by how much of my daily interaction was punctuated by laughter that was totally detached from what I was doing. I would buy some beer and cookies and give the clerk a twenty-euro note; inevitably, the clerk would ask if I had exact change, because Germans are obsessed with both exactness and money. I would reach into my pocket and discover I had no coins, so I would reply, "Um—heh heh heh. No. Sorry. Ha! Guess not." I made these noises without thinking. Every single time, the clerk would just stare at me stoically. It had never before occurred to me how often I reflexively laugh; only in the absence of a response did I realize I was laughing for no reason whatsoever. It somehow felt comfortable. Now that I'm back in the U.S., I notice this all the time: People half-heartedly chuckle throughout most casual conversations, regardless of the topic. It's a modern extension of the verbalized pause, built by TV laugh tracks. Everyone in America has three laughs: a real laugh, a fake real laugh, and a "filler laugh" they use during impersonal conversations. We have been trained to connect conversation with soft, interstitial laughter. It's our way of showing the other person that we understand the context of the interaction, even when we don't.

This is not the only reason Germans think Americans are retarded, but it's definitely one of them.

2B Part of what makes the notion of canned laughter so mysterious is the way it continues to exist within a media world that regularly rewards shows that *don't* employ it. Virtually every high-end, "sophisticated" comedy of the early twenty-first century—*Arrested Devel-*

opment, It's Always Suny in Philadelphia, Curb Your Enthusiasm, The Simpsons, 30 Rock—is immune to canned laughter, and it's difficult to imagine any of those shows supplemented with mechanical, antiseptic chuckling. Very often, the absence of a laugh track serves as a more effective guidepost than the laughter itself—audiences have come to understand that any situation comedy without canned laughter is supposed to be smarter, hipper, and less predictable than traditional versions of the genre. This comprehension began with the Korean War sitcom *M*A*S*H*, a series that started with the removal of canned laughter from scenes in the hospital operating room (so as not to mitigate the reality of people bleeding to death) and eventually excluded it from the entire broadcast altogether (in order to remind audiences that they were watching something quasi-political and semi-important). But this collective assumption raises two questions:

1. If TV audiences have come to accept that comedic shows without laugh tracks are edgier and more meaningful, is it not possible that the reverse would also be true (in other words, does removing the laugh track change the way a viewer preconceives the show, regardless of its content)?
2. If all the best comedies are devoid of fake laughter, why would anyone elect to use them at all (under any circumstance)?

What's interesting about these two queries is the way their answers are connected. The answer to the first question is, "Absolutely." If you watch a comedy that forgoes contrived laughter, you will unconsciously (or maybe even *consciously*) take it more seriously. Jokes will be interpreted as meaner, weirder, and deeper than however they were originally written. When Liz Lemon says something on *30 Rock* that isn't funny, there's always the paradoxical possibility that this was intentional; perhaps Tina Fey is com-

menting on the inanity of the "sitcom joke construct" and pur-
posefully interjecting a joke that failed, thereby making the *failure* of her joke the part that's supposed to be funny. *The Office* and
Curb Your Enthusiasm deliver "the humor of humiliation" without contextual cues, so the events can be absorbed as hilarious in
the present and cleverly tragic in the retrospective future. These
are things we all immediately understand the moment we start
watching a TV comedy without a laugh track: The product is
multidimensional. We can decide what parts are funny; in fact,
the program can even be enjoyed if *none* of the parts are funny,
assuming the writing is propulsive or unusual (this was the case
with Aaron Sorkin's *Sports Night,* an ABC satire that debuted with
a laugh track but slowly eliminated the chuckles over its two-year
run). We all take laughless sitcoms more seriously because they
seem to take *us* more seriously. They imply that we will know
(and can actively *decide*) what is (or isn't) funny.

Which directs us to the answer of question two.

The reason a handful of very popular sitcoms still use canned
laughter—and the reason why veteran network leaders always
want to use laugh tracks, even though doing so immediately ghet-
toizes their programming—is due to a specific assumption about
human nature. The assumption is this: Normal people don't have
enough confidence to know what they think is funny. And this,
sadly, is true. But it's not their fault.

2C *Friends* (at least during the early stages of its
ten-season run) was taped in front of a live studio audience. This, of course, does not make its
laughter (deserved or undeserved) any less fake: Studio audiences
are prompted to laugh at everything, *want* to laugh at everything,

and are mechanically fixed ("sweetened") whenever they fail to perform at optimal levels of outward hilarity assessment. *Friends* had a laugh track the same way *The Flintstones* had a laugh track— it's just that the prefab laughs you heard on *Friends* were being manufactured on location, in real time. For anyone watching at home, there was no difference.

Now, the best episodes of *Friends* were funny. The worst episodes were insulting to baboons. But the vast majority fall somewhere in between. Here is an example of a *Friends* script from season two; this episode was titled "The One Where Old Yeller Dies" and takes place when the series was still a conventional sitcom (as opposed to more of a serial comedy, which started during season three). The mention of a character named "Richard" refers to Tom Selleck, who played Monica's boyfriend for much of that season. This is the first scene following the opening credits . . .

> [Scene: Inside Monica and Rachel's apartment. Richard is on the balcony smoking and Monica is on the phone.]

> MONICA: Hey, have you guys eaten, because uh, Richard and I just finished and we've got leftovers . . . Chicken and potatoes . . . What am I wearing? . . . Actually, nothing but rubber gloves.

> [Chandler and Joey come sprinting into the apartment from across the hall.]

> JOEY: Ya know, one of these times you're gonna really be naked and we're not gonna come over.

> MONICA: Alright, I've got a leg, three breasts and a wing.

> CHANDLER: Well, how do you find clothes that fit?

JOEY: Oh, hey, Monica, we've got a question.

MONICA: Alright, for the bizillionth time—yes, I see other women in the shower at the gym, and no, I don't look.

JOEY: No, not that one. We're trying to figure out who to bring to the Knicks game tonight. We have an extra ticket.

The degree to which you find this passage funny is directly proportional to (a) how familiar you are with this show and (b) how much you recall liking it. Like almost all successful TV ensembles, the plots on *Friends* weren't a fraction as important as the characters and who played them—especially as the seasons wore on, the humor came from our familiarity with these characters' archetypes. People who liked *Friends* literally liked *the friends*. Audiences watched the show because they felt like they had a relationship with the cast. The stories were mostly extraneous. But there still had to be a story somewhere. There still had to be something for these people to do, so the show adopted a structure. This is the structure of the previous scene, minus the dialogue:

[Scene: Inside Monica and Rachel's apartment. Richard is on the balcony smoking and Monica is on the phone.]

MONICA: STATIC INTRO, PLUS JOKE

(small laugh)

[MOMENT OF PHYSICAL COMEDY]

(exaggerated laugh)

JOEY: JOKE BASED IN PREEXISTING KNOWLEDGE OF
    CHARACTER'S PERSONA

(laugh)

MONICA: SETUP

CHANDLER: OLD-TIMEY JOKE

(laugh)

JOEY: MINOR PLOT POINT

MONICA: UNRELATED JOKE

(laugh)

JOEY: BEGINNING OF STORY ARC FOR EPISODE

Using this template, it seems like anyone could create their own episode of *Friends,* almost like they were filling out a *Mad Libs.* And if those *Mad Libs* lines were actually said by Courteney Cox, Matt LeBlanc, and Matthew Perry, the result would probably be no less effective (were they especially absurd, the net might even be positive). The key to this kind of programming is never what people are saying. They key is (a) which people are doing the talking, and (b) the laugh track.

There are important assumptions we bring into the show as viewers; we are assuming that this is escapist (read: nonincendiary) humor, we are assuming the characters are ultimately good people, and we're assuming that our relationship to *Friends* mirrors the traditional relationship Americans have always had with thirty-minute TV programs that employ canned laughter. It's not always funny, but it's in the "form of funny." And because we're not stupid, we know when to chuckle. But we don't even have to do that, because the laugh track does it for us. And over time, that starts to feel normal. It starts to make us laugh at other things that aren't necessarily funny.

1B Earlier in this essay I mentioned how I've believed that canned laughter was idiotic for "(almost) my entire life." The key word there is *almost*. I did not think laugh tracks were idiotic when I was five. In fact, when I was five, I thought I was partially responsible for the existence of laugh tracks. I thought we all were.

At the time, my assumption was that the speaker on my parents' Zenith television was a two-way system—I thought it was like a telephone. When I watched *Laverne and Shirley* or *WKRP in Cincinnati* and heard the canned laughter, my hypothesis was that this was the sound of thousands of other TV viewers in random locations, laughing at the program in their own individual living rooms. I thought their laughter was being picked up by their various TV consoles and being simultaneously rebroadcast through mine. As a consequence, I would sometimes sit very close to the television and laugh as hard as I could, directly into the TV's speaker. I would laugh into my own television.

My family thought I just really, really appreciated Howard Hesseman.

And I did. But I mostly wanted to contribute to society.

3 In New York, you get used to people pretending to laugh. Go see a foreign movie with poorly translated English subtitles and you will hear a handful of people howling at jokes that don't translate, solely because they want to show the rest of the audience that they're smart enough to understand a better joke was originally designed to be there. Watch *The Daily Show* in an apartment full of young progressives and you'll hear them consciously (and unconvincingly) over-laugh at every joke that's delivered, mostly to assure everyone else that they're appropriately informed and predictably leftist. Take a lunch meeting with anyone involved in any form of media that isn't a daily newspaper, and they will pretend to laugh at everything anyone at the table says that could be theoretically classified as humorous, even if the alleged joke is about how airline food isn't delicious. The only thing people in New York won't laugh at are unfamous stand-up comedians; we really despise those motherfuckers, for some reason.

It's possible the reason people in New York laugh at everything is because they're especially polite, but that seems pretty unlikely. A better explanation is that New York is the most mediated city in America, which means its population is the most media-savvy—and the most media-affected—populace in the country. The more media someone consumes (regardless of who they are or where they live), the more likely they are to take their interpersonal human cues from external, nonhuman sources. One of the principal functions of mass media is to make the world a more fathomable reality—in the short term, it provides assurance and simplicity. But this has a long-term, paradoxical downside. Over time, embracing mass media in its entirety makes people more confused and less secure. The laugh track is our best example. In the short term, it affirms that the TV program we're watching is intended to be funny and can be experienced with low stakes. It takes away the unconscious pressure of understanding context and tells the audience when they should be amused. But because *everything* is laughed at in the same way (regardless of value), and because we all watch TV with the recognition that *this is mass entertainment,* it makes it harder to deduce what we think is independently funny. As a result, Americans of all social classes compensate by living like bipedal Laff Boxes: We mechanically laugh at everything, just to show that we know what's supposed to be happening. We get the joke, even if there is no joke.

Is this entirely the fault of laugh tracks? Nay. But canned laughter is a lucid manifestation of an anxious culture that doesn't know what is (and isn't) funny. If you've spent any time trolling the blogosphere, you've probably noticed a peculiar literary trend: the pervasive habit of writers inexplicably placing exclamation points at the end of otherwise unremarkable sentences. Sort of like this! This is done to suggest an ironic detachment from the writing of an expository sentence! It's supposed to signify that the writer is self-aware! And this is idiotic. It's the saddest kind of failure. F. Scott Fitzgerald believed inserting exclamation points was the literary equivalent of an author laughing at his own jokes, but that's not the case in the modern age; now, the exclamation point signifies creative confusion. All it illustrates is that even the writer can't tell if what they're creating is supposed to be meaningful, frivolous, or cruel. It's an attempt to insert humor where none exists, on the off chance that a potential reader will only be pleased if they suspect they're being entertained. Of course, the reader really isn't sure, either. They just want to know when they're supposed to pretend that they're amused. All those extraneous exclamation points are like little splatters of canned laughter: They represent the "form of funny," which is more easily understood (and more easily constructed) than authentic funniness. I suppose the counter-argument is that Tom Wolfe used a lot of exclamation points, too . . . but I don't think that had anything to do with humor or insecurity. The Wolfe-Man was honestly stoked about LSD and John Glenn. I bet he didn't even own a TV. It was a different era!

Build a machine that tells people when to cry. That's what we need. We need more crying.

Q: Is it true you literally sold ice machines to Eskimos?

A: I did. I was working for Manitowoc out of the Fairbanks office, and I would sometimes sell ice machines to the Yupik and Inuits. They were decent customers—more disposable income than you'd expect, mostly because of the PFD. Very willing to listen.

Q: How did it feel to embody a cliché?

A: Cold. Dark.

Q: Do you have any advice for aspiring salesmen?

A: People always say, "Don't take 'no' for an answer," but that's wrong. That's how rapists think. You'll waste a thousand afternoons if that's your attitude. However, never take "maybe" for an answer. Ninety percent of the time, "maybe" means "probably." Just keep talking.

It Will Shock You How Much
It Never Happened

1 There are new cans of Pepsi in the grocery store, and the cans look different. They're a deeper shade of blue, except for a few that are gold. The font is faux futuristic. These new aluminum cans look better, I suppose, although I know the old design will seem superior as soon as the new ones stop looking novel—it's the same process that happens whenever a sports franchise changes uniforms.

I don't drink Pepsi unless I'm flying on Northwest Airlines and they're out of Mountain Dew. Pepsi disappoints me. It makes me thirstier. But perhaps I'm wrong about this; perhaps I'm wrong about how I think and taste and feel. Perhaps I'm just not optimistic enough. Maybe if I had more confidence in the future of America, I would want to drink more Pepsi. Maybe if I believed Pepsi understood my lifestyle better, it would refresh me more.

Somebody working for Pepsi likes *Mad Men* too much.

2 The collection of words printed below this paragraph is from a press release. I'm not sure if I can legally reprint a Pepsi-Cola press release without their permission, but logic would suggest that I can. For one thing, this essay is (technically) media criticism, so copyright rules are tilted in my favor. More to the point, *this is a press release,* which means it only exists so that other people can republish whatever it pretends to argue. All things considered, having their propaganda available inside a library has to be a publicist's greatest fantasy. The press release is unnecessarily detailed, so I have placed the most interesting, least reasonable elements in boldface.

Purchase, N.Y., December 10, 2008—Despite a failing economy, employment woes and countless other concerns, a key segment of Millennials—people who were born between 1980 and 1990—remain confident about what 2009 will have in store for them. **According to an omnibus survey conducted by StrategyOne® on behalf of Pepsi, four out of five Millennials are hopeful about the future as the New Year approaches, and nearly all surveyed (95%) agree that it is important for them to maintain a positive outlook on life.**

More than 2,000 Americans were surveyed as part of the **Pepsi Optimism Project (POP), a new and ongoing study examining the mindset of Millennials. The survey comes as Pepsi launches a branding initiative that is part of a significant, multiyear reinvestment in carbonated soft drinks. The campaign starts with a new look for the trademark Pepsi packaging, which is now beginning to appear on store shelves across the country. An advertising campaign featuring a consistent theme of optimism that mirrors the current social climate will debut shortly.**

"Pepsi has always stood for youthful exuberance and optimism and we're pleased to learn through this survey that the positive spirit in youth culture is not only intact but growing," said

Dave Burwick, Pepsi's chief marketing officer. "Our new brand identity campaign reflects that optimism like never before—on shelf and in advertising."

"Children of the '80s and '90s inherently feel a strong sense of optimism in the future and their ability to shape it," says Lisa Orrell, generation relations expert and author of *Millennials Incorporated*. "This age group feels refreshingly unencumbered by history or tradition, a feeling that they can accomplish anything they resolve to achieve."

According to the POP survey, Millennials spend more time enjoying life than worrying about it and this group is most optimistic about their overall well-being and relationships with friends and family. Other findings include:

• With the season of good will upon us, 74% find that supporting causes makes them feel more optimistic.

• Despite recent job forecasts, 77% of Millennials report having a strong sense of optimism about their careers.

• Nearly all Millennials (95%) make positive associations when they think of the word "change," associating it with "progress" (78%), "hope" (77%) and "excitement" (72%).

• Two-thirds of Millennials (67%) say that the election of Barack Obama is making them feel optimistic about the future of the country.

Fueled by an excitement for change and an eagerness to shape their own destinies, Millennials are gearing up to make 2009 their year. Orrell concludes, "With so much to worry about over the next several months, maybe we would all be better served taking on this group's optimism."

It is not my intention to mock Pepsi for taking this approach to selling soda, particularly since (a) it's too easy to make fun of press releases, and (b) there's at least a 50 percent chance that this strategy is stupid enough to succeed. Labeling those born between 1980 and 1990 as "Millennials" might be a less-than-brilliant move (it kind of makes young people sound like garden shrubs), but weirder tags have stuck in the past. It's amusing to see someone named Lisa branding herself with the fictional title of "generation relations expert," not to mention how Lisa's paradoxically positive belief about Pepsi's target age group feeling "refreshingly unencumbered by history" indicates that Pepsi views its consumer base as a demographic of reanimated corpses who've consumed their own brain blood. But whether this "Refresh everything" scheme succeeds is almost beside the point; it really isn't that different from Coca-Cola's competing campaign, "Open happiness" (an attempt to connect drinking Coke with spiritual contentment). What I'm more intrigued by is the thought process behind Pepsi's decision. It appears to be something akin to this:

1. We want people to buy Pepsi. Unfortunately . . .
2. The country is struggling (and perhaps even collapsing). However . . .
3. Whatever beverage consumers are drinking does not really reflect anything important about society. Therefore . . .
4. If people need to be wrong about something, it's okay for them to be wrong about how they feel toward Pepsi. So . . .
5. Let's associate Pepsi with the exact opposite of everything happening in America, based on the premise that . . .

6. Young Americans would always prefer to be wrong and optimistic (as opposed to pragmatic and sad).

This is a brilliant application of profound cynicism—it actively tries to use people's misplaced optimism against them. It understands both how the media operates and how consumers are predisposed to distrust whatever messages they hear. It's the epitome of "high concept," which is another way of saying the strategy's genius is directly tied to the fact that it doesn't make sense unless you think about it in totally abstract, completely intangible terms. The fundamental premise essentially boils down to Al Pacino's explanation for drinking alcohol on a hot day in *Glengarry Glen Ross*: "I subscribe to the law of contrary public opinion. If everyone thinks one thing, then I say bet the opposite." It's that omnipresent notion that there's some deeper truth in business that's intentionally counterintuitive—you're never selling what you're actually selling. You sell people Pepsi by selling them Obama. That's the trick, and everyone knows it.

So what happens when everyone knows the trick? Does it still work?

It does. In fact, it works better.

3 As a piece of entertainment, *Mad Men* has done everything right. It's perfectly cast and brilliantly paced, and it uses symmetrical symbolism in a way rarely attempted on television—every plot point is mirrored by a minor, less overt story line in the same allegorical vein. No character is drawn without flaws. By placing itself in the "secret" 1960s that everyone now accepts as normative (i.e., the subversive and the damaged masquerading as suburban bliss), its white-collar characters are able to get away with living archaic, un-PC lives that (a) feel completely authentic but (b) would be impossible to depict in the present. Certainly, my opinion of *Mad Men* is not unique; with the possible exception of *The Wire,* I can't think of any contemporary TV show that's been more acclaimed by affluent audiences. And part of what we upwardly mobile, media-obsessed goofballs adore is the program's perverse glorification of the ad man. It makes advertising seem like the greatest career imaginable. Watching *Mad Men* makes me want to trick housewives into buying Tide.

Mad Men's protagonist is Don Draper, a pathological liar who charms women by grabbing their vaginas in crowded restaurants. He's not a good person, but he's kilometers beyond cobalt cool— and he's cool for unusual reasons. He's cool for being extraordinary at an office job. He's cool for keeping secrets and chain-smoking and cheating on his wife. He's cool for the way he talks to strangers. What follows is his extemporaneous description of how he intends to sell the Kodak Carousel (a circular slide projector for home movies) to the American public:

> Nostalgia . . . it's delicate, but potent . . . in Greek, nostalgia literally means the pain from an old wound. It's a twinge in your heart, far more powerful than memory alone. This device—it isn't a spaceship. It's a time machine. It takes us to a place where we ache to go again. It's not called The Wheel. It's called The Carousel. It lets us travel the way a child travels: around and around and back home again, to a place we know we are loved.

Within the environment of the episode, Draper is (obviously) not talking about projectors. He's talking about his own life and his own insecurities, and he's thinking about how his success as an idea salesman is irrevocably connected to his failures as a normal person. But try to think about that passage in nonmetaphorical terms; think about what those words would mean in a non-fictional, plotless workplace. Draper's espoused strategy is to confuse people; he's trying to make consumers associate a feeling (nostalgia) with a product (The Carousel) by artfully implying that the product *generates* that feeling. This is—I suppose—unethical. But not enough to hurt anyone: The net result of Draper's deception is that someone might purchase a slide projector they don't necessarily need. His motives are impure but not sinister. We all take for granted that this is how advertising works. And because this moment in *Mad Men* happens in 1960 (and because we're seeing this moment in 2007), the idea of intertwining emotion and commerce is entertaining: We assume this kind of advertising scheme would completely snow every target market from that era. Because it's happening in 1960, what Draper is proposing intrigues us because it seems *new*. It's like we're watching the invention of media duplicity. But now, duplicitous advertising is all that there is; it's what we expect from advertising all the time. The emotional transference Draper appears to be inventing is what we naturally anticipate from the promotion of any product. And that should make it fail. But it doesn't. And I think that's because people *like* recognizing that they are a target market. It makes them feel smart for figuring it out, and it makes them feel good to be viewed as desirable. And I suspect that advertisers are aware of this. Selling emotion is no longer a scheme: Pepsi-Cola can just send out a press release openly stating that Pepsi is now designed for optimistic young people, and optimistic young people make fun of that concept's lack of subtlety. But even as they mock, they think, "That's kind of interesting. That's kind of flattering. Is that who they think I am? I wonder how they came up with that?" Perhaps they imagine Don Draper in a room full of cigarette smoke, holding up a blue Pepsi can that looks like it was made in Tokyo.

Optimism . . . it's difficult but potent . . . on the Internet, optimism literally means the only answer to an unclear world. It's an explosion in your heart, far more powerful than common sense alone. This beverage—it isn't a refreshing treat. It's a hope machine. It embodies a taste we ache to experience later. It's not called Soda. It's called Pop. It lets us feel the way a child feels: out and away from reality, in a place we know we are loved.

People love advertising. They say they don't, but they do. And I don't just mean that they like clever commercials or reading *Lucky*; I mean they like the idea of a Draper (a) whom they'll never meet who (b) understands what they want and (c) views that wanting as important. It does not matter that this definition of import doesn't extend beyond their ability to pay for things. A feeling is a feeling is a feeling.

4 PepsiCo Incorporated has interesting problems. Around the same time they were making Pepsi less cynical, PepsiCo made a packaging change to another of their products, Tropicana Pure Premium orange juice. For whatever reason, PepsiCo changed the orange juice carton: Instead of an orange with a protruding straw, they featured the more literal image of a glass of orange juice. Immediately, orange juice drinkers lost their shit (not all of them, but enough to get attention). They were outraged; they could not believe that Tropicana had altered this essential image of an imaginary orange you could suck. A few weeks later, Tropicana switched back to the original design. This reversal was covered in the February 22, 2009, edition of *The New York Times,* and the angle of the story was that

PepsiCo was dealing with its own version of Coca-Cola's infamous 1985 introduction of New Coke.[1] However, there was at least one major difference that was mentioned in the story parenthetically, almost as an aside . . .

> (There are, it should be noted, significant differences between the two corporate flip-flops. For instance, the Tropicana changes involved only packaging, not the formula for or taste of the beverage.)

The orange juice was the same. As far as I can tell, the size and shape of the container itself was also identical—the only alteration was the picture on the carton. People were appalled because the same product (at the same price) was being presented to them in a slightly different way. If you're a person involved in the profession of advertising, this kind of scenario is the apotheosis of your vocation. It illustrates a rarified level of consumer appreciation: People aren't just buying something *because* of the advertising—they feel like they are *buying the advertising itself.* An essential piece of what they desire is the image on the carton, even though that image is only there to get attention and inform you of what's inside. It has nothing to do with juice. It almost never does.

This happens all the time: LeBron James does not sell Nikes; buying Nikes allows people to buy "LeBron James" (and whatever that's supposed to mean outside of itself). That cliché has been understood by advertisers for generations, or at least since Michael Jordan killed off Converse in the eighties. But—right now, today—*everyone* knows that this is how the game works. So how can a trick work when everyone knows it's a trick?

---

1. The failure of which, it should be noted, helped Coca-Cola immensely. The introduction of New Coke was either the smartest or luckiest marketing scheme of the 1980s.

Because the trick is the product.

On *Mad Men*, Draper tries to create a soft reality—he tries to trick housewives into thinking that Heineken beer reflects something about their level of class that Budweiser does not. Draper knows that this transference is a construction, but he knows how emotive construction works. As the audience for *Mad Men*, we intellectually relate to his task. We're sophisticated enough to imagine how beer can be sold as a lifestyle. And this is because the central mission of advertising has succeeded completely. What used to be its seemingly preposterous scheme—selling an emotion or a worldview through a disparate product—is now the actual, accepted motive behind why people buy things. It's the hard reality. There was a time when the only person who'd be crazy enough to argue that the visual image of an orange with a straw sticking from its side was "meaningful" was the artist who drew it; now everyone assumes this *must* be the case. It *must* have meaning. It's expected. So the advertiser's question is not "What do we tell people this product is supposed to mean?" The question is "When we tell people what this product is supposed to mean, how much will they accept and appreciate our transparently bullshit message?" In other words, Pepsi is not really trying to market soda pop to optimistic people. That's impossible and nonsensical. What they're hoping is that when consumers recognize that Pepsi is trying to amorphously tie soda to optimism, a segment of that audience will decide, "That's a good idea. It's ridiculous, but I see what they're doing. I'm willing to associate myself with this gimmick." It's the difference between a magician performing a trick to impress his audience and a magician trying to sell that trick to other magicians. There's nobody left for advertisers to fool. *We're all magicians.*

3A In the late nineties, a copywriter named Luke Sullivan published a book about advertising regrettably titled *Hey, Whipple, Squeeze This*. Part of the story was about how much Sullivan hated those "Don't squeeze the Charmin" commercials from the 1960s and '70s, regardless of how much toilet paper they moved along the way. To validate his point, he quoted a man named Norman Berry, an old-timey creative director for Ogilvy and Mather (the New York advertising agency that would eventually handle Kodak, just like Draper's fictional employer, Sterling Cooper).

> I'm appalled by those who [judge] advertisers exclusively on the basis of sales. That isn't enough . . . if sales are achieved with work which is in bad taste or is intellectual garbage, it shouldn't be applauded no matter how much it sells. Offensive, dull, abrasive, stupid advertising is bad for business as a whole. It is why the public perception of advertising is going down in this country.

Berry's point seems high minded and superficially levelheaded: He's arguing that the value of advertising isn't directly tied to its economic success. He thinks it should be socially uplifting and entertaining, and it should engage its audience. Berry's sentiments, it would seem, have now become the modern "perception of advertising," which is clearly *not* going down in this country. It's going up. When Americans watch Super Bowl commercials, they analyze them as pieces of art; they think about the message the images imply and they blog about what those implications are supposed to prove about the nation as a whole. We assume that commercials are not just informing us about purchasable products, because that would be crude and ineffective. We're smarter than that. But that understanding makes us more vulnerable. We've become the ideal audience for advertising—consumers who intellectually magnify commercials in order to make them more trenchant and clever than they actually are. Our fluency with the language and motives of the advertiser induces us to create new, better meanings for whatever they show us. We do most of the work for them.

Like all people who pretend they're smart, I want to feel immune to this. I avoid advertising. Since the advent of digital video recorders, I rarely watch[2] TV commercials (even when they come on during live sporting events I immediately change the channel, usually to a different live sporting event). I wrote a column in *Esquire* for five years, yet I can't think of one company who advertised alongside my work (I know they were there, but I can't remember any of them). I've never read a pop-up or a banner ad on the web. Does anyone? Even if I watch *Survivor* at cbs.com, I check my e-mail during the uncloseable commercial that precedes the episode. Obviously, I'm not the only person who does this. Yet—somehow—I still know about new things that are available to purchase. I can sense when I'm a target market. I knew that Pepsi was focusing on optimism long before I saw any new logos or press releases. So how could this be? How is it that ideas I never think about still burrow into my head? Why do I understand an ad campaign I completely avoid?

I enjoy Don Draper. He's got a lot of quality suits. But I'm afraid I might be his employer, and I don't even know it.

---

2. When I first wrote this sentence, it read, "Since the advent of digital video recorders, I never see TV commercials." But I suppose that isn't accurate; I don't *watch* commercials, but I do *see* them. I see them flicker across the screen at four times the normal speed, minus the audio. And maybe this is enough. Maybe all I need to do is see them, because I can figure out the rest on my own.

Q: So what new music are you listening to these days?

A: Not much. I like Neon Indian—they seem like the logical extension of democracy. I think Big Pink bring a lot to the table. I don't know if I can totally embrace the hype around Gonzaga Spread Eagle, but I thought *Otto Graham, Volume II* was a valid EP. That first Thad Holen album was pretty awesome. I used to like Melody Grove and the Movement, but I burned out on them after "New Blues." I suppose I'll always be a closet D'espairspray supporter. Ke$ha. Tooth Mouth. Moses Scurry. And while I didn't really appreciate Jay Reatard until he died, I loved his side project, Up In The Old House, immediately. I actually saw their first show in West Memphis. But you know what? If I'm honest, the music I truly dug the most—at least over the last half of this year—were those early two singles from Sinister Komodo. That was some Sabbath-meets-Elastica shit.

Q: That's a competent answer. But just out of curiosity, how many of those names did you totally fabricate right now, off the top of your head?

A: Oh, all of them.

All The Kids Are Right

1A How do you indicate that a new musical act is important? What is the most concise way to illustrate that a band is significant and modern and worth investigating? What's the shorthand way of saying any artist is culturally vital *right now*?

You say, "Listen to this song. This is what all the kids are listening to."

Okay, fine. But what if that's not your goal? What if you want to do the opposite? What if you want to disparage the value of an unknown band, even if you've never really listened to them yourself? What do you say if you want people to infer that a given artist is silly and insubstantial and shallow? How do you negate their existence?

You say, "Oh, don't listen to that crap. That's just what the kids are listening to."

So here's the obvious question: How can two identical sentiments be opposing ideas? Because they are. And they always will be, as long as rock music continues to exist.

1B If we concede that rock and pop and hip-hop are important (and—if you're reading this book—I'm going to concede that you do), we likely share a pretty rudimentary explanation as to why this stuff matters as much as it does: They are major art forms specifically designed and produced for non-adults. All other things being equal, a seventeen-year-old's personal perspective on T-Pain or the Japandroids is viewed as more valuable than the perspective of a forty-seven-year-old. This is not true in film or painting or theater or sculpture or architecture or even television; only pop music is irrevocably tied to youth. Now, logically, that perception no longer makes sense. It might have made sense when rock was new, but it doesn't anymore. Today, it's entirely possible that a forty-seven-year-old man and his seventeen-year-old daughter could both have the same favorite song.[1] Twenty-five years from now, the most popular music inside retirement homes will be the Beatles and *Physical Graffiti*. So the idea of rock 'n' roll being a young human's game should no longer hold H2O. At this point, we should think of rock the same way we think of film—as a technology-based art form that everyone experiences in the same way. But we don't. And I don't think we ever will. And that's good, because intellectual dissonance is what makes rock and pop and rap different from all those other art forms. As long as we all collectively *believe* something is supposed to reflect and enrich youth culture, that's how it will operate in practice, regardless of the reality or the content.[2]

But here's where an interesting problem emerges: The natural inclination of anyone old is to distrust the insight of anyone young. And this doesn't just mean an eighty-year-old Old World Man is going to be skeptical of a twenty-five-year-old New World Man; it also means that a person who's twenty-five believes he knows more than a person who's twenty-one, and that a twenty-one-year-old woman will always see herself as smarter than a high school sophomore. Second graders feel intellectually superior to

---

1. Probably something by U2 or John Mayer.
2. Easy example: *Jersey Shore*. Do you know people who act like The Situation? No, you don't. Oh wait—yes, you do. Or at least you do now!

kindergarteners. People tend to fixate on the physical downside of growing old, but everyone appreciates the aura of wisdom one inherits from staying aboveground. You live, you learn. That's how it goes. There aren't many situations where life experience is assumed to make you dumber. The ability to understand technology is one notable exception. The ability to understand popular music is another. And this creates a transfer of minor power: Teenagers—who almost always have a limited worldview and aren't supposed to understand *anything* essential about taste—will always retain exclusive command over one of the most transformative art forms on the planet. If young people view a pop song as important, it's important. There's no other element to that circular equation (if they like it, it matters, and it matters because they like it). If young audiences *don't* care about a certain pop song, it can still be amazing and insightful and artistically competent—but it can't be "important." Because that's the one thing they get to decide entirely.

2A Someday, My Chemical Romance will be classic rock. In fact, they already (kind of) are—their second-best song sounds like a combination of T. Rex's *The Slider* with Alice Cooper's *Billion Dollar Babies,* two albums that were What The Kids Were Listening To in 1973. The title of My Chemical Romance's second-best song is "Teenagers," and the teenagers they're talking about are people who are roughly twenty-one, because "Teenagers" was written in 2005 and I'm writing this essay in 2010. Like (proverbial) sand through the (metaphoric) hourglass, time makes all rock music dated the moment we realize it matters. But "Teenagers" will remain an excellent song to think about, partly because it stands up to multiple listens but mostly because it dwells on an eternal, essential question: At what point in one's life does it become acceptable to hate young people?

This is the chorus of "Teenagers," written by frontman Gerard Way:

They say that teenagers scare the living shit out of me
They could care less as long as someone'll bleed
So darken your clothes or strike a violent pose
Maybe they'll leave you alone, but not me

The first time I heard this song, I assumed Way was sarcastically writing from the perspective of the alleged establishment ("they") who hate teenagers in the traditional way we expect every establishment to despise its underclass. I liked the way the guitars sounded, but I thought the lyrical premise was cliché and thematically opportunist. But then I read an interview with Way, and he said this about the track: "That was the first time I felt old . . . I was nervous and I was a target. I felt like I had become a parent figure or part of the problem." This made the song more complicated; I liked the idea of someone twenty-eight years old feeling guilty about appealing to people half his age, because I know how that feels. Once I realized he was writing from his real perspective, I became obsessed with the chorus's last line: "Maybe they'll leave you alone, but not me." It's a line that can be taken in two totally different ways.

My initial interpretation was that Way was *advising* teenagers while accepting his role as cultural martyr. When he says, "Maybe they'll leave you alone, but not me," I thought he was essentially saying, "Adults hate what you symbolize and will try to marginalize your existence, so maybe consider becoming a Goth [*darken your clothes*] and feigning an interest in Columbine [*strike a violent pose*]. This won't make society accept you, but at least they will stop bothering you. But they won't stop bothering *me,* because I am the famous person acting as your leader." Yet the more I play his album, the more I suspect he's speaking from the perspective of how he honestly feels as a new adult. What he seems to be recognizing is that contemporary teenagers seem nuts, and that they will fuck with you if you don't intimidate them through their own illusionary tactics. He's actually advising *adults.* However, he also knows that teenagers will never stop fucking with him, because he is supposed to be one of their clan. "Teenagers" is Way realizing that he's trapped in his teenager self: because his job is to create What The Kids Are Listening To, he will be one of them forever. They will leave *you* alone, because you're not a pop star. But they won't leave him alone. And—as uncomfortable as that might feel to Way—he desperately needs that contradiction to remain in place. If teenagers lose interest in My Chem,[3] they will end up playing state fairs and rib festivals. So Gerard Way has to figure out how to be loved by people he cannot relate to (and who sometimes scare the shit out of him). Moreover, his emotional separation from youth culture puts the artistic content of this music in dire jeopardy; the band could still make albums that sounded great, but they probably couldn't make an album that was "important." This is because My Chemical Romance makes rock music, and rock music is only important when it's What The Kids Are Listening To.

---

3. One thing that might hurt My Chemical Romance long-term is that it's hard to abbreviate their name without seeming like a buffoon.

1C

INTERVIEWER: Maybe while you've been out of the country, you've watched the [*new teen idol*] phenomenon growing?

BRITISH SINGER: I saw him in L.A., when he played his so-called debut, which was about the fourth time he played L.A., actually. He played in a ballroom, which was quite nice. He was all right. He went down well. He looked nice. I thought he was best when he played his acoustic numbers, just sitting on a podium. He was good.

INTERVIEWER: What I wondered is how you reacted to what's happening. For the first time, there is something growing up underneath your generation. You're being displaced as the involuntary leader of that generation.

BRITISH SINGER: Well, I'm not nineteen and neither is he.

INTERVIEWER: But *he's* leading them.

BRITISH SINGER: Well, you're not really going to get a new thing until you get a new music.

The unnamed singer in this interview is Mick Jagger, although it could really be anyone who ever made a game-changing record before they were old enough to rent a car. The year is 1972, and Jagger is twenty-nine. He's promoting the upcoming release of *Exile on Main St.* on BBC2. The teen phenomenon he's responding to is Marc Bolan of T. Rex, who'd just put out *Electric Warrior*. In the thirty-plus years since, Jagger has been asked different versions of this same question over and over and over again. His answers have varied, but his core point never gets much different than the one he makes here: Jagger suggests that there can't really be a "new generational voice" unless the form that voice inhabits is its own original, autonomous creation. And—unless you erroneously view rap music as completely detached from rock and pop—that hasn't happened. Musically, we're closer to the 1950s than we are removed. But something else happened that might

be even better: Generational leaders have become less necessary, more temporary, and entirely interchangeable. Every year,
it feels like pop music becomes more and more celebrity driven,
but that's a media deception. That's just how music is covered and
sold and twittered, which isn't the same as how it actually is. It's
similar to how we follow politics—the current president always
seems epic and imperative, but he's never a fraction as important as *the presidency*. A president has tremendous power, but he's
mainly a placeholder for representative democracy. So whenever
you think about whatever new artist is most popular with the rul-
ing teenage class, don't focus on how he or she sounds. That only
matters half the time, and maybe less. What's important is that
such a person matters *at all*. The idea of someone becoming the
"American Rolling Stones" or the "New Bob Dylan" or even the
"Next Strokes" is no longer compulsory. The players will continually change, but the sport does not. Contrary to what you may
have heard, rock 'n' roll is not dead. It's a new kind of alive—it's
undead. Which technically makes it a zombie. But that's still better than the alternative.

2B People in 2010 refer to Lady Gaga as a "genius"
with surprising regularity, although almost never
as a straight compliment. When people call Gaga
a *genius,* they are usually talking about her media savvy and her
ability to (seemingly) fool people into embracing the stupidest
extensions of popular culture—she is, more than any other artist
I have experienced in my lifetime, "What The Kids Are Listening
To," even though the kids might have lost interest completely by
the time this book is released in softcover. People ask me about
her constantly, almost like she's some kind of unicorn and I'm

some kind of VH1 unicorn expert. There's never been a clearer manifestation of how the generation gap is now an information gap—Lady Gaga is the most famous pop star we've ever created whose music is completely unknown[4] by most of the country. Yet to reductively say she's "famous for being famous" overlooks the most compelling aspect of her persona: Lady Gaga is famous for making herself less substantial than her work warrants. She is famous for turning herself into the idealized version of What The Kids Are Listening To, even though I have no hard evidence that The Kids Necessarily Care If She Is Alive Or Dead.

Lady Gaga is like a fifteen-year-old Honor Student who gets drunk in the parking lot before school, but only because she wants to impress her weird English lit teacher. Her various bizarro antics—wearing a bee's nests on her head, performing inside a five-hundred-gallon drum of shark blood, dressing entirely in redwood bark and human bone shavings, dancing the Macarena on the summit of K2 without oxygen—are not done to impress (or shock, or inspire) the people who download her songs. All these things are done for the benefit of people who *don't* buy her music. It forces them to assume that this kind of hyperbolic, arty indulgence must be what adolescent Americans adore. She is actively trying to present herself as facile and disposable and unreal, as these are the assumed qualities of What The Kids Are Listening To. What makes this stance so confounding is that her music is actually . . . well, pretty good. Critics always think they're throwing Gaga a bone by comparing her to Madonna, but—at least structurally—Madonna's music was rarely this interesting. Much like David Bowie, Madonna's central skill was an innate ability to

___
4. And when I say "unknown," I mean fucking *unknown*—as in, the overwhelming majority of America can't name one song title, abstractly identify a song like "Paparazzi" by its melody, or even hypothesize about what one of her tunes might sound like if they were forced to guess.

adopt and mainstream whatever was happening on the fringes of musical culture just before that specific novelty disappeared (this was most obvious on an album like *Ray of Light*, which co-opted trance and electronica in the spring of '98). But Lady Gaga has so many disparate influences (some popular, some unknown) that her songs can sound both original and indistinguishable at the same time. In simplest terms, Lady Gaga makes a brand of time-less world disco that lyrically emphasizes the precise moment she inhabits. Her voice is decent and she makes interesting decisions. She's both consciously funny and consciously dumb, and she does not see either of those qualities as positive or negative. As a result, Gaga is a mystery to people who don't want to care about her but feel as though they must. Most of the time, the only thing non-fans understand about Lady Gaga is that she must be (somehow) important, because she's What The Kids Are Listening To.

And she *is* important. She is. It's just that nobody can explain why, including me. Her importance is not generated from her music (which is underrated), nor does it come from the War-holian nature of her persona (which is overrated). It seems to emerge solely from the fact that normal adults don't understand what she's supposedly doing, mostly because she isn't doing all that much of *anything*. She's making records and dressing a lit-tle pervy. That's the formula for her existence. Everything else is what an illusionist refers to as "misdirection"—except in this case, the misdirection doubles as the payoff. Lady Gaga doesn't seem interested in representing anyone except herself; she is not polit-ically threatening or authentically transgressive (within Gaga's core audience, a pro-gay agenda is a given). Whenever she's on TV, she just seems like a lithe transsexual. But it's this unspecific "modern otherness" that makes all those unengaged with her fame both alienated and impressed. They're certain something complex must be going on here, even though (a) they don't know what it is, and (b) they're positive they want no part of it. It's a fame puzzle. Case in point: Lady Gaga refers to her fans as "little monsters." Now, here's what *New York Times* theater writer Jason Zinoman thinks that means: "At first it seems to be a term of affection, especially when she contorts her hand into a claw in a show of solidarity with her army of devotees,[5] decked out in mirror-ball earrings and wielding glowing disco sticks. But when she flirts with her fans, expressing her love for them, the standard pop star clichés clash with the macabre story of the show, which acts out more of a dysfunctional relationship." These are excellent, sophisticated thoughts. But they also feel like blind guesses at a deeper, darker meaning. That's her strategy. Lady Gaga understands the most essential element of embodying What The Kids Are Listening To—she knows how to be taken more seriously by the people who don't love her than by the people who do. She's important because *we don't know* how to argue that she's not. And even if we did, we're not in a position to try.

1D "You really need to stop writing about rock music," my friend Nick Chase sometimes tells me. Nick Chase is a federal prosecuting attorney who has likely sent several of my former drug dealers to prison. "You're too old to be writing about rock bands. You're going to become the forty-year-old Fonzie, and nobody wants to see that. Nobody. Not even the fifty-year-old Fonzie."

Nick Chase is probably right. I probably am too old to be writing about someone like Lady Gaga, and I have a sinking suspicion

---

5. Also, I have to admit—calling your own fans "monsters" and then making a little monster claw with your hand is pretty goddamn brilliant. It's almost as brilliant as naming yourself "The Situation"!

that my appreciation of My Chemical Romance might prove that they suck. As I'm writing this very essay, I'm listening to the song "Swim (To Reach the End)" by Surfer Blood, and a key stretch of the chorus sounds like the 1985 single "Your Love" by the Outfield. The fact that I am making such a connection means I am not the intended audience for Surfer Blood, even though I needed to be thirty-seven years old in order to recognize that such a connection exists. This is the underrated ecstasy—and the tragic paradox—of staying alive: I love getting older, because it allows me to remember things I once needed to learn. I feel like I understand music more today than I did yesterday, and yesterday I understood it more than I did two days ago. But yet, I wonder: Does this understanding only serve to signify that this part of my life is supposed to be over? Is "understanding" an emotional, unserious art missing the point entirely? Maybe. But I can't stop, even if I should. I'll always be interested in What The Kids Are Listening To, even as that interest becomes the sonic equivalent of looking at animals inside a zoo. I see a zebra, and I know what it is. But you know what I can't see? How zebras look to a zebra. And that, I realize, is what matters most.

Q: How did that make you feel?

A: No idea.

Q: Oh, come on. How did it make you feel?

A: I don't know. I know what you expect me to say, and I know what kind of response you're hoping I'll give you, and I know how other people might feel if they were in my position, and I know that I'm supposed to feel *something,* because this was a very traumatic event. But I don't know how I feel, even though I know there are feelings somewhere inside me. It's just that I can't possibly verbalize what that feeling feels like.

Q: Why don't you just try? Who cares if you're wrong? What is the harm in being wrong?

A: Because why would I want to get something wrong just so it will make more sense to you? It still won't make any sense to me.

T Is for True

1 *Put me in a special school*
'Cause I am such a fool
And I don't need a single book to teach me how to read
Who needs stupid books?
They are for petty crooks
And I will learn by studying the lessons in my dreams
— Weezer, "Troublemaker"

2 Every morning upon waking, I always feel something of a deficit. "Again! Why have I not dreamt?" This may be one of the reasons I make films. Maybe I want to create images for the screen that are so obviously absent from my head at night . . . I have never set out to imbue my films with literary or philosophical references . . . Film is not the art of scholars but illiterates. You could even argue that I am illiterate.

— Werner Herzog, *Herzog on Herzog*

3 Every time I see something terrible, I see it at age 19.

—Ralph Nader, speaking to *Esquire*
at the age of forty-nine

4 Irony, as we all know by now, is not interesting. We have all talked about irony for twenty years, and now we're done talking about it. But *lying* is still interesting. And these two things remain connected, even though they feel so utterly different. An ironist is someone who says something untrue with unclear sincerity; the degree to which that statement is funny is based on how many people realize it's false. If everybody knows the person is lying, nobody cares. If nobody knows the person is lying, the speaker is a lunatic. The ideal ratio is 65–35: If a slight majority of the audience cannot tell that the intention is comedic, the substantial minority who do understand will feel better about themselves. It's an exclusionary kind of humor. It's also the dominant humor of this era and (arguably) the only kind of humor interesting young people are still able to understand. It's become so central to modern communication that anything smart Americans enjoy is described (or misdescribed) as *ironical*. Either the product is being consumed ecstatically and with detachment (such as *American Idol* or Lil Wayne's nonmusical pursuits), or it's supposedly serving as a wry commentary on the straight, mainstream world—sometimes intentionally (Jason Bateman, Beck, *Harold and Kumar Go to White Castle*) and sometimes accidentally (*Sex and the City, Us Weekly,* Susan Boyle). To varying degrees, almost every new cultural invention is built on (a) an overt suggestion of partial dishonesty or (b) the universal inference that the artist *must* be lying, even if he or she insists otherwise. This is why we become so disoriented whenever someone tells the truth in a forthright manner; it always seems ridiculous, precisely because it is not.

1A

People are generally disappointed by Weezer albums. It's become the band's defining ethos— they consistently disappoint the people who love them most. It's an insular version of disappointment that makes no immediate sense: Weezer distresses the exact same people with every record they release. This should be impossible. If *every* new record a certain band makes disappoints its base, one would assume chagrined consumers would eventually give up. But people have a different kind of relationship with Weezer, and it's due to the songwriting of front man Rivers Cuomo: He writes completely straightforward lyrics, presented through music devoid of irony. He *exclusively* presents literal depictions of how he views the world, and he (almost exclusively) plays guitar riffs that he'd personally want to hear as a fan. There are no other major elements to his work. The tone of his guitar is an attempt to replicate the tone of guitarists he appreciated as a teenager, particularly Ace Frehley and Carlos Cavazo. He employs metaphors, but the metaphors are hyperobvious stand-ins for his own confessionals; he tosses around stilted hip-hop language that makes it seem like he's mocking all the affluent white kids obsessed with superficial blackness, but he used to be one of those kids. His lyrical fantasies (such as living life as a professional surfer) are faithful, expository descriptions of what he fantasizes about. In 1994, he wrote an unreleased rock opera called *Songs from the Black Hole* that involved six separate characters (one of which was a robot), but he later admitted the entire narrative was really about his own experience on tour. Artistically and motivationally, Weezer makes completely unaffected music—more authentic than Black Flag or Bright Eyes or Janis Ian. But because every other aspect of Cuomo's public life seems constructed and self-aware—and because he displays all the usual qualities we've come to associate with kitsch and irony—audiences are unwilling to view Weezer's music as a reflection of Cuomo's autobiography. They think it must be about something else; they think it must have something to do *with them,* and with *their* experiences, and with *what they want* from pop music. They are disappointed that Weezer's post-*Pinkerton* music doesn't sound honest; it often strikes them as lazy or self-indulgent or unfinished. But the reason it sounds that way is because it's *only* honest. It's so personal and specific that other people cannot relate to it. And—somehow—that's assumed to be Cuomo's job. For some reason, he's supposed to make music that his fans can connect with and live through. But he can't do that (or won't do that) on purpose. He can only do that by accident, and only intermittently. As a musician, he does not lie for the benefit of other people, and that keeps his fans terminally disappointed.

In 2006 I delivered a lecture at Boston University, and a person in the audience wanted to know what I thought of the Weezer album *Make Believe.* This man, for whatever reason, was extremely upset about it. "Is Rivers trying to fuck with us?" he asked. "That album contains three of the worst songs ever recorded." I mentioned there were at least three songs on the album I liked: "Beverly Hills," "We Are All on Drugs," and "Freak Me Out." The man in the audience immediately lost his mind. "Those are the three songs I was referring to!" he exclaimed. "They're terrible. It's almost feels like he's trying to make fun of me for buying his music."

This is a strangely common sentiment; since returning from a self-imposed musical exile in 2001, there has often been a sense that Cuomo is mocking the kind of utterly earnest person who loves Weezer the most. Weezer's relationship to the emo movement is central to this problem: They're not an "emo band" in any sonic respect, yet they're the most important group the genre has ever produced. Weezer defines what emo music is supposed to do— if Sunny Day Real Estate's "Seven" is the emo "Rock Around the Clock," then Weezer's 1996 sophomore effort *Pinkerton* is the emo *Sgt. Pepper*. The concept of a confessional male songwriter directly emoting to the audience about his own paralyzing insecurities is perfectly realized on *Pinkerton,* and that makes it the defining document of the idiom. But here's the twist—traditionally, emo musicians draft a metaphorical contract with their fan base. The message is this: "I am telling you exactly how I feel, even if that feeling is problematic and embarrassing and temporary, because we are ultimately the same people. We have all the same feelings, even if some of those feelings aren't real." For hard-core Weezer fans, that experience happened when they listened to *Pinkerton.* What they failed to realize was that the connection was accidental. Cuomo did not write those words to connect with other people. He did not make a conscious attempt to help confused teenagers understand themselves. It just worked out that way. But the assumption was that Cuomo had constructed this level of empathy and that this construction *must* have been, to a certain degree, unreal. It had to have been—at least partially—a career move. No realistic human ever expects absolute authenticity from any musician; that expectation would feel naïve, and it contradicts everything we know about how art is presented in the postmodern world. So when someone actually does this— when someone doesn't fabricate feeling for the sake of artistic purpose—we misread the motive. Rivers Cuomo is such a solipsistic writer that his fans cannot accept that he's giving them *exactly* what they claim to want. Whenever he examines the process of being alive, he really isn't thinking about anyone except himself. He is beyond emo, and he's not lying about anything.

This is what the question asker in Boston did not understand: He could not fathom that a person he believed to be working for him had never considered his needs at all. When he listened to a song about the desire to possess a swimming pool in Beverly Hills, it seemed to be the opposite of what he identified as his own desires. He thought it must be cheap sarcasm. When he listened to the song "We Are All on Drugs," it seemed like Cuomo was making a joke that did not have a punch line. In truth, there isn't even a joke. "We Are All on Drugs" is intended to be taken literally, except for the specific use of the word *drugs*. That was the only abstract aspect of the entire track.[1] "Freak Me Out" struck him as the single stupidest moment on the album, particularly since the band had started claiming in interviews that the lyrics were about Rivers being frightened by a spider. To the question asker, this explanation made sense; *of course* it had to have an inherently facile meaning. Except that it clearly does not. Go on the Internet and read the lyrics—they are amazingly self-evident. It's not about a spider. It's a song about Cuomo walking down the street at night, only to have some random bozo jump in his face and say, "Hey! You're the guy from Weezer! Your band kicks ass! But your albums disappoint me! Can I take your picture with my cell phone?" The song is called "Freak Me Out" because it's about being freaked out (and then feeling guilty about your own reaction). The question asker from Boston hated "Freak Me Out"

---

1. "Some fans have told me that their children hear me saying 'we are all on drugs' and they take it literally because they don't know any better," Cuomo later told *Spin*. "And that makes me feel horrible . . . In my mind, love and drugs are the same thing—we're all numbing ourselves or stimulating ourselves with intense relationships or TV or movies or music and we use these like drugs." In other words, this is a figurative phrase that requires a literal reading, which is not the same as irony.

because it did not seem to match any feeling he'd ever had. This is because the inquisitor has absolutely nothing in common with the protagonist who wrote the song. He is not like Rivers Cuomo; he is more like the weirdo in the shadow.

2A German film director Werner Herzog sometimes talks about truth being "elastic," a modifier that should indicate his definition of honesty does not have much to do with being literal. His persona is built around fictionalized mythologies: He's perceived as an egomaniac who supposedly pointed a loaded rifle at an actor in order to make him perform. While making the 1976 Bavarian glass-blowing epic *Heart of Glass,* Herzog hypnotized members of the cast to make them seem zombie-like on-screen. His singular cinematic achievement is 1982's *Fitzcarraldo,* a movie where hundreds of Peruvian natives drag a 320-ton boat up the side of a mountain, entirely shot without the use of special effects. The dragging of the boat is a fictionalized version of a semi-historical event; in the late nineteenth century, a Peruvian rubber baron pulled a smaller steamship over a South American mountain, but even that craft was disassembled before it was moved. In other words, Herzog faked the reality of the event, but he did not fake the event itself: What happens in *Fitzcarraldo* is actually more unbelievable than the story it's based upon. What was fabricated for the sake of the film was considerably more difficult than the factual achievement. To quote Herzog: "Facts create norms, but they do not create illumination." He once said he would only touch truth "with a pair of pliers." This sounds like a metaphor, but maybe it isn't.

So what does this mean? For one, it tells us that Germans are bizarre. But it also shows how truth is easier to accept when it's

stridently unclear. We can watch *Fitzcarraldo* and see its legiti-
macy precisely because Herzog is bending all sorts of lies for that
final purpose. The situation is fake and the motives are fake, but
the boat and the gravity are real. This makes us comfortable. It's
the way we're now accustomed to consuming honesty in any
film—tangential details are manipulated for the benefit of one
Big Truth, which we are supposed to unspool upon retrospection
(and also from the cognitive, preexisting understanding that this is
a real fucking mountain and a real fucking boat, as no one who's
ever watched *Fitzcarraldo* was not aware of those facts before seeing it—very often, they're the *only* things people know about this
movie). In other words, this seemingly fanatical episode from
Fitzcarraldo is among the most normal things Herzog has ever
done as a filmmaker. He has constructed truth through standard
(albeit complicated) cinematic means. But this is less interesting than when Herzog delivers truth without construction. That
happens less often, but when it does, it's way crazier. This is a
man who once consumed his own leather shoe, simply because
he promised Errol Morris that this is something he would do.[2]
Sometimes Herzog is literal in a manner so straightforward that
almost no one pays attention.

There's a moment like this in *Grizzly Man,* Herzog's fascinating
2005 documentary about bear fanatic (and eventual bear entrée)
Timothy Treadwell. Mostly assembled from Treadwell's own
video footage, *Grizzly Man* is the story of an idiot (Treadwell)
who—upon being rejected for the role of "Woody" on *Cheers*—
decided to spend the next thirteen years of his life living with
Alaskan grizzly bears, videotaping his experiences for a series
of nature films. Treadwell views the bears as human peers and
talks to them like children, constantly overstepping the (seemingly obvious) boundary between goofball human and 1,200-

---

2. Hence the 1980 short film *Werner Herzog Eats His Shoe.*

pound killing machine. Eventually, Treadwell and his girlfriend are killed and eaten by a bear. But along the way, Herzog quietly (and fairly) dissects the psychology of Treadwell; he spends a stretch of the documentary showing how Treadwell would often reshoot scenes of himself in order to control his own perception. He also points out how Treadwell fundamentally lied about a core aspect of his public persona—his girlfriend would sometimes accompany him on these trips into bear country, but Treadwell always insisted (directly into the camera) that he was alone. In many ways, *Grizzly Man* is about the very idea of truth. But that shifts when we get to a scene where Timothy discovers that a male grizzly has killed a few innocent bear cubs in order to have sex with their mother. Treadwell is shattered by this event and decries how the world is confusing and painful. But then the camera cuts directly to the face of a bear and the image freezes. And as we look into the frozen, empty eyes of a bear, Herzog's voice-over says this:

> Here, I differ with Treadwell. He seemed to ignore the fact that in nature there are predators. I believe the common denominator of the universe is not harmony but chaos, hostility, and murder.

Because this pronouncement is so dramatic (and—quite frankly—because Herzog's voice and accent are so goddamn funny), it always makes viewers laugh. It's impossible to watch the scene without laughing, especially since you're staring into the face of a motionless bear who seems to be emoting those same sentiments through mind bullets. It's not a moment most people remember from the film. Yet could there be a more unambiguous thesis for how Herzog views existence? There is no irony here. It is, in many ways, the core of his entire creative career. I can't rephrase his sentences with any greater clarity than what already exists on the page. *But this is funny to people.* It makes us laugh, because it's disturbing to take literal thoughts literally.

"I am someone who takes everything very literally," Herzog has said.[3] "I simply do not understand irony, a defect I have had since I was able to think independently." That defect, however, is more an issue for his audiences than it is for the director himself. Most of us have the opposite defect: We *only* understand irony, even when it is not there to be understood.

3A "I can spend all day listing the mistakes the Democrats made both before and during Florida, but I don't care." This is political writer Eric Alterman, speaking into the camera in the documentary *An Unreasonable Man,* analyzing the 2000 presidential election. "[Ralph] Nader professed to be standing for one thing when in fact he was deliberately causing another thing. The Democrats were just incompetent. Nader was dishonest . . . To me, he's a very deluded man. He's a psychologically troubled man."

The reason Alterman hates Ralph Nader is obvious and well documented: He feels that by running for the office of president and getting 2.7 percent of the vote, Nader cost the 2000 election for Al Gore and subjected the United States to the most reactionary presidential administration in recent history. Many Americans feel this way; had 10 percent of the 97,421 people who voted for Nader in Florida supported Gore by default, everything about this country would be (in some way) different. There is no mathe-

---

3. Most Herzog quotes in this essay are coming from the aforementioned book *Herzog on Herzog* (edited by Paul Cronin), simply because it is one of the few examples of the director speaking in an unfiltered context.

matical way around this. Alterman's essential point is true—in practice, Nader's decision to run for the presidency was bad for America. But his perception of Nader as a person is completely wrong. To people like Alterman, Nader seems delusional and troubled and dishonest. But this is because people who follow politics closely cannot comprehend people who aren't partially lying. They are intellectually paralyzed by literal messages.

While running against Hillary Clinton in the race for the 2008 Democratic nomination, eventual U.S. president Barack Obama came under fire for his long-standing spiritual relationship with the Chicago Reverend Jeremiah Wright, a preacher who claimed the U.S. government created AIDS in order to destroy the black race. Wright had been the officiant at Obama's marriage and baptized Obama's children; when first pressed on the issue, Obama said he could no more disown Wright than he could disown his own grandmother.[4] But the reverend refused to shut up; he kept making crazier and crazier statements. A few weeks later, Obama disowned him completely. This was seen as a totally rational, wholly acceptable move. I would have done the same thing. When Obama compared Wright to his grandmother, no one had really believed him; when he cut Wright loose, only the most partisan Republicans labeled him a hypocrite. What he did was normal, understandable, and nonliteral: It's what makes Obama a reasonable man and a (potentially) good president. We immediately recognize that his literal comparison of Wright to his grandmother is different than his actual feelings. Yet this is precisely the kind of unwritten dichotomy Ralph Nader would never accept. Nader might be the most stridently literal man who has ever gained traction in the modern political arena. Werner

---

4. In fact, he briefly suspended his 2008 campaign (in late October) when the aging woman fell ill. She ultimately died one day before her grandson's election.

Herzog says he cannot understand irony, but at least he can create it for other people; Nader is a perpetual sincerity machine. His critics insist that he's a megalomaniac, and that's almost certainly true—but it's *sincere* megalomania. His arrogance is not misplaced. He lives in an inflexible world of complete moral certitude. He authentically believes that all of his values are 100 percent correct. Granted, this is an oddly common perspective within partisan politics; it's always shocking how much blind confidence people absorb from party propaganda. But the difference is in how people present that certitude. When Obama[5] or Sarah Palin or Rachel Maddow or Glenn Beck speak, we take for granted that—at the very least—they are partially (and consciously) lying. They are asking us to view their sentiments through preexisting filters we have all inherited through media; we take the verbatim sentences, consider the person's larger motive, search for code and subtext in the specific words and phrases, and triangulate the true meaning. But Nader doesn't work like this. Nader speaks literally, and that makes him superfluous.[6] He delivers accusations in an unpackaged, unbendable manner: "The auto industry is killing people. Power has to be insecure to be respon-

5. Immediately after Obama's feel-good victory in fall of 2008, writers as sensible as Joan Didion expressed the fear that this might push America into an "irony-free zone" where "innocence, even when it looked like ignorance, was now prized." This was similar to the "Death Of Irony" that was supposed to happen following the terrorist attacks of 9/11. In both cases, the Death Of Irony lasted roughly five weeks. Irony is like Jason Voorhees.

6. The day after Obama was elected president, Nader said the key question that would be facing the new leader was whether he would be an "Uncle Sam" for the American people or an "Uncle Tom" for giant corporate interests. This was essentially the end of Nader's TV career. But what's even crazier about the content of this statement is that Nader was not using the term "Uncle Tom" the way 99.9 percent of Americans perceive it; he was using it as it strictly applies to the character from Harriet Beecher Stowe's 1852 novel, which did not necessarily depict Tom pejoratively. Nader doesn't understand how the nonliteral world operates. That's his paradoxical value.

sive. Game six of the 2002 NBA Western Conference Finals was illegitimate." That type of talk is antithetical to the thinking of all political animals. This is why Eric Alterman hates Nader so much, even though they fundamentally agree on many, many points. Alterman cannot fathom that the motives a man gives for running for the presidency could be identical to whatever his true motives are. Nader's reasons for running in 2000 (and in 2004) were unvarnished extensions of what he claimed to represent. He was not psychologically troubled. He was literal, which is received by the public as the same thing.

2B *Cinema verité* literally translates as "cinema of truth." Herzog, of course, hates cinema verité, claiming it's "devoid of *verité*." In 1999, he wrote a ten-point manifesto titled "The Minnesota Declaration," probably the only document in film history that attacks cinema verité techniques while complimenting Jesse Ventura. His essential point was that cinema verité provides "the accountant's truth" and that cinema verité auteurs are like tourists. Keeping this in mind, I think it would be very interesting to see a Herzog movie about an accountant on vacation.

Any film consumer recognizes cinema verité the moment they see it, even if they're unfamiliar with the term: It's the kind of naturalistic, shaky, provocative camera work that feels like orchestrated news footage. You often see it employed in exceptional rock documentaries (*Don't Look Back, Gimme Shelter*), but also in fictional narratives dependent on the aura of reality—*Cloverfield, The Blair Witch Project,* the opening combat scenes from *Saving Private Ryan,* most of the mumblecore movement, the 1971 dissident project *Punishment Park,* and both the U.S. and UK versions of *The*

Office.[7] Whenever we watch cinema verité movies, we unconsciously think of them as more lifelike than conventional film, simply because they're made to look cheaper and more amateur than they are. This is why Herzog hates cinema verité: It's more realistic, but it's not remotely literal. It's the least-literal filmmaking there is.

I am a huge fan of the NBC program *Friday Night Lights,* despite the fact that I don't like what it does to me. I don't like the way it manipulates my emotions. Here is a show about a high school football team in Texas, packaged as a melodramatic soap opera. While certain aspects of the program are legitimately well done by any standard (most notably the relationship between the head coach and his wife), much of the action involves implausible characters doing unbelievable things (showing up to football practice drunk; accidentally murdering people; winning or losing every game on the final play of the fourth quarter, etc.). But even when the on-screen action is ridiculous, it always has a *physical* impact on me—the combination of the music and the imagery consistently makes me feel like I'm on the verge of tears. *Friday Night Lights* can make my stomach hurt, even when my mind says, "This is silly." So I wonder: How much of this reaction is simply a product of the show's relentless use of cinema verité style, fused with my own self-imposed confusion over what truth is actually supposed to look like?

I suspect almost all of it.

Maniacal Slovenian monster-brain Slavoj Žižek once made a

---

7. Here's an unasked question about *The Office*: In both the American and British versions, the program is shot as a documentary. The characters are directly interviewed and often acknowledge the camera crew with knowing glances. But why is this office being filmed? Why is someone making an around-the-clock documentary of these ordinary people, even when they leave the building? What is the purpose? And when, in theory, would the filming conclude?

perverse, semi-relevant point about the movie *Titanic*; he argued that people are so out of touch with their true feelings that they mentally construct fantasies they don't even want, simply to feel like they have control over their unknowable desires. "How is the catastrophe [depicted in *Titanic*] connected to the couple, the rich upper-class girl and the poor lower-class boy?" Žižek asked. "After making love, they go up on the deck and embrace again and then she tells him, 'I will stay with you and abandon my people.' At that moment the iceberg hits the ship. What's the point? I claim the true catastrophe would have been for them to stay together, because it wouldn't work and they would split. It's in order to save that impossible dream that the ship must sink."[8] Žižek is essentially arguing that because we cannot understand what we want from ourselves and from other people, we construct fictional placeholders that help us feel secure within our emotional confusion. We assemble and embrace false feelings in order to feel normal. In the same way, our inability to comprehend literal messages prompts us to pick arbitrary versions of media that become stand-ins for truth.

The cinema verité on *Friday Night Lights* only works because I know what it is (and because I have pre-accepted what it signifies). I know its self-reflexive flaws are supposed to indicate that what I'm seeing is closer to reality, so I automatically make that jump with my consciousness. In other words, this entire style of filmmaking only exists to remind me that what I am watching is supposed to be life. And I'm used to this; I am used to things that are constructed solely to make me feel like I am experiencing something natural. State parks and zoos are like this. The personality of Michael Moore is like this. The small talk made between

---

8. This is from an interview conducted by Jennifer Wallace for the book *Predictions*.

strangers, the noises people make during intercourse, and compliments given to small children are all like this. I don't know if I could enjoy a genuinely literal TV show about high school football, or if I could spend my life with a wholly literal person.

4A

There are many aspects about Ralph Nader that intrigue me, but none more than this: As far as anyone can tell, he's never had a single romantic relationship in his entire life. None. No ex-wife, no former girlfriends, no secret gay lover, no hookers, no one-night stands with savvy nineteen-year-olds who are hot to take down the Federal Trade Commission. You cannot even find a photograph of Nader that someone might misconstrue. There's just nothing there. And people have certainly tried to find this information. In fact, people have tried to *make this* happen: When he was fighting the auto industry in the 1960s, it's rumored that General Motors hired women to accost Nader in grocery stores and attempt to seduce him, all in the hope of discrediting his single-minded efforts to ensure that new cars didn't explode on impact. With the possible exception of Morrissey, I cannot think of a higher-profile figure so adamant about appearing asexual.

This makes sense.

It makes sense that Nader could not function inside a romantic relationship, as those are always nonliteral relationships. All romantic relationships are founded on the shared premise of love, a concept defined differently by all people. Conversations between couples are theatrical and symbolic; the first thing anyone realizes the moment they enter a serious relationship is that words (especially during fights) never represent their precise definitions. Nader would be paralyzed by the content of wedding vows—he would want to qualify everything. "In sickness and in health" would become "In sickness, with the possible exclusion of self-contained vegetative states, and in health, assuming neither party has become superhuman or immortal." It would be a deeply wonkified ceremony, probably held in rural Oregon.

Rivers Cuomo is not asexual, but he has had a lot of relationship problems (or at least he used to). I assume those problems were manifestations of his literalism. Love songs from Weezer usually paint Cuomo as a self-deprecating doofus, and they feel commercially smart because the main character seems like an idealized reflection of the bespectacled hipster nerds who buy his albums. But if the Weezer consumer ends up being a reflection of Cuomo, it's purely an accident—he's usually just explaining himself in very specific ways. He does (or at least did) look like Buddy Holly. He did, at one point, grow tired of having sex with people. His interest in Asian girls is not affected —those are the women who consistently arouse him. In the song "Across the Sea," Cuomo explains how he received a letter from a female fan in Japan[9] and became obsessed with the paradox of being loved by someone who was completely absent from his life (at the time, he was depressed and attending Harvard). He sings, "I've got your letter, you've got my song." He's having a one-to-one communication with this woman in a public setting, which is why everyone thinks he's so emo. But it's more than that. Cuomo is ignoring the basic principle we all assume is part of the creative process; he is not "creating" anything. If someone wants to analyze the nonsonic elements of "Across the Sea," they are not performing music criticism; they're psychologically profiling Cuomo in a totally clear-cut fashion. The only thing that can be decon-

---

9. The one detail in the song that was changed was the age of the real-life letter writer: In the lyrics, she is described as eighteen. She was actually fourteen.

structed is the person himself.[10] This is why Weezer songs are not taken seriously, or at least not as seriously as they deserve to be. People don't want to think about singers as humans; they want to think of them as entities who create songs *for* humans. Moreover, they want to decide how sincere the creator is supposed to be—and the only way to do that is to start with the premise that the message is not the message. It cannot be literal. If it's literal, the process is already over.

5 "And make no mistake: irony tyrannizes us," wrote David Foster Wallace in 1993, long before this kind of problem had occurred to someone like me. "The reason why our pervasive cultural irony is at once so powerful and so unsatisfying is that an ironist is impossible to pin down. All U.S. irony is based on an implicit, *I don't really mean what I'm saying.* So what does irony as a cultural norm mean to say? That it's impossible to mean what you say? That maybe it's too bad it's impossible, but wake up and smell the coffee already? Most likely, I think, today's irony ends up saying: *How totally banal of you to ask what I really mean.*"

When I began writing this essay, Wallace was still alive. And because he was still alive (and because I wanted to write about the absence of literal messages instead of the proliferation of ironic

---

10. I suspect Cuomo now realizes this and is somewhat uncomfortable with what that means. He has taken to giving conflicting reports about what happened in the wake of this recording. In 2006, he claimed he had never contacted the girl who wrote the letter and knew nothing about her. In 2008, he said the woman was actually receiving royalties from "Across the Sea," due to his use of specific lines from her original note. I suppose it is possible both of these things are true, but highly unlikely.

ones, and because I knew I could never compete with the intellectual intensity of his work), it was my original intention to not mention him at all. But then he killed himself. In the wake of his suicide, it seems wrong to neglect referencing his views on what people mean when they say anything in public. Yet I suspect that the (very real) problem Wallace saw in '93 has evolved into something else entirely. It's not that we all collectively agree that asking someone what they really mean is banal; it's that we now assume that the real meaning of every statement is hidden by default. We assume that *all* statements must be mild inversions of the truth, because it's too weird to imagine people who aren't casually lying, pretty much all the time.

Every time I publish a book, I get asked if what I wrote is actually how I feel. If I write a review about *Chinese Democracy*, people will ask if I really like Axl Rose as much as I claim and if I'm being honest in the way that I describe liking his music. The same thing happens when I write about *Saved by the Bell* or ex-girlfriends in Minnesota or fictional characters with no ties to reality. The subject matter is irrelevant. My response to these questions is never the same. Sometimes I say, "Yes." Sometimes I say, "Sometimes." Occasionally I argue that the things I write are "thought experiments," or that I am only concerned with the technical practice of writing (with little care for the content), or that I am *only* interested in forwarding my ideas (and artistically unattached to the manner in which they are presented). Now, all of these answers are partially true. But the deeper reality is that I'm *not* sure if what I do is real. I usually believe that I'm certain about how I feel, but that seems naïve. How do we know how we feel? I'm likely much closer to Žižek's aforementioned description of *Titanic*: There is almost certainly a constructed schism between (a) how I feel, and (b) how I *think* I feel. There's probably a third level, too—how I *want* to think I feel. Very often, I don't know what I think about something until I start writing about it.

However, I do know this (or at least I think I do): When I am in the active, physical process of writing, I am writing literally.

It is always a literal, present-tense depiction of what is cognitively happening in my mind. Now, once a given sentence exists, that might change. Sometimes it changes just four seconds after I type it. But I still believe that sentence should be read in the literal context of its creation. I often wonder if we would all be better off if we looked at all idioms of art in a completely literal fashion, all the time. It would be confusing as hell for the first twenty or so years, but I suspect the world would eventually make more sense than it does now. At least we could agree on whatever it is we're pretending to understand.

I am no longer afraid to believe what I read, so I will go first.

Q: A lot of the criticisms regarding your work have been tied to its length. How do you feel about that?

A: I'm never sure how to respond to this question. There are certain accepted lengths that works of fiction and nonfiction are supposed to be, and almost everyone sticks to those general parameters. Some writers will go slightly further and some writers will write slightly less, but almost no one exits the format entirely. Those kinds of restrictions never bothered me, but they never interested me, either. I am exclusively interested in New Thoughts. I only care about ideas and notions that no one else has ever thought before—not reactions to other media, but unique creations that come exclusively from one source. So if I can get to that New Thought in twenty-five or thirty words, that's all I write. But it usually takes longer. And it's generally impossible.

FAIL

1 There are certain rules I try to follow as a writer. One rule is to never place the word *and* directly following a semi-colon. Another is not to write positively about diabolical mathematicians who murder people through the U.S. mail. As a consequence, I'm nervous about saying anything non-negative (or even neutral) about Ted Kaczynski, simply because there are always certain readers who manage to get the wrong idea about everything. For most of the world, the fact that Kaczynski killed three people and injured twenty-three others negates everything else about him. There is only one socially acceptable way to view the Unabomber: as a hairy, lumber-obsessed extremist whose icy brilliance was usurped only by a sinister lack of empathy. Writing about Kaczynski's merits as a philosopher is kind of like writing about O. J. Simpson's merits as a running back—at first it confuses people, and then it makes them mad. I would advise against it. You absolutely cannot win.

But who wants to win?

Like so many modern people, my relationship with technology makes no sense whatsoever: It's the most important aspect of my life that I hate. The more central it becomes to how I live, the worse it seems for the world at large. I believe all technology has a positive short-term effect and a negative long-term impact, and—on balance—the exponential upsurge of technology's social import has been detrimental to the human experience. Obviously and paradoxically, I'm writing these sentiments on a laptop computer. And because I've felt this way for years (and because I've e-mailed these same thoughts to other people), there are those who tell me I'm like Ted Kaczynski.[1] The only thing everyone knows about Kaczynski (apart from the violence) is that he was an enraged hermitic technophobe who lived in the woods. His basic narrative has been established: He left academia for rural Montana, he spent seventeen years sending anonymous letter bombs to innocent people he'd never met, he demanded that his thirty-five-thousand-word manifesto be published in *The New York Times* and *The Washington Post,* and he was apprehended in 1996 after his brother and the FBI deduced that Kaczynski was the Unabomber. All of that is true. This is why the Unabomber matters to historians: He's a fascinating, unique crime story. But the problem with that criminal fascination is how it's essentially erased the content of his motives. Kaczynski believed he had to kill people in order to get his ideas into the public discourse. He was totally upfront about this: "If [I] had never done anything violent and had submitted the present writings to a publisher, they probably would not have been accepted," he plainly writes in *Industrial Society and Its Future.* "In order to get our message before the public with some chance of making a lasting impression, we've had to kill people." On the most primitive level, this goal succeeded. But not the way he hoped. Because Kaczynski sent bombs to people, nobody takes anything he says seriously (they might in three hundred years, but they don't right now). Despite the huge circulations of *The New York Times* and *The Washington Post* and its ever-present availability on the Internet, the "Unabomber Manifesto" is an unread, noninfluential document. And that's regrettable, because every day, the content of *Industrial Society and Its Future* becomes more and more interesting. It's like an artless, bookish version of the Kinks song "20th Century Man," amplified by a madman who's

---

1. My physical appearance might play a role in this.

too smart to be reasonable. I will grant that it contains a lot of problematic fascist ideology (not surprising, considering that the author was a problematic fascist who shared both the good and bad qualities of Martin Heidegger). But it's not nearly as insane as it should be, at least relative to how we view its author. I can easily imagine a distant, dystopic future where it's considered the most prescient work of the 1990s.

As I read it now, three things strike me:

1. As it turns out, I am nothing like Kaczynski. In fact, I represent precisely what the Unabomber hates about humanity, as do most of the people who embody the target audience for this book.
2. Just about everyone who hasn't read *Industrial Society and Its Future* assumes it's a screed against technology, and sometimes it is. But it's mostly about the concept of a specific type of political freedom. Kaczynski is not interested in *feeling* free; Kaczynski is interested in a kind of freedom most people don't even realize is possible.
3. *Industrial Society and Its Future* was written by an isolated man living in a cabin without electricity during the 1980s and early '90s. The text mentions the Internet several times, but one has to assume it was impossible for him to fully understand what the Internet would eventually become. Yet Kaczynski's core ideas about this specific technology are competitive with those of virtually everyone who's written about it since. He couldn't have fully understood what he was writing about and his language is often unsophisticated, but his sense of the web's inherent problems is natural and spot-on.

He was a bad person, but sometimes he was right.

2 The psychological profile of Ted Kaczynski reads like an origin story for someone who'd eventually become one of the Watchmen: Born in 1942, he's smart and weird. His IQ in fifth grade is 167. He's so smart that they skip him from sixth to seventh grade, and this ruins his life. He's teased constantly and has no friends. The socially retarded Kaczynski is accepted into Harvard at the age of sixteen and immediately excels at math, specializing in the field of geometric function theory. But something unorthodox happens while at Harvard—he takes part in a psychological experiment that's based on deception. Participants in the study believe they are being asked to debate philosophy with a collegiate peer, but the "peer" is actually a lawyer whose sole purpose is to aggravate and attack the unwitting applicant; Ted has unknowingly volunteered for a stress test. When the reality of the hoax is eventually explained to Kaczynski, he feels betrayed and outraged. This experience seems to change him. At his eventual trial, Kaczynski's lawyers will argue that this was where his hatred of authority truly began.

After earning a PhD from the University of Michigan, Kaczynski takes a post as an assistant mathematics professor at the University of California–Berkley in 1967, but he leaves the position in '69 without explanation. Two years later he starts living in a remote Montana cabin; six years after that he starts mailing homemade bombs to people. Because his early targets were either universities (*UN*) or airlines (*A*), authorities dubbed him the Unabomber. Part of the reason he was able to avoid apprehension for almost twenty years was his ability to embed the bombs with misleading clues: He kept using the code word *wood* in the missives, sometimes inscribed the random initials "FC," and once included a note to a nonexistent person named "Wu." Since these were the only clues the FBI had, they always pursued them to the ultimate extreme (which was always a dead end). Our only visual aid was the most recognizable police sketch of the twentieth century, a preposterously generic image that suggested (a) the Unabomber didn't like the sun in his eyes and (b) he owned at least one hooded sweatshirt. Had Kaczynski's own brother[2] not figured out who the Unabomber was after the manifesto's publication, it's plausible that Kaczynski would never have been caught.

Now, before I go any further, I want to stress that I am not a "fan" of the Unabomber. None of the bombs he sent were justified. Every person who was hurt was hurt for no valid reason. But I still want to think about the reasons why he sent those bombs, and those reasons are found in *Industrial Society and Its Future*. He became a domestic terrorist so that people would consume this document. In and of itself, that relationship is immaterial (a manifesto doesn't become important just because its writer is merciless and desperate). The main thing one can deduce from Kaczynski's willingness to kill strangers is that he is an egotist. That said, the fact that a document's creator is an egocentric murderer does not preclude the work from being worthwhile (Phil Spector shot a woman in the face, but that doesn't make the harmonies on "Be My Baby" any less beautiful). The fact that Kaczynski has a deeply damaged psyche doesn't mitigate its value at all: Not all crazy people are brilliant, but almost all brilliant people are crazy.

3 Cultural criticism is a temporary kind of art. Works of this variety sometimes experience massive spikes in popularity at the time of their release, but the shelf life is short. If a

---

2. Kaczynski's brother David deduced that the Unabomber was probably Ted when he noticed that several of Ted's pet phrases were used in the manifesto, most notably the term "cool-headed logicians."

piece of cultural criticism truly succeeds, its ideas and theories are completely absorbed by mainstream society (which means that the book itself becomes unnecessary). This has happened with lots of influential books from the past forty years that are now rarely purchased by new audiences—*The Closing of the American Mind*, *Within the Context of No Context*, the novel *Generation X*, and other works in this vein. One of the most fascinating examples of the phenomenon is Jerry Mander's *Four Arguments for the Elimination of Television*. Part of what makes this book so entertaining is the laughable impossibility of its nonmetaphorical goal: The author seems to have written this book with the hope that everyone in America would read it, agree with all its points, and literally destroy their television sets with sledgehammers. This did not happen. But there are still tons of great ideas in *Four Arguments*, and it's amazing that Mander came to these realizations in 1978, before the advent of cable or the inception of the web. When Mander rails against his version of mediated culture, he's really just railing against three networks and PBS. But three channels and *Sesame Street* were all he needed to see the truth, which is this—TV takes away our freedom to have whatever thoughts we want. So do photographs, movies, and the Internet. They provide us with more intellectual stimuli, but they construct a lower, harder intellectual ceiling. The first time someone tries to convince you to take mushrooms, they often argue that mushrooms "allow you to think whatever thoughts you want." This sentiment makes no sense to anyone who has not taken psychedelic drugs, because everyone likes to assume we already have the freedom to think whatever we please. But this is not true. Certain drug experiences *do* expand a person's freedom of thought, in the same way that certain media experiences make that freedom smaller.

On page 243 of *Four Arguments for the Elimination of Television*, Mander lists a variety of scenarios and asks the reader to imagine them inside their own mind. These are things like "life in an Eskimo village," "a preoperation conversation among doctors," "the Old South," "the flight of Amelia Earhart," or "the Old West." This is very easy to do, and you can do it right now—pick any one of those situations and watch it inside your mind's eye. But once you've done so, consider what Mander says about the process:

> It is extremely likely that you have experienced no more than one or two of [these situations] personally. Obviously, these images [inside your head] were either out of your own imagination or else they were from the media. Can you identify which was which?

In all likelihood, *all* of your internal images did (at least partially) originate from television. Your supposedly unique mental picture of a Georgia plantation during the Civil War is just an interpretation of what you unconsciously recall from *Gone With the Wind* or *Roots* (or some other show that used the same set). Mander goes on to make an even more troubling request—he asks the reader to imagine a basketball game. Do that right now. Close your eyes and imagine a basketball game in your head. What did it look like? One can assume that virtually everyone in the United States has attended a live basketball game at some point in his or her life, and almost as many have played in a basketball game for real (at least for five minutes at recess in sixth grade). I played organized basketball for thirteen years. So why is my first mental image of a basketball game a moment from game four of a Celtics-Lakers championship series I saw on CBS in 1984? Why is *that* my immediate, galvanized definition of a sport I actively played?

It's because we really can't differentiate between real and unreal images. We can describe the difference, but we can't manage it.

Decadent French critic Charles Baudelaire made a comparable point about photography way back in 1859, but the process is accelerated a thousand fold when applied to images that move and talk and morph. Mander's point is that technology evolves much faster than we do physically or mentally, and the consequence is that vague sense of alienation expressed by Thom Yorke on *OK Computer*. Humans have existed for 130,000 years. *The Great Train Robbery* was made in 1903. For roughly 129,900 years, any moving image a human saw was actually real. It was *there*, right in front of you. If a man in 1850 saw a train chugging toward his face, it was actually a train. For 129,900 years, we were conditioned to understand that seeing something in motion had a specific meaning. But that understanding no longer exists; today, we constantly "see things" that aren't actually there. Intellectually, we know that there's a difference between *The Great Train Robbery* and a real train. Intellectually, we know there is a difference between a living person and a Facebook profile. We know that *The Sopranos* and our own life are different. But is there any possible way that 129,900 years of psychological evolution can be altered within the span of a single century? Is it any wonder that people feel paradoxically alienated by the mechanical devices they love?

We do not have the freedom to think whatever we want. We don't. And until we accept that, it's useless to think about anything else.

2A I don't expect consumers of this book to read *Industrial Society and Its Future*, or even to spend more than two or three minutes scanning it on Wikipedia. I know how this works. But just to make things a little more collectively cogent, here is the document for Matt Damon fans who prefer the editing of *The Bourne Ultimatum* to *Gerry*:

1. The first line of the introduction is "The Industrial Revolution and its consequences have been a disaster for the
human race." The important thing to note here is that the
words *Industrial Revolution* have been capitalized. Kaczynski's complaint with society starts around the year 1760,
almost two centuries before he was born.

2. The next sections discuss "the psychology of modern left-
ism," which is an attack on a certain kind of person—not
necessarily a *political* liberal, but people whose worldview
and morality are marked by "feelings of inferiority" with
characteristic traits that include "low self-esteem, feelings of
powerlessness, depressive tendencies, defeatism, guilt, self-
hatred, etc."

3. A big chunk of the manifesto is about the desire for power
and socialization. He argues that modern people are so
obsessed with socialization that they deceive themselves
about everything—about what they feel, why they do things,
or what their true morals are. It's weird to take moral advice
from a guy who sent bombs to strangers, but his thoughts
are not invalid: Basically, the Unabomber believes modern
people have no idea how they're supposed to think or feel,
so they convince themselves to care about whatever rules
the rest of society seems to require. It's something of a rudimentary loop—people conform to the status quo because
the status quo validates the conformity they elected to
adopt.

4. Kaczynski was obsessed with autonomy. "For most people, it is through the power process—having a goal, making an *autonomous* effort and attaining the goal—that self-
esteem, self-confidence and a sense of power are acquired."
This is the root of his hatred of technology—he could not
be a singular individual if his livelihood was dependent on
machines.

5. In a section titled "Sources of Social Problems," he argues that conservatives are "fools" for complaining about the deterioration of values while supporting economic and technological growth. This is a key point for Kaczynski. He sees these things as interrelated.

6. Science, the Unabomber argues, is the ultimate "surrogate activity." This is the term Kaczynski uses in reference to pursuits that give people an artificial goal and a constructed meaning to their lives. As applied to the Internet, the argument is almost unassailable.

Now, here are the three points that matter most:

7. The manifesto outlines five principles of history. Only the fifth principle is important: "People do not consciously and rationally choose the form of their society. Societies develop through processes of social evolution that are not under rational human control."

8. Technology is a more powerful force than the desire for freedom.

9. We cannot separate good technology from bad technology.

If you mention these last three statements to most normal people, they will say number 7 is usually true, number 8 is possibly true, and number 9 is probably false. But they're all equally accurate.

3A While writing this essay I read Lee Siegel's *Against the Machine*, a 2008 book subtitled *Being Human in the Age of the Electronic Mob*. One of the author's central thoughts involves the way the Internet has negatively transformed people's sense of self and about how widespread anonymity on the Internet has inadvertently lowered the level of American discourse. These are good points. But *Against the Machine* is ultimately an unreliable book, simply because of Siegel's motive for writing it.

The author describes all this in the book's introduction: In 2006, Siegel wrote a piece for *The New Republic* that questioned Jon Stewart. When the article was posted online, dozens of people hurled childish, ad hominem insults against Siegel in the comment section—a phenomenon that now happens when almost anything interesting is published in public. But Siegel responded in the worst possible way. He created a fake profile for himself and wrote self-aggrandizing attacks directed at his critics. (He injected insights like "You couldn't tie Siegel's shoelaces.") Siegel was suspended by *The New Republic* for doing this. According to the author, the debacle prompted him "to write the book on Web culture that I'd long wanted to write," which turned into *Against the Machine.*

I believe Siegel is lying, at least to himself. I don't think *Against the Machine* was the book he'd been waiting his entire career to publish. The whole tome reads like an ill-advised reaction to the controversy on *The New Republic*'s website. He wasn't against "the machine" until it personally wounded him.[3] Had the commentators only praised his arguments, it's easy to imagine Siegel writing a completely different book about how the Internet is saving the American intellectual. This is why reading about the social mean-

---

3. I would never argue that Siegel isn't a smart guy, nor would I expect him to take my criticism of his work seriously. However, much of this book is inundated with weirdly transparent explanations for his cultural values. At one point in *Against the Machine,* he attacks Malcolm Gladwell, insisting, "Back in high school, people like him were the reason you drank, brooded over Kierkegaard's *Fear and Trembling,* and imagined which celebrated public figures would speak at your (imminent) funeral." I halfway assumed the next sentence was going to be "And you know what else—Gladwell thinks his hair is so cool, but it's totally not."

ing of technology tends to go nowhere: Such works are almost always written for wholly personal reasons. The only people who think the Internet is a calamity are people whose lives have been hurt by it; the only people who insist the Internet is wonderful are those who need it to give their life meaning. Web philosophy is an idiom devoid of objective, impersonal thinking. In 2008, the *Columbia Review of Journalism* interviewed a man named Clay Shirky about the pitfalls of modern Luddism and the meaning of information overload. Shirky teaches interactive telecommunication at NYU and wrote a book about social media called *Here Comes Everybody*. In the *CRJ* interview, Shirky said things like "I'm just so impatient with the argument that the world should be slowed down to help people who aren't smart enough to understand what's going on." This is the message net-obsessed people always deliver; the condescending phrase most uttered by frothing New Media advocates is "You just don't get it." The truth of the matter is that Clay Shirky *must* argue that the Internet is having a positive effect—it's the only reason he's publicly essential. Prior to 1996, no one wanted to interview Clay Shirky about anything. He used to be just another unassuming intellectual (of which the world has many). Now he's the prophet for a revolution. By promoting online media, he promotes himself. And this is not uncommon—the reason so many bloggers fixated on the TV show *Gossip Girl* was because inflating the import of *Gossip Girl* amplified the significance of blogging itself. The degree to which anyone values the Internet is proportional to how valuable the Internet makes that person.

This is why *Industrial Society and Its Future* feels so different. Unlike just about everyone else who writes about technology, Kaczynski doesn't have a horse in the race. Had he elected to embrace the trappings of the modern age, there is no doubt he could have been wildly successful—I suspect he could have been one of the Internet's architects, were that what he wanted.

It wasn't that he was frozen out or ostracized—he *chose* not to be involved. Moreover, he was ultimately able to live separate from the electronic age as successfully as any American could expect; it wasn't tangibly impeding him at all, unless you count the occasional airplane coasting twenty-eight thousand feet above his head. Technology wasn't damaging him in any real way. Were he not a sociopath, he could have stayed in his cabin and avoided the advancing world forever. He made things personal by mailing bombs to strangers, but his complaints were not about himself or his career or what anonymous cretins might be saying about him on *The New Republic*'s website. His ideas were too radical, but at least they were his own.

2B The Unabomber writes that society evolves irrationally, which is probably how he justified mailing people bombs. But what would a rational society look like? He never explains that part.

When it's warm out, I like to sit inside air-conditioned rooms. This feels rational to me. It seems rational to want to be comfortable. But is it rational to expect to be cool when the outside temperature is 95 degrees? I suppose it isn't. But why would it be irrational to build and use a machine that makes things cooler? Here again, that seems rational.

Yet what am I giving up in order to have a 70-degree living room in July?

Nothing that's particularly important to me.

For the air conditioner to work, I need to live in a building that has electricity, so I have to be connected to the rest of society. That's fine. That's no problem. Of course, to be accepted by that society, I have to accept the rules and laws of community living. That's fine, too. Now, to thrive and flourish and afford my electric bill, I will also have to earn money. But that's okay—most jobs are social and many are enriching and unnecessary. However, the only way to earn money is to do something (or provide something) that is valued by other people. And since I don't get to decide what other people value, what I do to make a living is not really my decision. So—in order to have air-conditioning—I will agree to live in a specific place with other people, following whatever rules happen to exist there, all while working at a job that was constructed by someone else for their benefit.

In order to have a 70-degree living room, I give up almost *everything*.

Yet nothing that's particularly important to me.

When Kaczynski wrote, "Technology is a more powerful social force than the aspiration for freedom," I assume this is what he meant.

3B When I was younger, people would often ask what my political affiliations were. These days, I find that people will just tell me what they assume my political affiliations *must be,* usually based on something I've published that wasn't remotely political. Everyone I've met in New York or California tells me I'm conservative. The rest of America tells me that I'm almost comically liberal. I feel good about this. I enjoy writing about my own life, but I don't like people knowing anything about me.

However, the Unabomber knows me. He knows me better than I know myself.

I would never have guessed that I am a Modern Leftist; I've never been involved in a Parisian riot or aligned myself with a black bloc or campaigned for Russ Feingold. But I embody at least half of Kaczynski's Modern Leftist criteria. Here (once again) are the qualities he assigns to the Modern Leftist: "feelings of inferiority," "low self-esteem," "feelings of powerlessness," "depressive tendencies," "defeatism," "guilt," and "self-hatred." Granted, some of these traits are amorphous. *Low self-esteem* is a totally meaningless designation, simply because there's no extension of human behavior that doesn't qualify. If you have no self-confidence, you are believed to possess low self-esteem; if you have an abundance of self-confidence, it's assumed your arrogance is an attempt to overcompensate for a lack of self-esteem. I don't think I've *ever* met a person with the "correct" level of self-esteem. But some of Ted's other designations are more telling. To me, it seems naïve *not* to feel as though one is powerless, a sentiment that probably proves that I also possess a feeling of inferiority. I'm depressed a lot, usually for no reason (although sometimes I'm just hungry, which often feels the same). I'm extremely defeatist about anything that doesn't come easily to me. I don't have much guilt (in fact, my wife claims I don't have enough), but I do hate myself. In fact, I can't relate to people who *don't* hate themselves, which might mean I have low self-esteem (or, I suppose, the complete opposite). Another trait of the Modern Leftist (according to Ted) is someone "interpret[ing] as derogatory almost anything that is said about him." I understand how this feels, too: I always suspect people are saying negative things about me, even if they are being friendly and flattering. But I'm sure I make other people feel this way, too. For years, I tried to avoid overused words like *nice* and *cool* whenever I made small talk. I'd always try to offhandedly compliment strangers with less predictable phrases, like "Wow! That's an unorthodox haircut." As it turns out, most people—and especially most women—hate this. They typically respond by hiding in the bathroom, trying to get drunk, or (on one occasion) attempting to get drunk *in* the bathroom. This used to bother me.

But now I realize I was simply partying with too many Modern Leftists. I should have spent more of my social time with Post-modern Leftists; they never care what you say to them, as long as you don't criticize architecture or Girl Talk.

My point, basically, is this: Even though I am defending several of Ted Kaczynski's ideas, I'm the kind of human he hates most. It was people like me who made him mail bombs to university professors he'd never meet. I suspect that if you went to his supermax prison cell in Colorado and asked Kaczynski who most represents the problems he outlines in his manifesto, he would say something along the lines of "People who know the truth, yet still refuse to accept what they know to be true." That's who I am (and—if you're reading this—you probably are, too). Even though he deserves to die in jail, Kaczynski's thesis is correct: Technology is bad for civilization. We are living in a manner that is unnatural. We are latently enslaved by our own ingenuity, and we have unknowingly constructed a simulated world. The benefits of technology are easy to point out (medicine, transportation, the ability to send and receive text messages during Michael Jackson's televised funeral), but they do not compensate for the overall loss of humanity that is its inevitable consequence. As a species, we have never been less human than we are right now.

And that (evidently) is what I want.

I *must* want it. It *must* be my desire, because I would do nothing to change the world's relationship to technology even if I could. My existence is constructed, and it's constructed through the surrogate activity of mainstream popular culture. I understand this. And because I understand this, I could change. I could move to Montana and find Ted's cabin and live there, satisfied in my philosophical rightness. I could go the Christopher McCandless route and shoot a moose for food and self-actualization. But I choose the opposite. Instead of confronting reality and embracing the Experience of Being Alive, I will sit here and read about Animal

Collective over the Internet. Again. I will read about Animal Collective *again*. And not because the content is important or amusing or well written, but because the content exists. Reading about Animal Collective has replaced being alive. I aspire to think of myself as an analog person, but I am not. I have been converted to digital without the remastering, and the fidelity is appalling.

A few hours ago, someone asked me if I thought it would be good for the world if the Internet spontaneously went black and never returned. It was a hypothetical, so I said, "Yes." It would be a positive insurrection for the world. We would have less access to information, but we would not be any less informed about reality. People like to assume the democratization of media is a wonderful concept, but that's only because most Americans are childishly obsessed with the word *democracy*: They want to believe anything becomes better if you make it more democratic. This may be true for governments and birthday parties, but not for everything else. Should we democratize the world's supply of uranium? Should we democratize guns? Should we democratize cocaine?[4] The Internet is not improving our lives. It's making things (slightly) worse. But because I'm not free—because I am a slave to my own weakness—I can no longer imagine life without it. I love the Internet. *I love the Internet*. And I will probably love whatever technological firebomb comes next. My apologies, Ted. Your thirty-five-thousand-word document makes sense to me, but I cannot be saved. You'll have to blow up my hands.

---

4. Well, maybe.

Acknowledgments

As always, the existence of this book is primarily due to the work of Brant Rumble and the acumen of Daniel Greenberg.

Others who deserve mention for specific suggestions and meaningful changes: Kyle Anderson (particularly for his assistance with "Oh, the Guilt"), Bob Ethington (who has quietly and aggressively edited every book I've ever written, without compensation), Rob Sheffield, Greg Korte, Michael Weinreb, David Giffels, Ben Heller, Jon Dolan, Brian Raftery, Jennifer Williams, and the University of Leipzig.

The title for the tenth essay was stolen from John Hodgman without his permission. I likewise borrowed an old joke about wildebeests from Jack Sullivan. Half of the essay "Going Nowhere and Getting There Never" originally appeared in *The Believer* magazine and was edited by Ed Park. The other half was edited by Zoe Wolff.

I would also like to thank Melissa Maerz for marrying me, for allowing me to be crazy, and for keeping the batteries inside the remote control.

Index

INDEX

INDEX

INDEX

New York Dolls, 118
New York Yankees, 79n6
New York Observer, 4, 5
NFL, 79n3, 80, 150n2, 153–55, 165, 166
NFL Films, 154–55
NFL Network, 153–54
Nicholson, Jack, 125
Nike, 207
Nine Inch Nails, 108
Nirvana
    "Aero Zeppelin," 34
    "All Apologies," 45–46
    Bleach, 28
    greatness of, 36–38
    guitar smashing by, 27–28, 44, 49–50
    Incesticide, 34–36
    In Utero, 27, 28–30, 33, 34, 36, 38–40, 39n3, 44, 45, 47, 48, 60
    "Lithium," 39
    "Molly's Lips," 34
    Nevermind, 29, 39
    "On a Plain," 39
    "Rape Me," 39
    "Sliver," 34
    "Smells Like Teen Spirit," 39
    With the Lights Out, 36–37
Nixon, Richard, 3, 164
NME, 38, 100
no-huddle offense, 159
Notre Dame University, 152
Novak, Kim, 92–93
Novoselic, Krist, 29
Nutt, Houston, 162n12

Oakland Raiders, 150, 154
Oasis, 117
Oates, Warren, 135

Obama, Barack, 112, 201, 203, 231, 235, 235n4, 236, 236n5, 236n6
Odyssey (Homer), 125
Office, The (television series), 190, 237–38, 238n7
Office Space (television show), 103
Ogilvy and Mather, 209
Ohio State University, 164
OK Computer (Radiohead), 253
Olajuwon, Hakeem, 75, 85n10
Old Joy (film), 137
Ole Miss football, 162n12
"On a Plain" (Nirvana), 39
O'Neal, Shaquille, 102n3
On the Road (Kerouac), 124, 129
Oprah (television show), 115
orange juice repackaging, 206–07
Orrell, Lisa, 201, 202
Ortmayer, Steve, 80
Orwell, George, 55
Outfield, 223
Ozzfest, 47

Pacino, Al, 203
Packers, 81, 158
Page, Jimmy, 111
Paisley, Brad, 112
Palahniuk, Chuck, 59
Palin, Sarah, 236
Palm, Carl Magnus, 171, 173
Parcells, Bill, 164
Payton, Walter, 44
Pearl Jam, 31
Penn football, 151
Pennington, Chad, 147
Pepsi, 199–203, 205
PepsiCo Incorporated, 206–07
Perfecting Sound Forever (Milner), 39

276

A Scribner Reading Group Guide

Eating the Dinosaur

Questions for Discussion

1. The first essay in the book features a conversation between Klosterman and filmmaker Errol Morris, in which they discuss the significance and nature of interview responses. Klosterman and Morris disagree about the importance of narrative consistency versus truth. If you were to be interviewed on a national stage, would you lie in an attempt to present a better image of yourself, or would you tell the truth because you think truth is always the better story?

2. Klosterman devotes much of the second essay to analysis of Nirvana's *In Utero,* which he defines as "guilt rock." Can you think of other examples of popular bands, singers, actors, writers, etc., who, after achieving commercial success, purposely produced or participated in "bad" art? Why did they do so? Did they have the same motives that Kurt Cobain is argued to have had?

3. Consider Klosterman's comparison of Kurt Cobain and

David Koresh. Do you think he makes a valid case? Did *Eating the Dinosaur* change your perception of either man?

4. Ask yourself the question that Klosterman likes to ask when he's 5/8 drunk. If you could phone your fifteen-year-old self, but only talk for fifteen seconds, what would you say?

5. Do you agree with the assertion that "Seeing the secret lives of others removes the pressure of our own relative failure while reversing the predictability of our own static existence" (page 103)? Why or why not? Think of a scenario from your own past in which you enjoyed peeping in on someone. Why did you engage in that voyeurism? Can you recall—if it ever occurred—the first time you actively sought out an opportunity to spy on other people?

6. The essay titled "The Best Response" features statements meant to exonerate people who have gotten themselves into embarrassing, illegal, or career-ending crises. Do you think these are the best responses? In your opinion, which is the most successful, and how does your response to this question demonstrate your own ethical values to the rest of the group? Come up with a few "best responses" of your own—to being caught shoplifting, to your best friend whose birthday you forgot, to your boss who has discovered that you didn't do the work you told him or her you did.

7. Klosterman contends that football changes more than any other sport and can therefore be characterized as liberal. Do you agree? Can you make a case for why another sport plays a more significant role in American culture and history?

8. Before having read the chapter entitled "'Ha ha,' he said. 'Ha ha.'," had you ever contemplated what response the existence (or lack thereof) of canned laughter was supposed to elicit? What is your reaction to canned laughter in television shows?

9. What do you think the second "It" in the essay titled "It Will Shock You How Much It Never Happened" refers to?

10. In the final essay of the book, Klosterman states, "My existence is constructed, and it's constructed through the surrogate activity of mainstream popular culture" (page 262). What does he mean by this? Consider your own existence. Would you draw the same conclusion?

11. What role did the Q&A's at the end of each chapter play in your reading experience?

12. The book description asks if there is a larger theme within *Eating the Dinosaur* and suggests that it is something about reality. What other themes are present in this book? Do you think there's an overarching message that Klosterman wished to convey?

Enhance Your Book Club

Filmmakers Errol Morris and Werner Herzog are featured in this book. View their films, such as *The Fog of War, The Thin Blue Line, Grizzly Man,* or *Encounters at the End of the World* with your book club.

If you haven't already, read Klosterman's previous books, which include *Downtown Owl; Chuck Klosterman IV; Killing Yourself to Live; Sex, Drugs, and Cocoa Puffs;* and *Fargo Rock City.*

Visit Chuck Klosterman's website, www.cklosterman.com.

A Conversation with
Chuck Klosterman

You use the concept of eating dinosaur in an aside that illustrates the absurdity of our desire to travel through time, but the concept, by virtue of being used in the book's title, seems to have been assigned more significant meaning. Who is "eating the dinosaur"? You? The media? Society as a whole? Is this good or bad?

A: The short answer is that I just liked the way that phrase sounded. The long answer is that I am particularly interested in all the versions of media that are regularly defined as "dinosaurs"—the newspaper industry, the music industry, network television, unmediated sports, etc.

How has your perception of authenticity changed over time?

A: When I was young, I never thought about it. In my late twenties, I came to the conclusion that authenticity (at least as it's applied to art) did not matter and was not important. I now feel like it still does not matter, but it's probably the *only* thing that's actually important.

How, if at all, has your career as a journalist changed the nature of personal conversations you have?

A: I can no longer tell the difference between interviewing someone and talking to them. But that was probably always the case.

As a pure consumer of entertainment, and not from the standpoint of a music critic, do you enjoy listening to ABBA? Is it possible to even answer this question within this boundary?

A: This is an easy question to answer. I love listening to ABBA.

What advertising campaign have you attempted to feel immune to but found yourself wanting the product nonetheless?

A: Every infomercial I've ever seen. I feel like no genre of advertising is more effective than the infomercial.

Did you employ the numbered-outline structure in *Eating the Dinosaur* to facilitate the read or make it more complex?

A: Probably the former, although the main idea was to reflect the structure of how modern humans think about problems. I would never consciously try to make a book more complex than it naturally was. That seems crazy to me. Clarity is my primary goal.

Can you tell us who is featured in each Q&A within the book? At what point during the writing of this book did you decide to include the Q&A's and how did you select each of them?

A: None of those are real. I decline to answer the second part of the question. Although I will concede that it's a good question.

You recently wrote your first novel, *Downtown Owl*. How different was that process from writing nonfiction? Which narrative form engages you more deeply with reality?

A: It took more time. It was harder. It was less engaged with reality. I guess I've kind of stopped thinking about that book, actually. Maybe I'll think about it again when I write another novel.

You write that being a journalist is a "tremendous way to earn a living." If you could have any profession other than your own, what would it be?

A: Private investigator or crisis management consultant. Or are you including dream jobs, like playing in the NBA or being Tony Iommi or something? Could I be a cult leader? Does that count?

You admit to having openly lied in interviews. How do we know that you've told the truth in these responses?
A: How would *you* know? How would *I* know?